Navigating the Dissertation

Strategies for Doctoral Advising Faculty and Their Advisees

Second Edition

by Marianne Di Pierro, Ph.D.

NEW FORUMS

NEW FORUMS PRESS INC.

Published in the United States of America
by New Forums Press, Inc. 1018 S. Lewis St.
Stillwater, OK 74074
www.newforums.com

Copyright © 2021 by New Forums Press, Inc.

All rights reserved. No part of this publication may be reproduced or transmitted in any form or by any means, electronic or mechanical, including photocopy, or any information storage or retrieval system, without permission in writing from the publisher.

Library of Congress Cataloging-in-Publication Data Pending

This book may be ordered in bulk quantities at discount from New Forums Press, Inc., P.O. Box 876, Stillwater, OK 74076 [Federal I.D. No. 73 1123239]. Printed in the United States of America.

Cover designed by Dionna Marie Di Pierro.

ISBN 10: 1-58107-353-4
ISBN 13: 978-1-58107-353-9

Table of Contents

ACKNOWLEDGMENTS ix
PREFACE xi

CHAPTER
1   Dissertation Advising: The Need for Collaborative Training Models 1
2   The Rules of Engagement 17
3   Defining Editing Expectations: More Rules of Engagement 31
4   The Toxic Committee 39
5   Considerations When Forming a Committee: For Advisees 53
6   Selection of the Advisee: For Faculty 69
7   Other Considerations for the Advisor as Leader 79
8   Vetting the Committee 83
9   Discovering the Dissertation Topic 85
10 The Concept Paper and the Quality Circle Review 99
11 Implementation of Editorial Commentary and Technology 121
12 Naming Conventions for Maintaining Draft Files 131
13 Working Against the Grain: For Advisors 137
14 Working Against the Grain: For Advisees 151
15 Dissertation Proposal and the Human Subject Institutional Review Board (HSIRB) Protocol: Symmetry in Design 165
16 Preparing for the Oral Defense of the Dissertation: 17 Easy Steps 177
17 Bill of Rights for the Advisee/Advisor 185
18 Combating the Dissertation Blues: Comprehensive Examinations—The Prelude 189
19 The Dissertation Writing Blues 195
20 The Dissertation Aftermath Blues 203
21 Debriefing: An Essential Final Step in Doctoral Education 213
22 New Forms and New Paradigms 219

23	Personalizing Academic Misconduct: An Approach for the Graduate Classroom	227
24	A Visionary Perspective for an Academic Resource Matrix	243
25	Blurred Lines: Ethical Considerations for Committee Members	253
26	Quick Takes	273

About the Author 283

Index of Book 285

About This Book

This book examines the intricacies of the doctoral educational process and delineates a pathway for continuous improvement designed to shape and enhance better professional relationships between dissertation advisors, new and seasoned, and their advisees. Thus, its objective is to cultivate opportunities for increased retention and graduation. The book includes critical principles, interwoven with students' and faculty's real life experiences which serve as illustrative vehicles. Moreover, its innovative approach departs from other books that provide generally only a one-dimensional view, usually from the student's perspective. The titles of many of these are couched in metaphors of survival and overcoming a threat, rather than centered in strong initiatives that lead to timely graduation in a supportive and encouraging environment. This book offers innovative leadership approaches to transport advisors and advisees to successful outcomes.

Dedication

To the guiding force in my world, my husband, John, who
transforms possibilities into realities
through love, inspiration, and encouragement.

Acknowledgments

Gratitude, appreciation, and love to my daughter, Dionna Marie Di Pierro, for her endless encouragement and support and whose rare excellence makes her an exemplar in her own right, *nihil nisi perfectio.* Much love to my son, John Peter Di Pierro, whose amazing sense of humor, courage, and persistence teach the valor and beauty in the attainment of life goals.

To my parents, Paul and Natalie Rose Furfaro, whose lives embraced the majesty and privilege of education, a conduit to all possibilities.

To Douglas Dollar, *New Forums Press*, my publisher, who saw the value in this project and supported its publication.

Research is contingent upon a vast history of forebears whose work precedes our own and whose efforts serve as beacons lighting the way for others to make their own contributions: Chris Golde, Barbara E. Lovitts, Maresi Nerad, Maya Angelou, Orlando Taylor, Gary A. Olson, Miguel Roig, among many others. Much appreciation to Sylvia Fiore, Elton Smith, Joseph Bentley, Van Cooley, Eileen Evans, Sonia Foss, William Waters, Julien Kouame, Ilse Schweitzer VanDonkelaar, Alee Sleymann, Ronald Davis, Donald Thompson. Special gratitude and appreciation to Norman Carlson, who recognized my potential and whose vigilance advanced my career in graduate education. In appreciation to Hope Smith for lending her expertise to the finalization of both editions of this book.

To those dedicated graduate faculty who, by their example, selflessly cultivate generations of emerging scholars.

Last, but certainly not least, I acknowledge the steadfast efforts of the many doctoral students with whom I have worked during these years. You have taught me well. It has been my privilege to enter into your worlds, and I thank you for placing your trust and confidence in my ability.

Author's Note: The names and identities of certain individuals referenced in this book have been changed. Others granted permission for their actual names to be used, and in those instances their names appear. Situations and examples cited are not necessarily restricted to any one institution. This book is intended as only one of many resources for graduate faculty and their advisees and provides practical information to steady the course.

Preface

Graduate education is becoming more highly nuanced and complex over time. Students have more diverse needs and expectations than ever before, and universities and colleges must respond accordingly. When I began my work over 20 years ago, I asked two questions: (1) What do graduate students need to know in order to be successful in their trajectories to the Ph.D.? and (2) What do graduate advising faculty need to know in order to help students achieve success in their trajectories to the Ph.D.? The answers to these two questions have framed my work during more than two decades, and they continue to serve as viable parameters as we move forward. As educators, we must continue to ask and answer these questions.

It is a well-known fact that institutions of higher education are indeed faced with complex, compelling issues. Challenges to enrollment, decreases in state appropriations, fewer available graduate assistantships, and declining faculty ranks, in light of institutional imperatives to meet accreditation standards and Carnegie rankings, represent just a few of these. To this, add the ramifications of COVID-19 and the drastic changes in educational delivery modalities that confront all universities and colleges, let alone the vast array of sociological and psychological problems that have disrupted the lives of many students and faculty. Protracted doctoral time-to-degree as well as doctoral attrition figure prominently against this significant contemporary backdrop. Research indicates that the longer Ph.D. students remain in their programs of study, the more the opportunities for them to attrite. Economic and financial challenges, as well as those phenomenological issues confronting students within domestic and professional spheres, exert their own intense pressures. Couple all of this with declining university and college student enrollment and rocketing student loan debt and it becomes readily apparent that our graduate students are too frequently enmeshed in uncertainty and hesitancy regarding their futures, which include degree completion and access to viable careers in their disciplines.

As educators, we must be cognizant of the ethical responsibility to examine variables in the doctoral educational process that pose logistical barriers to degree completion and to career access and then implement ameliorative strategies. If we endorse continuous process improvement and related quality standards, then we must move past rigid ideas that create normative standards out of current practices and the "it is what it is" notion. In like manner, we must also be aware of the ethical responsibility to reform the curricula in a manner that aligns with the expectations of the dissertation, as well as to *counsel out* students who cannot complete their programs of study, who have decided not to complete them, or who have demonstrated an inability to complete them. Students require training and support through this process, as well. Permitting students to *time out* as a mechanism to separate them from their degree endeavors is not acceptable. Neither is it acceptable to remain apathetic to the need for faculty training in the dissertation process, to fail to educate faculty about the *counseling out* process, to ignore the inherent difficulties in understanding when and how to initiate it, or to withhold support to faculty as they manage these challenges. We cannot help our students without first addressing the challenges that confront our faculty.

Doctoral students deserve the absolute best of every educational opportunity for success that we can provide, and it is our charge to honor them by doing so. It is their charge to reach for our extended hands.

Chapter 1

Dissertation Advising: The Need for Collaborative Training Models

It is not important to change. Survival is not mandatory.
W. E. Deming

It was initially difficult to begin this book and equally so its second edition for a variety of reasons that have less to do with actual content and more to do with the realization that not much in doctoral education has changed during the course of the 17 years that I served as director of the Graduate Center for Research and Retention at Western Michigan University. Despite abundant research and the often-echoed affirmations that something must be done to quell doctoral attrition, progress is essentially hampered by a reluctance to recognize that advising faculty cannot continue to work with doctoral advisees by replicating models that are passé. Some of those models worked to a certain degree, but others failed in navigating students successfully through the arduous dissertation process. Losing half of all doctoral students to attrition is a fact that years of research still have not yet ameliorated. Half of the nation's most intelligent and hard-working doctoral students do not complete the Ph.D., a goodly number of them *stuck* at the dissertation stage. This percentage has remained constant for a number of years, from the days of Berelson, who was among the early researchers to address high doctoral attrition rates, to more contemporary researchers such as Lovitts, Golde, and Nerad, among others. In addition, these echoes reverberate in the almost decade-long findings of the Council of Graduate Schools (Council of Graduate Schools, 2009).

All in all, the problem is perpetuated from generation to generation of scholars, without significant changes witnessed via research projects that focus on the doctoral education process and the variables that impact time-to-degree and attrition. We have done a good job of unearthing factors that lend to attrition, but not much in actual problem solving. Moreover, the claims that students who are proficient enough to be admitted to a graduate program *a priori* qualify for award of the Ph.D. cannot stand against the reality of what we understand about the graduate education process and what it takes to complete the degree. False illusions to account for attrition must be re-examined. We need to pay more attention to the voices of the students whose experiences frame their existential landscapes: they tell us what they need. *Are we listening? Are we responding?* If half of the patients admitted to all hospitals in the United States died, there would be a national outcry, a protest of the highest order. We would react: explore patient safety issues, medical education and training, equipment performance, among other factors. But half of our doctoral students are *dying* en route to the Ph.D. and sustained inquiries, accompanied by action plans to avert these statistics, are not in place. If the statistics alone do not startle us, then the absence of solutions surely should. This edition of the book will examine these and related observations, discuss a strategic approach to enhance the advisor–advisee relationship, provide a progressive model for dissertation advising, as well as explore ethical considerations that interface with students' critical transition.

Lack of Training

For the most part, universities do not invest resources in the formal training and preparation of graduate advising faculty for the dissertation advising/mentoring responsibility. Faculty may experience some cursory interventions, such as initial service on a dissertation committee or shadowing a more senior faculty advisor; however, more often than not, faculty are enmeshed in an isolated advising journey, relying frequently on their own often-solitary dissertation experience, the model that many will replicate with their own advisees. This fact accounts for one of the reasons why poor models are perpetuated: unless dissertation advisors make concerted efforts to implement purposeful change into the model from which they emerged and may even have found dysfunctional, they will tend to replicate it with their own advisees because it appears normative. In essence, they say, "This was my experience, and now it will be yours, too." Alternate perspectives or questioning of the entire process from which they emerged do not always resonate, perhaps because they have escaped through graduation and no longer have to reflect on a misalliance that may have almost eclipsed their success. Perhaps having emerged on the "other side of the Ph.D."—in other words, having survived—and now confronted by the prospects of becoming tenured faculty, they think of themselves as being less in opposition to their advisors and more in league with them; they have set their sights on the next phase, employment, and cannot risk cultivating untoward relationships with dissertation chairs and committee members at this increasingly vulnerable stage.

The lack of formal training imposes a limitation on the advising process because it does not provide a groundwork for the expertise required, does not discuss best practices in advising, nor does it interpret or define "advising" as a term critical to an understanding of the expected duties and responsibilities of this position. What actually qualifies an individual to lead a dissertation is not clear, aside from having graduate faculty status, centered more in publications and conferences and being a faculty member in a department. This fact of ill-defined roles and lack of training plays out in continuous ways, as we will see.

A component of the lack of faculty training in dissertation advising also resides in the fact that graduate program directors (GPD), those who sit at the helm of the graduate experience in their respective departments, may not be necessarily well recruited or trained, and further, these vitally critical positions may not even reflect a position description from which to draw a robust candidate pool. Often, GPDs simply inherit the role, and there may be only slight carry over or succession planning from program advisor to program advisor and little in the way of transitional interactions; worse yet, there may perhaps be nothing at all in terms of specific training. In addition, they may not understand or be aware of the array of graduate education policies and procedures that could assist them in their roles as advisors not only to students but to their faculty colleagues as well.

These considerations are gradually coming to the forefront of graduate education: a Council of Graduate Schools listserv communication in November and December 2020 revealed that educators from various institutions sought information regarding the availability or use of position descriptions for GPD and, perhaps for the first time, understood that this is not a position into which just anyone should be randomly assigned.

Qualified individuals who occupy this role can be pivotally important in operationalizing faculty training, not only in dissertation advising but also in conveying the logic and power of graduate education policies and procedures. The role itself requires interconnectedness with vast campus resources, understanding the mission of these offices and the identities of the individuals administrating them—the admissions office, ombudsman, financial resources, legal office, graduate college/school, and other departments and offices—instead of residing within the more restricted and somewhat siloed department environment. Yet, a major disconnect exists between institutions' understanding of the importance of defining the GPD role and its intersection with graduate student/graduate advising faculty success.

Recent progressive and commendable efforts by Missouri State University to execute a job analysis of the GPD role "affirmed the [Missouri State University] Graduate College's perspective that little information existed specifically for the role of graduate program directors in higher educational settings nationally" (Missouri State University Graduate College, 2017, p. 4). Further, research conducted by Missouri State University indicates the "seeming undesirability of the job role and the ambiguity of the GPD role in some departments" as two obstacles that inhibited certain department heads from an accurate performance evaluation of the individuals who occupied those roles. The lack of hard data gave way to an "informal performance appraisal process for a GPD" based upon subjective assessments and personal histories (Missouri State University Graduate College, 2017, p. 9). The lack of a position description necessarily negates evaluation and lends to the idea that the position itself is not worthy of a description in the first place: a person can make the position his or her own, and at that point the work produced appears valueless and unpleasant.

Interestingly enough, although the Missouri State University study revealed that "no uniform training need [for the GPD position] presented itself in interviews or survey responses," it is curious that department heads indicated that "training resources in a number of content areas, both technical and 'soft' skills, would certainly provide value to faculty serving as GPDs, as well as department heads, overseeing graduate programs," a finding that cannibalizes the very notion that "no uniform training need" was identified (Missouri State University Graduate College, 2017, p. 21). The word *uniform* draws my attention: needs may not have been *uniformly* presented, but even diverse needs certainly qualify. The idea that department heads "typically select faculty members who, [*sic*] they believe, possess the skills and abilities required to fulfill the role of GPD" (Missouri State University Graduate College, 2017, p. 21) lends to a certain subjectivism that does not account for the true demands of the position and that assumes a level of qualification that an individual may not necessarily possess.

Lastly, while it is important for departments to consider course release time and stipend payments for GPD, as expressed in the study, these are not the overriding matters that they should deliberate. The questions are these: "What is the role and responsibility of GPDs? What specifically do GPDs need to know to ensure effectiveness of their position? How can their universities support them in these roles and provide the necessary resources and training, including succession training to incoming GPDs?"

If the GPD role, perceived on a national level as "thankless, poorly defined, or suffering from inadequate resources" (Missouri State University Graduate College, 2017, p. 10) and as a role that can be filled with less-than-qualified individuals because "no one else would do the job instead" (p. 11) gives us pause, it should. However, we should not be startled at the outcome, nor should we be startled at ancillary outcomes when we extend this idea of lack of qualification, training, and assessment to any other individual associated with doctoral education: committee chairs and committee members, for example.

What other jobs out there do you know of that require no training, no job description, and no performance evaluation procedures, and that reflect debatable remuneration packages? In other words, how can you be well paid if your boss doesn't really know what you do, in the first place?

Reflection on the Advising Process: Complications and Complexities

Important questions for graduate advising faculty to ask are the following: "How effective was my advising model? What did I learn from this model in terms of the personal/academic interrelationship between advisor and advisee? What elements protracted the completion of my degree? If I could do this over again, how would I improve upon this model?" This "student's perspective" is an invaluable tool that faculty can use to pierce into the complexities of the dissertation process from their own personal experience, as former advisees. Thus, the process can open up to continuous process improvement, a quality tool that remains critical to any educational practice but yet, for some reason, does not always inhere within the dissertation advising process to the degree necessary to reverse substantially the attrition rates that are decimating graduate education on the doctoral level.

Yet another aspect of the advising dilemma stems from overtaxed schedules that do not permit advising faculty to spend the time upfront that is required to hone, shape, and conceptualize the research focus. Some faculty hold to philosophical views that suggest it is the student who should define a research agenda, in isolation. The advisor will *know* it when he or she *sees* it. I have encountered students mired in proposal development for years, without success. It wasn't until they reached beyond the impasse that they were able to regain themselves, and their dissertations. But that risk is substantial and, in certain instances, not always fruitful. An enormously talented Ph.D. student in statistics battled with his topic for two years, unable to satisfy his advisor, who refused to intervene in the conceptualization process: he held to the view that the student must work out the complex factors surrounding the study himself. At the suggestion of his advisor, the student departed his program and began to work as a researcher at a prestigious university, during which time we both considered his potential transition to that university's statistics degree program, an unsuccessful endeavor for this ABD (all but dissertation). We then coordinated his readmission to his original program. One additional year of struggling with the same advisor ensued with no progress noted, and the student eventually abandoned the pursuit of his degree.

Advisors may hold firm to their philosophical views and refuse to consider alternate approaches, as in this instance. In addition, they are not always skilled in conceptualization and therefore may experience difficulty in organizing the components of the dissertation in a cohesive, integrated manner, a difficulty that harkens back to the lack of advising training. Whereas it is true that the more frequently we do something, the better we will become at it, it is also true that some targeted training will net more effective results. Another related factor is professional bias: those who serve on committees frequently bring with them their own particular brand of disciplinary bias, which may often bleed into a dissertation concept, tending to confuse rather than enlighten the student's topic.

Training goes beyond the critical leadership aspect of the advisor–advisee relationship, which, sadly, is also too frequently not addressed but includes the technical aspects of conceptualization, conceptual editing/writing or sustaining the research focus across the complexities of the entire dissertation, methodological acumen, statistical support, and various other elements that are part of a complicated scholarly process. It also encompasses the ethics of advising, timeliness of returning editorial commentary, relevance of editorial feedback so that the student understands the nature and context of the comments and knows the mechanisms for successful implementation, and is assured of the advisor's commitment in fostering a successful and rewarding dissertation journey. In too many instances, students do not arrive at this culminating experience with a sense of confidence, accomplishment and anticipation, but with agitation, stress, and uncertainty. Together the lack of time, lack of availability to the student, lack of training, and overloaded faculty schedules presents a formula that undermines opportunities for success.

Moreover, the staid notion that the dissertation is a solitary activity that occurs between advisor and advisee also undermines success. Collaborative models, whether in science, business, medicine, or law, have proven to be some of the most successful models but are not always present in academe. Instead, there are many committees that place the advisor as sole authority over the dissertation, working with students who are clearly at a disadvantage because of the power differential. Committee members may also discover a similar proclivity, even among themselves, to demonstrate deference to the chair and his or her decisions, regardless of logic. Despite the veneer of an egalitarian atmosphere that many advisors would like to create, this is not necessarily a relationship of equals.

Wearing the Mask

In this guarded environment, students exercise great caution with their advisors in addressing their own frailties or lack of knowledge or expertise in research and writing. Unmasking of any deficiency is regarded as costly, despite an advisor's kindly demeanor. The name of the game is survival, and displaying any vulnerability is a primordial mistake.

Advisors, too, ironically enough, fall into this same category in which insecurity wins out over common sense notions of help-seeking. Consider the often-abstruse pathways to the tenure track and think of the numbers of those individuals who fail to secure the prize. In addition, the politics of the department frequently play into this notion: faculty are sometimes left to their own devices to ferret out solutions to difficulties and/or to downplay their problems or to find their own ways through the morass. Carrying the imprimatur of *faculty*, they are regarded as beings with autonomy, in-depth knowledge, and expertise, despite a wide array of indicators that may suggest otherwise. No one has all the answers—one of the reasons why there are dissertation committees. The dynamics of the department hold great sway, and faculty may not always ask for the assistance they deserve. Further, even offers of assistance from fellow colleagues may be perceived as potential effronteries to be avoided assiduously. The result is a growing tendency to play the *waiting game* for emergent problems to be put to rest, rather than to confront them directly. Too often, problems exist on a continuum, perpetuated across time, from student to student, with little change enacted to enhance the advisor–advisee relationship and with questionable intervention from department chairs or faculty colleagues. Avoidance of the stepping-on-toes philosophy at times wins out over exercising good common sense.

What we see, then, is a certain reticence on the parts of both advisors and advisees to disclose their own frailties within the dissertation process.

Compensatory Collaborative Dissertation Advising

So, where are doctoral students going for dissertation and advising support today? Some certainly emerge on the other side of the Ph.D. without difficulty. To be certain, there are dedicated faculty who know their business and have emerged with solid advising reputations, ushering many successful candidates across the graduation stage.

However, some students remain haplessly united with uninformed advisors and stumble upon graduation as a result of hanging around long enough and sticking through the bad times. Others seek out their peers for advice and avoid the risk of unveiling flaws to an advisor or dissertation committee. A Ph.D. process, years in the making, is a high-stakes enterprise that can leave nothing to chance, and so opportunities outside of institutions of higher learning have sprung up to provide students with the support they need to ensure success. Private dissertation coaching and writing retreats, once the bastion of creative writers, are now being sought out by graduate students who are hungry for guidance as well as a quiet place to think and write; dissertation writing boot camps and scholars retreats all offer the promise of a completed dissertation. Some students, like Laura, one of my mentees, steal away for a few days to a solitary bed and breakfast and escape professional as well as domestic responsibilities to find the solace necessary to academic writing.

Confidential settings replete with dissertation coaches provide students with comfort outside of the advising circle. Students learn to navigate between their advisor's guidelines and recommendations, with the assistance of a dissertation coach who is adept at traversing the tumultuous landscape of written language and who sometimes serves as interpreter of an advisor's undecipherable editorial suggestions.

Some universities have created graduate centers designed to provide support in the form of proposal development, statistical consultation, and sustained one-on-one interaction throughout the dissertation process, and even beyond, as students prepare for interviews, conference presentations, publication in peer-reviewed journals, and even salary negotiation. The center that I formerly directed served as an example. But what I learned over the years is that doctoral students require more assistance than ever before, and from a variety of investors, an idea that, unfortunately, runs anathema to the traditional ways in which academicians think about doctoral education: the student should know everything about the dissertation and be well versed in all nuances of the process; only department faculty are able to cultivate the dissertation.

Experience teaches us that this is not so and that students frequently suffer from the lack of knowledge, as well as the lack of support, mentoring, guidance, and advising to which they are entitled. Yes, I use the word *entitled* here, and I agree that it is a strong word, but universities and colleges that offer doctoral programs need to consider the level of their commitment to student and faculty success. The old saying "Put your money where your mouth is" holds sway where the success of graduate education is concerned. Deficiencies in institutional commitment and resources thwart the potential for that success, undermine students' self-confidence, and erode the satisfaction that is naturally derived from working diligently toward a goal and accomplishing it. Further, an unfortunate outcome of graduate education is that students may not understand the purpose of the dissertation and have not been taught its heuristic value, its ability to cultivate their potential as emerging scholars and not to function as a simple branding of an undefined expertise. When considering the concept of what he refers to as Motivation 3.0, Daniel H. Pink (2009) writes of the importance of *autonomy*: the desire to direct our own lives, "acting with choice" (p. 88); *mastery* as a mindset: the urge to become better at doing something that matters to us; and *purpose*: the yearning to do what we do in service of something larger than ourselves. If our doctoral programs do not infuse these philosophical values into each and every course as an overarching philosophy, then it is small wonder that students approach the dissertation as the simple checking of a box, without understanding its transformative power, on both the existential and the disciplinary levels, and without the motivation to engage. We will return to this idea later in the book. Progress is critical to success, and advisors must realize the emergent repercussions when progress is halted or compromised, either philosophically or pragmatically, for themselves, for their advisees, and for their institutions.

Let's go back to the collaborative model for a moment because there is truth and wisdom in that paradigm. I hold to the view that as long as a dissertation coach understands the vision and direction of the advisor, that individual can assist the student in following those directions and can reinforce the pathways to completion. Sometimes just hearing the words from another party solidifies the advisor's advice. The student is more apt to interact with an individual who is not there to judge or criticize but whose role is more interactive, congenial, and based on the *discovery* of ideas through creative engagement. Skilled coaches/conceptual editors move a wandering student back into the advisor's vision and then keep the student in place by focusing the writing in that very direction. Sustaining the momentum and the writing acumen across the vast sometimes-several-hundred-page territory of the dissertation can be daunting to a doctoral student who may have little formal writing experience or whose longest research project was just 25 pages in length. (We will come to modular writing in another chapter.) Assistance in this critical area is essential, and it is far better for all of us to work together, knowingly, collaboratively, as a team, rather than furtively. This approach may be an ideal, however, as the territory of the dissertation is often sacrosanct, closely guarded, protected, and off limits to transgressors. Here is one example.

Advising Insecurity: Backlash

Jenna, one of my advisees, came to me several years ago, troubled by the complexity of her research as well as by the unavailability of her advisor. Jenna complained that her advisor, a busy administrator, was unprepared for their meetings and would read a draft of the concept paper in front of her but generally not before the scheduled meeting. Thus, Jenna's perceptions were that the advisor was ambivalent about the project. Moreover, her sense of the meetings was that the advisor appeared rushed and in a hurry to send her along. Often, *follow on* meetings would be delayed excessively or cancelled at the last moment, without warning. "When I can pin her down," Jenna said, "I can get something out of her in terms of what to do next [on the dissertation], but I can't always get her to work with me consistently."

Jenna and I worked together for months and, finally, after many stops and starts, concluded that she had produced a concept paper that was ready for presentation to her advisor. In place now were highly defined research questions, as well as components for the literature review, which were not present in the draft the student presented to me initially and also not present in the draft that her advisor had first reviewed. Smoothened writing with clear transitions replaced the parataxis that had characterized her work. This progress was the result of continued drafting based on sustained editorial commentary and further revisions. In between were regularly scheduled meetings with me so that we could further refine the concept. I remained confident in the scope and dimension of the concept paper; however, I reiterated that the advisor had "final say" in this matter and could accept the paper, implement additional changes, or simply reject it altogether, which I thought unlikely. We would have to wait for her response, and whatever the outcome we would continue according to the task at hand and work in the direction the advisor recommended. After Jenna's meeting with her advisor, Jenna came to see me for additional advice. I was pleased that her advisor concluded that Jenna had made progress, but then, the following email arrived later the same day:

> Thanks for a great meeting today . . . I feel weird saying this, but I have been thinking about it since our last meeting today . . . when I told [Professor X] that we were working together at our last meeting, her reaction was not great. I got the impression that she is not comfortable with her grad students working with people outside the committee. Is it possible to keep our meetings between us? I am really sorry if this puts you in a weird position and if it does, please let me know. Thank you again for your time today.

This instance of advisor intolerance, as well as student insistence on support, makes a critical point: students are going to seek assistance wherever they can find it, and especially within centers for success (like the one I directed) that their own universities institutionalize as support structures designed originally to assist, retain, and graduate their Ph.D. students. The old model of the scholar-in-isolation is a dead model, as it often leaves students vulnerable to attrition. The notion is "sink or swim," and too many students fail to tread water, let alone swim to shore. The wisdom and economy of the collaborative advising model clearly does not remove the advisor from the process at all. Instead, the model, as I have used it, holds to the primacy of the advisor but also places doctoral advisees within the context of supportive, professional environments in which they can discuss their ideas, clarify the research initiative, and write up a series of decent drafts for presentation to their advisors, who make the ultimate decisions.

Rigidly guarded advising circles through which students detect that they are not permitted to confer with others will not serve and, quite frankly, will be vanquished as students transgress boundaries and reach for the assistance that advisors fail to provide. The point in dissertation research is to cultivate researchers. Speaking *with* and listening *to* doctoral students as they *talk through* their ideas are keys to success. They need to think about the feasibility of their projects; need to listen to their own thoughts, voiced aloud in conceptual conversations as well as reflected in their writing; and need to consider whether they are writing from an intellectually engaged perspective or just moving through the steps, checklist style, in completing their dissertations.

Advisors like Jenna's, whose dichotomous actions barricade students from help-seeking, while they simultaneously and deliberately make themselves unavailable, should avail themselves of Robert Sutton's (2010) book *The No Asshole Rule: Building a Civilized Workplace and Surviving One That Isn't*, a splendid little tome packed with sage observations and advice for anyone who holds to inflated views of themselves and their positions of authority, as well as those suffering from the effects of such people.

The New Momentum: Change

Embracing change in the doctoral advising process is critical to the survival of doctoral students, and embracing the concept of formal training for doctoral advisors and committee members is an integral part of that very process. In addition, the evolution and expansion of the dissertation committee from restricted enclave to collaborative resource circle will usher in the tools, the philosophy, and the cultural change necessary to successful completion of the degree.

The prospect of change is already evident in the many brands of interdisciplinary doctoral degrees that are currently emerging. Many of these programs are creating a welcome stir within the configuration of the dissertation committee, which must embrace multiple disciplines, in multiple concentrations, *across* institutions of higher education, *not* merely *within* them. These new program models will influence and perhaps compel much-needed changes critical to innovative dissertation advising models. Necessarily, this will include new and innovative team members with diverse professional experiences, who will be invited to lend their skills in unprecedented ways that benefit the student, the committee, the discipline, the university. Many years ago, the University of Michigan, for a period of time, compelled faculty in its Department of English to serve on dissertation committees and to oversee the writing process, and thus, a collaborative model such as this one proved highly successful in the monograph's organization, its highly professional appearance, and its proficiency in rhetoric. In addition, collaboration with the committee's content experts ensured symmetry and accuracy between the research and its linguistic presentation.

Epilogue on Jenna

I continued to work with Jenna behind the scenes for a period of time. Within one year of our working together, Jenna defended her dissertation and graduated. The momentum that we had established helped her to overcome an obvious impediment in her progress and deliver a viable dissertation proposal. Although I will not take credit entirely for the successful outcome, I will say that without this intervention and continued support, it is reasonable to conclude that the advisor's pattern of unresponsiveness and unpreparedness would have prevailed for an extended period of time. Was this enough to thwart Jenna's graduation? I can't say for certain. But in my view, the substantial progress and the quality of the three-chapter proposal that we produced served to encourage the advisor to move the student forward with the research phase of the monograph and to defend and graduate.

~ The Take Away ~

1. Be aware that dissertation training models have changed and are moving in the direction of collaborative, integrative, interdisciplinary styles. The old model of the student as *scholar in isolation* is passé.
2. Know that, generally, formal advising training for faculty to serve as dissertation directors is not a standard in place, and

too often faculty are relegated to self-reliance in terms of figuring out this process.
3. Understand the fundamentally critical role of graduate program directors as a conduit to best practices in graduate education for both graduate students and graduate advising faculty. This role is currently undervalued.
4. Understand that dissertating students will find ways to compensate for what they do not receive in the dissertation advising circle.

References

Council of Graduate Schools. (2009). *Ph.D. completion and attrition: Findings from exit surveys of Ph.D. completers.* Retrieved September 2, 2014, from https://cgsnet.org/phd-completion-and-attrition-findings-exit-surveys-phd-completers-0

Missouri State University Graduate College. (2017, November). *A report on the job of graduate program director at Missouri State University.* Springfield, MO: Author.

Pink, D. H. (2009). *Drive: The surprising truth about what motivates us.* New York, NY: Riverhead Books.

Sutton, R. I. (2010). *The no asshole rule: Building a civilized workplace and surviving one that isn't.* New York, NY: Business Plus, Hatchette Book Group.

Chapter 2

The Rules of Engagement

The problem with communication is the illusion that it has taken place.
George Bernard Shaw

Conversations that clarify the dissertation process and that guide and oversee the procedures are necessary. Yet, these do not always happen to the level commensurate with student needs. Committee members and students too frequently are catapulted into the dissertation without the benefit of understanding the process by which they will interact and essentially *live* with each other for an extended period of years. Imagine lawyers trying to plan for a client's defense without the benefit of in-depth discussions among them, or consider a surgical team about to perform a challenging procedure without the benefit of consultation and research. Too often this is what happens with dissertation committees. The process has begun, but the framework to guide the process is not secure, and under these circumstances progress becomes questionable, at best.

It is savvy to begin with the idea that the dissertation is indeed a collaborative project. The student advances the research agenda, but with the explicit interactions, guidance, and advice of the advisor and, of course, the committee and any others brought into the advising circle. Again, the team concept constitutes an ideal approach that must work pragmatically as well as philosophically.

A schism in this perspective, however, can dismantle the solidarity of the team, especially when the unarticulated responsibility for cultivation and design of the proposal, for example, shifts to the student alone, who, in reality, is a novice in the process. Advisors must engage in discussions through which they establish the *Rules of Engagement* or the expectations that will gird the dissertation experience: Who is responsible for proposal design? How will the committee work together as committee members? What are the roles, duties, and responsibilities of the committee, as delineated by the advisor? What are the committee's expectations of the advisee? What are the advisee's expectations of the committee members? How will the committee members interact with the advisee and the advisor, as well as each other? How will the quality of the dissertation be assessed? Successful committees should engage in carefully articulated conversations regarding these procedures so that all members of the advising circle remain similarly aligned in common goals, and it is the role of the dissertation chair to manage this process. *The dissertation is project management raised to an entirely new level.*

Doctoral programs are widely divergent, nuanced, and complex. Procedures will vary accordingly; however, excellent communication, dispensed not only *just in time* but also as part of a continuous, ongoing process, is not negotiable. Repetition and the testing and implementation of ideas are driving components of the dialogue.

The following are some additional elements that constitute the Rules of Engagement for both dissertation committee members and their advisees:

1. *Who is the primary person(s) responsible for the cultivation of the concept paper or Chapter I of the dissertation or the dissertation proposal?*

   Many advisors prefer to oversee this initial point in the process themselves and will work one-on-one with the advisee to shape the direction of the topic. Then, once the document reaches the appropriate stage of development (concept paper or Chapter I or chapters that constitute a proposal, usually three), the advisor generally invites input from the other members of the committee. With sufficient conceptual and editorial revision, the document advances to the point where the committee clears the advisee to continue to hone and shape the dissertation proposal, in preparation for its defense. The proposal defense can be formal, an event to which other students are invited. In this capacity, it serves as a heuristic, imparting important information to students who will soon enter into this phase. In many instances, the formal proposal defense is a nascent precursor to the actual dissertation defense. Students should prepare a Microsoft PowerPoint presentation, complete with handouts for the committee members, and they should be attentive to the advice provided, taking notes, and then implementing corresponding revisions and submitting the revised proposal to the committee on a date acceptable to all parties. However, the proposal defense can also be informal, taking place with the committee members, advisor, and advisee only. Advisors should make this process clear to the advisee. Advisees should make appropriate inquiries to ascertain the specific procedures used by their respective departments, since practices and procedures vary widely across disciplines.

2. *At what point in the process do the other committee members become involved in conceptualizing and editing?*

   Advisors need to clearly communicate the point at which the committee members will be brought into the conversation. As indicated in the example above, some advisors will cultivate the concept paper, Chapter I, or the entire proposal directly with the student, and then will signal the readiness of this document for dissemination to the committee. Other advisors prefer that the entire committee work together throughout the conceptualization and editing process, reviewing all chapters and providing input from the onset of the process. Still others bring specific committee members into the advising circle to oversee only specific points or aspects of the research and writing of the dissertation. Whatever the procedure used, it is critical that an advisor consider the dissertation management strategy that works best for him or her and then communicate clearly that approach to the committee members so that expectations are articulated. In addition, advisees need to understand these procedures so that they remain in league with their advisor's approach and do not inadvertently send chapters to other committee members, when doing so clearly violates the procedures outlined by the advisor, or the reverse: to fail to disseminate chapters to the committee members because the procedures have not been explained. Throughout, advisors must "close the loop" between and among themselves, the committee members, and the advisee.

3. *What is a reasonable "turn around" time required for returning edited chapters?*

   In order to keep the dissertation process moving fluidly, it is necessary for the advisor to engage in a conversation with the committee members to ascertain their response time. This may elicit some discomfort on the part of the advisor, as advisors are keenly aware of the constraints on their colleagues' time. However, *not* having the conversation opens up to the interpretation that the reading/editing task is something to be fit into already-taxed schedules and therefore is not necessarily a priority.

We know that unless there is sustained productive activity throughout the dissertation process, it will lead to a deadly inactivity that results in a contagion to the advisee, as well as to the other committee members. In other words, it is possible that inactivity or complaisance on the part of a committee member can become an untoward signal, whether conscious or unconscious, to other committee members that this project is simply not a priority, not worth the time or effort. Students can easily fall into this abyss. Protracted turnaround times from committee members can dismantle the motivation of even the most stalwart of students. Without the clarity of an agreement regarding the management of chapters and editorial feedback, delays can become normative, and dissertation completion can languish.

One of my colleagues conducted a dissertation seminar for inducting newly dissertating students into the dissertation process. She posed this question: "What do you think is a reasonable time for committee members to return your chapters?" One student replied, "Well, they should do that soon," and so my colleague pushed further to inquire about the meaning of "soon," and the student replied, "Several months or maybe even a semester." The phenomenon to bear in mind here is that students will absorb a great deal of inconvenience, and in some instances even maltreatment, before they raise an objection. Simply put, they have not traveled this road before, and they have limited expectations regarding appropriate procedures or interactions. What civilities are they entitled to? Committee members who take months to respond with editorial commentary send an unfortunate signal to each other and to the student that the advisee's work is not important. In effect, their actions become normative or par for the course, and students who perceive their own limited power accept these behaviors although they often resent them. With the emphasis on timely completion of the dissertation, it is necessary for dissertation advisors to establish the groundwork for editorial turn-around, for both committee members and advisees.

Let's turn this dynamic around: committee members submit editorial feedback, and the advisee takes months to implement changes and return the next draft. This too creates a backlog of work for committee members, who can lose momentum as well as the keen insight and intellectual command of the document that is sustained only through continued and timely writing and drafting. The advisor, as process manager, must bear in mind that the street runs both ways, and he or she must protect the committee members as well as the advisee.

4. *Are edited chapters to be shared by the entire committee and sent to the advisor first for approval or sent directly to the student? Are these to be in hard copy or electronic?*

It is important to establish the order in which this activity occurs. Committee members contribute to the process in invaluable ways, their ideas shaping and honing arguments, refining points, creating logical connections, and smoothening language. There are various ways to approach such procedures. The advisor may choose to engage in such editorial work first, and then he or she will forward the document directly to the student for implementation. However, there are other times when the advisor will ask committee members to send their chapter reviews directly to the advisee. Sharing of edited chapters among the committee members offers the best advantage to sustaining quality. The most advantageous model is to group edit, using Microsoft SharePoint, Google Docs, or some other type of software that permits all editors to view each other's work. This approach saves time and avoids a duplication of effort: Three people addressing the same editorial issue just wasted their time; if two members observe that an issue has been rectified, they can move on to other editorial tasks, knowing that another colleague has taken control of the problem.

The issue of hard copy versus electronic file is a matter of personal preference. Many committee members eschew the idea of editing in "track changes" or in any sort of electronic environment. They prefer the hard copy/pen-to-paper approach and will print edited hard copies to be either mailed to or collected by their advisees. Also, for some committee members, electronic dissemination is easily achieved through scanning and sending documents as attachments via email. Others are technologically astute and prefer working in a technical environment. Again, it is necessary that this point be discussed so that the advisee as well as committee members articulate their preferences and their working methodology. The advisor has to establish a reasonable level of comfort for the team players.

5. *What is the best mode/time frame of communication between and among committee members and the advisee: email, phone, text, Zoom, Webex, etc.?*

    This appears to be somewhat forthright, but actually the methods that we select can be fraught with difficulty, and for a variety of reasons. With technology as advanced as it is, we can reach each other anywhere, anytime, and maybe we all don't want to allow that accessibility into our worlds. However, it is advisable to establish the best mode of contact. If by email, then should everyone be copied on an email? If via phone, is the voice mailbox on the cell phone or office phone full, so that messages cannot be left? Are phone calls or email inquiries being ignored or returned promptly? Are cell phones turned off for the majority of the time, making access impossible? Is it permissible for a student to contact a professor at home or only during office hours? Establish early on the methods and modes of communication.

6. *Are faculty available for continued work on the dissertation during the summer sessions or only during the fall and spring semesters?*

    Students need to understand the parameters that surround their interactions with committee members. In addition, committee members need to understand the expectations delineated by the advisor, as well as to respect the needs of the student. If committee members are not available during summer sessions, then a planning agenda by the end of the spring semester is in order to take the student through the summer sessions up until fall when the faculty return. In this manner, students can continue to make progress, despite the fact that their committee may not be available for feedback. The delineated plan will keep them focused, on track, and making progress. Herein lies the value of a dissertation coach who oversees the process, even during the down time of summer.

7. *How often should the dissertation committee meet?*
Dissertation committees need to meet as often as necessary. The frequency should be determined by the advisor, in concert with the committee members. If the dissertation process is difficult or has become protracted, then more frequent meetings will be necessary, especially if there are specific issues that must be addressed. Similar to any working body of professionals with a specific goal to reach, the committee must be engaged with each other in terms of a physical, intellectual, and ethical presence. It is a team aligned with the common goals of producing a quality dissertation and moving the student through to graduation.

8. *Who sets the agenda for the dissertation committee meeting?*
The agenda can be established by all members of the committee who raise particular concerns or simply want to affirm that the student is making progress. Meetings for the latter purpose are just as important as meetings for the former. These issues can be centered in difficulties that hold the potential for protracting the process: data collection or analysis, for example; poor academic writing skills; delays in securing appropriate research compliance approvals; or difficulties with statistics, among others.

9. *When discrepancies in the editorial feedback are provided to the student, who is responsible for negotiating these discrepancies?*
Another element for advisors to consider is the manner in which to resolve contradictory editorial suggestions. Students who receive contradictory signals are generally not equipped to contend with these issues, either pragmatically or politically. In addition, they do not always know where to go for support or how to determine the direction they should

take. Logic would tell us that they should take the issue to the dissertation chair or directly to the committee members, and that makes sense, but not necessarily to the dissertating student who wants to avoid causing trouble on any level. And so, they live in a kind of paradoxical stasis—in other words, *stuck*. They are caught by the need to implement a recommended change, but also by the inability to negotiate between the two contradictory impulses of their committee members. In these instances, the advisor can carefully monitor all editorial feedback to ensure that such contradictory elements are resolved in a way that does not exacerbate the issue for either the student or the committee members.

10. *What is the timeline that the dissertation advisor and committee members set for the student's completion of the dissertation and graduation?*

    The work to be accomplished must follow a particular order, and generally it is important that everyone work according to the projected graduation date. Failure to work toward this goal will result in an excessive and unnecessary flexibility that simply defers the important steps that must be taken. Parkinson's Law will rule supreme: work will expand to fill the time available for its completion.

    Expanding and shifting timelines threaten degree completion: defense dates that are set and then broken, graduation dates that sit on the calendar more as wish fulfillment rather than a viable target, and chapters with a turn-around time of months can undermine advisees' ability to succeed. Most faculty members are conservative when it comes to setting a defense or graduation date; they know full well that the semester or session in which a student plans to graduate is actually quite short. By using a *Backward Calendar* (see Table 1), based on the intended date of graduation and then moving back from that date to account for all the elements that must be accomplished prior to graduation, it is clear that the student does not have the advantage of a full semester's time, and less so during a summer session. For example, at my university, a student graduating in the fall semester (December) may need to have scheduled a dissertation defense by the end of October, with the first week in November as the last date to actually hold the defense. Defended dissertations, in final form, must be submitted to the Graduate College by the middle of November, a full month prior to the actual graduation. This schedule does not at all reflect the timetable necessary for the committee review of the dissertation, as well as the student's preparation for the defense, nor does it account for post-defense implementation of any revisions that the committee suggests.

The fall semester then becomes easily cannibalized by an intensive, demanding process that is better served if the final draft of the dissertation is prepared in the summer session prior to the intended date of a fall graduation. In fact, some programs operate by this more flexible timeline so that the committee members and their advisees are not rushing breathlessly to the defense and graduation. Students generally fail to appreciate the complexities of coming to the finish line; the end of the process may hold more difficulties than ever imagined, and so it is imperative that the team work together to coordinate these end-of-process efforts.

Table 1. The Backward Calendar for Doctoral Students

Action Plan	Intended Graduation Date
Defended dissertation submitted to Graduate College/School	One month prior to graduation
Dissertation defense	One month prior to submission of final dissertation to the Graduate College/School
Deadline to schedule defense	One month prior to dissertation defense
Secure committee approval to defend	At least 2 weeks prior to deadline for scheduling defense
Suggested time for submission of completed dissertation draft to committee	At least 3 months prior to scheduling dissertation defense
Apply for graduation	Apply 4 months prior to the intended graduation date
Complete forms: Committee Appointment, Proposal Approval, and Doctoral Candidacy	Submit each form to the Graduate College/School as soon as it is completed at the respective step

11. *How committed are the dissertation committee members to the dissertation process?*
    Do the members have sufficient time in their schedules to accommodate the demands of serving on a committee? This is an important question for prospective dissertation advisors and committee members to ask themselves. The question is not benign. Academic and personal demands can be overwhelming at times, and these, set within the continuous demands of a dissertation experience that can be years in the making, may not make for a viable engagement. It is critical that the advisor and committee members ascertain the time available to them to invest in the advisee's progress. Ph.D. students require more time, not less time, and many will require sustained guidance and mentoring. In addition, prospective committee members may already be working on several other committees, thereby reducing the time available to assist new advisees. Faculty must consider their own resources, as well as remain aware of the time that dissertating students will certainly require. Different students will have different needs. For example, some students are exceptionally independent, self-motivated, and self-directed and will not require the same investment in time as a student who requires extensive oversight.

    Tenure-track faculty are taxed by publication, service, and teaching demands, an academic triathlon of significant proportion that tests expertise, endurance, and persistence. In short, they must consider the time available before committing to a student who asks them to chair or serve on a committee. Once the commitment is made, it must be honored. Committee members who take these obligations without cognizance of the time commitment often place their advisees and themselves at risk.

12. *For the advisor or chair: Is there sufficient expertise among the committee members to sustain their presence on the committee and their contributions to the content of the advisee's dissertation?*
    A qualitative dissertation without the benefit of a qualitative expert; a student writing a dissertation on quality assessment without the benefit of a quality expert; a student writing a

dissertation on interdisciplinary, international evaluation without a content specialist in this area; a quantitative dissertation without the benefit of a skilled statistician—all bode poorly for the outcomes of a viable dissertation. Although it is true that in many non-scientific fields the advisor's expertise does not have to match precisely the student's research interests, certainly the committee must be configured in a manner that encompasses purposefully the content area or area of expertise necessary to evaluate, guide, and assess the student's progress in research, as well as the contribution to the field. I will continue this discussion later in the book.

13. *How will the dissertation committee assess the student's progress, as well as the quality of the dissertation?*
This is a complex question that may well be teased out or determined as the student builds toward the dissertation. Yet, it is an evaluative question to bear in mind throughout the conceptualization, research, and writing processes. The question harkens to the idea of the *quality indicators* established by individual departments regarding dissertation quality, research design, and scholarly presentation. Are there carefully delineated dissertation standards in place on the department level that are also well represented within individual dissertation committees? In addition, are advisees aware of these standards so they tailor their efforts to meet these objectives? Certainly, such standards account for the quality of the writing, the fulfillment of the purpose of each dissertation chapter, the cohesiveness of the presentation of information, the logic in constructing an academic narrative, the quality of the research and the research method, and the significance of the research and what the research intends to accomplish as it informs the discipline and contributes to the field in innovative ways, among other factors.

It is critical that the dissertation not exist as a mere exercise in a long checklist of program requirements. It is the litmus test that demonstrates the student's scholastic capability to stand squarely as a researcher in the field. By no means the student's *magnum opus*, it is nevertheless, as Gary A. Olson and Julie Drew (1998) write, "the last major project that a scholar completes as a 'student'" but with the expectation that this is an initial stepping stone on the scholar's evolutionary pathway. Paul Cantor (1989) writes, "You are your dissertation," a statement that blends the student's monograph with career potential and desirability in a complex and challenged hiring economy, and so a standard of excellence is requisite. With these ideas as guiding factors then, what is the identity of the dissertation and how does it reflect on the identity of the student, the advisor, the committee, and the respective university? Advisors must think in global terms about these factors in order to meet their advising obligation and, in good conscience, sign the dissertation approval forms signaling the advancement of the student to the Ph.D. Writing from the perspective of English studies, Olson and Drew caution that "a dissertation that most resembles a professional scholarly monograph in both form and content is likely to serve the candidate best." However, the idea of appropriate form, content, and accessibility is true for all fields. For additional information, please refer to Barbara Lovitts' (2007) work, "Making the Implicit Explicit."

14. *Will the work of the committee be incorporated into the student's Annual Review of Progress?*

    Many institutions of higher education have enacted an annual review policy, which is a policy that applies to academic review and assessment of graduate student progress. It considers both students' accomplishments as well as problematic concerns and provides a balanced perspective, certainly not a "doom and gloom" odyssey. Whether departments and programs actually comply with the policy is yet another story; however, the philosophy that guides the policy concerns students' rights to be appropriately advised of their continued academic progress, as well as to anticipate an opportunity to remedy any perceived shortcomings in attaining their goals. Yes, we live in a litigious society and must be aware of potential lawsuits: universities must provide such assessments as part of due process and must consider the potential legal ramifications of not doing so. However, we should consider less the concept of lawsuits and more the concepts of student success and retention, in my view, so that we remain appropriately aligned with quality and best practices.

The policy considers not only academic progress but also encompasses ethical considerations. In addition, it takes into account time-to-completion: 6 years for master's students and 7 years for doctoral students at my university. These stats may vary from institution to institution. The purpose of such a policy is actually centered in retention initiatives, as it is critical that students are apprised of not only the elements that lend toward success, but also those elements that may protract timely completion of the degree or that threaten entirely the completion of the degree. At my university, students admitted to a graduate program are supposed to be advised, from the onset of their admission, to read the student code, as well as to familiarize themselves with the requirements of their respective programs as delineated in the program handbook. These include sections of the graduate catalogue that concern students' duties, responsibilities, program expectations, and other pertinent information necessary for their successful trajectories to the graduate degree. As part of the annual review process, students first provide a written self-assessment of their progress to degree completion, and this document is reviewed by an annual review committee, configured by respective departments as deemed appropriate. Among those are the following configurations: faculty mentor and committee, dissertation committee, faculty committee, training committee, program committee, and committee of the whole. In this manner, the dual assessment process creates an ongoing dialogue through which expectations and continued progress come to the table, so to speak. If any disparities or any lack of cohesiveness becomes apparent, then remediation of difficulties ensues. Barring academic misconduct issues or academic insufficiency (low GPAs) or ethical concerns, students generally have one academic year in which to address issues. The policy, as my university has crafted it, permits for three options: continuation, continuation with reservation, and dismissal.

However, in my opinion, it is important to emphasize the necessity of including progress on the dissertation into the annual review. Moreover, it is imperative that the one-year policy (or the recommended time period) for remediation of concerns be revamped for students at this particular advanced stage, as review every semester or at least once in a six-month period is necessary. Dissertating students should not be left to their own devices for extended periods, as continued oversight and management of the process are requisite for student success. When this process is built into an annual review, the department faculty and the student are joined in league with the common goals of timely degree completion. Elements of the dissertation process that are problematic or that protract degree completion rise to the forefront, and the committee as a whole (if other than the student's dissertation committee) can intervene, establish communication with the advisee and his or her dissertation chair and committee members, and work together toward the common goal. If not, the student's lack of progress remains invisible, and this invisibility opens up to the potential for non-completion of the degree.

~ The Take Away ~

1. Dissertation advisors should establish and communicate a carefully arranged set of guidelines that serve as parameters for dissertation committee members and doctoral advisees. Doing so ensures heightened awareness of the dissertation process and its objectives.
2. Use a Backward Calendar to keep track of student progress in meeting graduation timelines.

References

Cantor, P. (1989). The graduate curriculum and the job market: Toward a unified field theory. In A. Lunsford, H. Moglen, & J. E. Slevin (Eds.), *The future of doctoral studies in English* (pp. 9–14). New York: MLA.

Lovitts, B. (2007). *Making the implicit explicit: Creating performance expectations for the dissertation.* Sterling, VA: Stylus.

Olson, G. A., & Drew, J. (1998). (Re) Reenvisioning the dissertation in English studies. *College English, 61*(1), 56–66.

Chapter 3

Defining Editing Expectations: More Rules of Engagement

The expectation that the doctoral student should be familiar with the internal workings of the committee or with the rigor of research, know how to write within an academic frame, and come to the academy equipped with a vast array of problem-solving skills is misplaced. This perspective must be reexamined. All of their intellectual brilliance and capability aside, such students actually are quite vulnerable within the foreign contexts of the dissertation landscape. Ongoing communication from the inception of the process and throughout, until the culmination of the degree and even beyond, is critical. And yet, given the extensive visual and verbal communication stimuli to which we are exposed each day, it is perplexing that many of us, including advisors and their advisees, are frequently poor communicators.

Highlight and Delete

Committee members, as well as the advisor, may assume that the advisee understands their editorial commentary on a dissertation chapter, or their instructions, or their advice, only to learn later that the student may have missed the point altogether. Faced with a returned chapter that seems to bear scant trace of improvement, they bristle, their time seemingly wasted. They discover that a problematic paragraph or sentence that requires further clarification has been conveniently excised from the chapter, neatly eliminated so as to eliminate the need for editorial revision. *Highlight and delete* often becomes the advisee's response to addressing an editorial concern. I noticed this behavior when I taught undergraduate writing and literature courses, but I had not been aware of this proclivity among doctoral students until I began working with them; it was disconcerting to learn that so many had not acquired strategic editorial skills at this advanced stage of graduate study. Cognizance of this facet of students' editorial behavior can save a great deal of time later, when sustained writing and editing through continuous drafting and revision are requisite.

Leave Well Enough Alone

The editorial process is a delicate one, but it is clear that if a committee member does not touch a particular area of the text, he or she is communicating that that section is fine, *as is*, and does not require further work. At least, that would be my interpretation. However, this statement, simple as it may be, often sets up a series of oscillating, contradictory impulses between advisor and advisee, as the advisee may continue to initiate ongoing changes and revisions, even at those points in the text not identified as being problematic. This penchant results in a series of drafts that are perpetually changing and that have no constancy. This means that the advisor and the advisee are continually revising a draft that will never advance to the next level of development; hence, it remains only a nascent entity, expiring at its birth. *The threat to completion of the monograph is clear: we have a series of firsts only and will produce no final product as long as this activity continues.*

Advisors and committee members need to clearly announce: "If I haven't touched that part of your work, leave it alone." As conceptual editors, committee members try to *build* to a finished product, with all of the ideas, points of logic, and arguments woven together like threads in a fine tapestry. If the threads are continuously being pulled out, the threat to the integrity of the whole is obvious, a fact not lost on Odysseus's enterprising wife Penelope and, eventually, her unwanted court of suitors.

Use This One, Not That Other One

(The subject line of an email sent to me by a student)

Committee members may well read and edit an entire chapter and return it, only to check their email and discover that the student asks them to review a *new* version, which the student has just updated, but without receiving the committee members' most recent editorial commentary. This *new* one is the *real* one he or she wants commentary on, because of a sense of insecurity perhaps and also disenchantment with the one *already* sent. Caught up in a tenuous process, students behave in a tentative manner, second guessing themselves and somewhat impatient to move things along. They are not aware that they are wasting their own and their committee members' time. They must be taught the Rules of Engagement regarding the submission of chapters for review and the process for implementing changes, without intervening draft chapters thrown in willy-nilly. They should be instructed to *walk away* from the document and let it *cool down* prior to dispatching it to the committee. Distancing themselves from it provides much needed objectivity and also permits them to proofread, without emotionalism. In this manner, they establish a certain rapport with their own writing style and come to understand the value of stepping back from the narrative. This step enables them to dedicate themselves to the writing process, as well as spares committee members' valuable time and energy. Simply put, you don't have time to read countless iterations of a draft that is not worthy of your time in reviewing because it has been poorly prepared. Advisees need to be taught to value *your expertise* and avail themselves of *your time* productively.

Advisees certainly want to make a favorable impression, and so submission of a draft is somewhat risky and carries with it the unfortunate concern that it will be judged and found lacking or determined to be insufficient, worthy of criticism. That is a frightening feeling, alleviated only if advisors explain that continual drafting *of an evolving document* is the only way to reach the kind of excellence that will stand a scholar in good stead and that will uphold the quality of the monograph. Committee members' time is a valuable commodity that must be respected.

Advisors could emphasize to their advisees that once a draft is submitted for the committee's review, advisees must wait for and implement the committee's revisions or recommendations for *that* particular draft of *that* chapter; the submission of intervening chapters is not, nor should it ever be, part of the editing process, as such actions throw off the entire process and largely waste everyone's time. Concomitantly, elements of the monograph that have not drawn untoward criticism from the committee should be left intact and not subjected to elimination or revision until or unless such changes are warranted. Lastly, advisors who clarify or explain their own editorial process from the beginning of their interactions reach a stage of agreement early on with their advisees regarding their working style and their working process.

They should ensure their advisees understand the elements of a working editorial style so that everyone remains focused on a common goal. In essence, "This is how I am going to edit your chapters and work with you, and this is what I expect you to do with my commentary. If you have questions or concerns about anything, let me know and we'll discuss it so that you are clear." The idea of having an open door policy is critical: students need to know that their questions and/or the need for clarification of ideas are always welcome. Students may hint at their needs but often are never as direct as they would like to be or think they are.

Brent's Story: Blurred Lines

One advisor with whom I worked drew long and convoluted lines with arrows through and around the narrative texts of chapters that he edited in his own handwriting. In addition, many of these arrows ended up in question marks and also cryptic comments that were undecipherable in terms of content and meaning. Brent, his advisee, seldom understood the rationale behind the question mark: Was the advisor disagreeing with a particular critic that the student had mentioned, or was he disagreeing with the student's argument, or was a particular theory problematic, or was the sentence not grammatically correct? Which? All? Some? He struggled to understand, voicing his frustration to me, but he would never consider asking the advisor for clarification, despite my numerous entreaties. On the other hand, the advisor was not particularly enamored of his advisee's seeming reticence to implement critical changes to the text. Because Brent did not exactly understand what the advisor wanted, he resorted to guessing, which was not a satisfactory way to address the advisor's editorial concerns and did not win him any points: his drafts never seemed to improve. At times, with his own frustration surely mounting, the advisor resorted to the use of the exclamation point, a signifier that Brent could not discern whether it was a positive reinforcement of an idea he had expressed (*Right on!*) or a negative commentary (*Come on, now—really?*).

In the end, as a member of Brent's committee, I had to make educated decisions about how best to address the advisor's concerns. These had mounted considerably and resulted in the advisor's understandable refusal to let Brent proceed to a defense; the dissertation was not well written and therefore could not be approved. To use an oft-quoted saying, Brent and his advisor passed each other like two ships in the night, dangerously close to a collision. This unhappy process continued throughout their association. You can well understand the impact of a failed editorial process in this one small example of misaligned communication. Ironically, the advisor's familiarity in associating with this student over a course of many years seemed to have obscured the fact that English was not Brent's first language and that Brent had been struggling painfully to maintain academic rigor in his writing. His math and stats skills were solid and well represented in histograms, charts, and tables, but reflected through the narrative prism of another language, his skills seemed quite modest.

Brent would often lament, "If only I could write this in French!" The vague presence of the question marks, exclamation points, and terse commentary had served only to increase his level of anxiety, not prompt him into a more progressive writing style. It was not until Brent had finally approached the painstaking advent of the eventual dissertation defense that the advisor realized the extent of Brent's language issues. In his view, his comments were direct and clear; in Brent's view, the advisor's comments were abstruse and calculated to create frustration. The problem was exacerbated by the fact that the advisor, according to Brent, sometimes canceled meetings without warning, was sometimes unprepared for the meetings he did show up for, and essentially appeared disinterested in Brent's progress. And so the editing issues were simply one dimension of a much larger misalliance between them that was rooted in a questionable advising model, but not in personal dislike. Actually, outside of their advisor–advisee roles, they had a congenial relationship and got along splendidly. It is important to note, however, that advisees will put up with a great deal and suffer many frustrations, inconveniences, and hardships in order to win the coveted Ph.D. and, in many instances, their advisors will never know these hidden stories.

~ The Take Away ~

Assumptions, then, on the part of the advisor or the advisee frequently pose threats to the integrity of the process. Relying on the routine ways in which people work together, whether effectively or ineffectively, can dismantle professional relationships. Routine behaviors yield the continuity of the routine only, not necessarily the continuity of progress, and certainly not quality. Dissertation chairs and committee members may find themselves enmeshed in unsatisfactory behavioral patterns that do not necessarily yield student productivity or advancement in completing the degree. Brent's case serves as a good example.

1. *Advisors*: If it appears that your advisees are not making sufficient progress or are taking an extraordinarily long time to complete the dissertation or are not implementing the editorial improvements to the text that you expect, it is time to reflect upon your communication process. If you are not taking into account the *reader's perspective*, the way that your advisee interprets your commentary and makes sense of it, your suggestions may be more "hit or miss" rather than productive. Consider that, although Hemingwayesque editing may be *your* style, it may not serve your *advisee*. Some students may need a more interactive, hands-on editing process: detailed writing in the margins, so to speak; dialogue within the text; or scheduled meetings to explain problematic elements or even to address how to implement editorial suggestions. In certain business and Institutional Review Board (IRB) circles, this is known as a "facilitated review," during which highly complex editorial and procedural details are explained to a writer. It is not a given that students know how to employ your comments to enhance the narrative.

2. *Advisees*: On the other hand, if you are a doctoral student struggling with the same recurrent editing issues when working with your advisor or committee and failing to make progress, it is time to cease and desist. Edging close to the time-to-degree (TTD) policy set by your university but without consistent progress is a signifier of difficulty. If you find yourself tackling your advisor in hallways in order to have a meeting, your progress is already compromised. It is time to

reevaluate these circumstances and contemplate alternative mechanisms for success, such as actually *talking* with someone who can provide guidance and mentorship. Remaining in place, repeating the same actions over and over again, failing to communicate, and remaining stuck in an editing quagmire are tantamount to a metaphoric death or, at least as Einstein observed, insanity.

Chapter 4

The Toxic Committee

Change—or Die!
Gordon Ramsay

The definition of insanity is doing the same thing over and over and expecting a different outcome.
Albert Einstein

Many individuals fall into the mode of behavior observed by Albert Einstein and, more recently, Gordon Ramsay, whether it be unsatisfactory careers, precarious businesses, woeful supervisors, disappointing spouses/significant others, or empty friendships. Many of us continue to cling to what we know best, even if the experiences are not necessarily pleasant or rewarding. Some remain stuck in place, committed to the possibility of an alternate outcome that is almost always chimerical, a fantasy.

In the case of the dissertating student, the outcomes of excessive delays in degree completion can be deadly. Consider the fact that protracted time-to-degree frequently results in loss of employment opportunities, which, if the student has taken out educational loans, can result in compromised financial standing and overwhelming debt, delays in purchasing a home or car, even getting married and having children, the standard entrees to adulthood. Consider fields such as the humanities, where it is not uncommon for time-to-degree to expand to 9 years or more for history, or, in the case of English, 8 to 10 years on average. With student enrollment rates plummeting, faculty lines being reduced or cut altogether, and current faculty maintaining their positions and postponing retirement, it becomes apparent that the employment picture for recent or soon-to-be graduates is somewhat foreboding. If you have noticed a certain sense of *dis-ease*, angst, and uncertainty among your doctoral students as they consider their futures, you would be right in your assessment. Life on the other side of the Ph.D. is questionable in terms of deliverables and outcomes.

Companies such as *The Versatile PhD* are all too familiar with the lack of possible employment opportunities in academe and have devised ways to cultivate awareness of alternate careers for Ph.D.s. By helping them to cast wide nets into the employment oceans in the hopes of garnering positions in related or similar areas of expertise, The Versatile PhD helps doctoral graduates position themselves for lives outside of the academic arena. Considering the numbers of Ph.D. graduates who are relegated to adjunct faculty positions or those unemployed/underemployed entirely, it is clear that the philosophical and business orientation of such an enterprise as The Versatile PhD is centered in the reality that not only is the academic job market not the prosperous horizon it once was, but the entire national economic prospect may be significantly challenged by the imbalance between Ph.D. preparation and the array of corresponding employment opportunities.

It is not surprising then that The Versatile PhD arrives just in time as an anodyne of sorts. William Bennett and David Wilezole (2013), in their book *Is College Worth It?*, question the relevance of securing secondary and postsecondary educational degrees in a world challenged by a dearth of employment opportunities in fields that may be obscure or highly limited in terms of potential, such as "medieval studies" or "anthropology," or in fields such as the humanities that have an overabundance of graduates balanced precariously against a restricted number of positions. Newly envisioned degrees designed to bolster student enrollment sometimes fall into this category. One program was aborted almost at its onset. An interdisciplinary master's degree in sustainability at one university never made it to program launch and most likely for good reason: despite the fact that the topic itself is of global importance, the alignment with the labor market remained ambiguous, a fact borne out by the enrollment of not one student. Poor program marketing may also have contributed to the demise of the program, as well as the fact that the design of a certificate may have constituted a more viable and financially accessible alternative to a two-year master's degree.

Let's integrate a few ideas to gain a more cogent perspective of this issue. Take the concept of an overproduced Ph.D. field, a reasonable expectation of unemployment or underemployment, the toxicity of a fractured dissertation committee whose actions result in the near possibility of degree non-completion, and place all of these factors within a student's lived educational experience.

Jack's Story

I'll begin with the good news: Jack is a Ph.D. graduate in a field known for its protracted time-to-degree, but his arrival to degree completion was fraught with stress and uncertainty.

By the time Jack came to me, he had accrued over 70 dissertation credit hours (12 were required for his degree) and was $100,000 in debt and on the verge of divorce. His full-time job and his full-time worries were centered in completion of his degree, but he was not making progress and had become, as he himself describes it, "desperate."

Background

Jack had entered his program in 2004 and completed his comprehensive examinations and configured his four-member committee by 2008. Several months after the committee had been convened, one of the members suffered an untimely death, an event that disrupted the momentum that had been established. The professor who died was replaced, and despite the tragic loss, Jack seemed on track for timely degree completion. But by 2013, he still had not graduated. According to his estimate of the situation, his dissertation was not suffering from lack of academic rigor nor did it reflect an inability on his part to conduct research and write. Jack felt secure moving forward because no one on his committee claimed anything to the contrary at that point in time.

Pathology of Committee

The difficulty lay in the pathology of his dissertation committee, which had, like a chameleon, been figured and reconfigured several times, with faculty members joining, serving for a period of time, and then by force of fate finding themselves unable to continue their service for a variety of reasons. These changes did not incorporate new paperwork by which reconstituted committees should be convened, and thus no formal process or paperwork trail existed. This lack of continuity proved to be the fatal flaw, one that characterized the committee's interactions with a sense of randomness and contingency. This was a group without a plan of action and with shifting commitments to their advisee, a world in which anything can happen, or not.

After a great deal of tussling, Jack received approval for the prospectus, although initial comments from one committee member (Professor A) signaled concern regarding the rationale for the study, but in the end this individual approved the prospectus, and so over the course of the next two years Jack began to research and write in earnest. During this time, Jack noticed what he deemed to be increasingly long periods from the time he submitted drafts to the committee and their turn-around time for submission of edits back to him. Eventually, Jack had to request an extension to complete his doctoral program because he had inched too close to the period allocated for completion of the degree. By 2012, one committee member (Professor B) informed him that his dissertation was on the "home stretch," and another (Professor A) indicated that he was on his last set of revisions. Professor C, who had replaced the professor who died, provided editorial input but also appeared to share his colleagues' view that essentially the dissertation was progressing.

False Assumptions

Jack interpreted these comments to mean that he would soon defend the dissertation and graduate. But then, without informing Jack in advance, one committee member (Professor A) went on sabbatical for an entire semester and was unavailable to respond to email or to provide continued editorial commentary. Around this same time, Professor B began to experience schedule constraints and indicated that time was not available to read Jack's drafts, as other professional obligations required more immediate attention. Jack, sensing that he had no authority to complain or to press the issue, concluded that he had no other recourse but to wait.

And then, a glimmer of hope emerged, and it seemed that the defense would be scheduled, but abruptly Professor A, who had taken the sabbatical, decided that his area of expertise did not actually align with the student's topic, and so he withdrew from the committee. At this same time, Professor C experienced personal issues and subsequently resigned, leaving only Professor B and the dissertation advisor as committee members.

Riding the Committee Carousel

At this point, the dissertation advisor decided to replace Professor C with Professor D, an external committee member. Professor

B, indicating that Professor D lacked scholarly expertise in the advisee's topic, objected to the new addition to the committee, and so Professor D was not added to the committee. Professor C, who was the content expert but who had resigned from the committee due to personal issues, decided suddenly to rejoin the committee, but indicated that other projects would take precedence. In addition, he stated that his stamina had declined. More blurred lines.

By the time Jack sought out my assistance, a chilly silence reigned. Jack, who initially had been told he could proceed to a defense in the previous year, after implementing revisions, was now told by Professor B that he could not. In the interim, Jack did not receive any editorial feedback from Professor B or from any committee member for the drafts produced in the year prior. His dissertation was at a complete standstill.

The Apex

Jack revised his dissertation as best he could and sent the draft to Professors B and C, both of whom continued to claim they had no time to read, as other projects required their attention. Jack, recognizing that he was in trouble, complained to his advisor, who dismissed Professors B and C from committee service and attempted to replace them. Professor E, a professor external to the department but internal to Jack's university, joined the committee and was satisfied with the dissertation, its concept, and Jack's research and writing acumen. Professor E was joined by Professor F, a professor from Jack's department. At this point, Jack attempted to put into place the paperwork to convene his new committee. The chair of the department, greatly disturbed at the flawed nature of the entire process, refused to sign the paperwork and route it for the additional signatures required. Instead, he thought that some form of communication between the original committee and the reconfigured committee should take place to determine next steps in this problematic process; the second committee needed to learn of the first committee's critical objections to Jack's dissertation and to ensure that those problematic elements were addressed. If all of this sounds like the coming together of the North and the South during the Civil War, you would be correct. A meeting never took place, but correspondences ensued.

Complicating the issue was that Professor F's graduate faculty status was due to expire, making Professor F ineligible to serve as a member of the committee. This obstacle was overcome with a simple waiver enacted, the appropriate paperwork convening the new committee put into place, and official signatures gathered. The second committee conferred directly with Jack and reviewed and returned draft chapters in record time, and Jack proceeded to his successful defense. The storm had passed.

Epilogue

It is important to note that while circumstances such as this one are rare, nevertheless, the details serve as harbingers of complications that can thwart successful outcomes. Although most committees stay together and succeed in their efforts to graduate their advisees, some do not. This one serves as a good example of a dysfunctional committee that could well be described as toxic.

This committee never worked fluidly as a team united with a common purpose, and its willingness to surrender the advisee's needs to second-place status undermined Jack's ability to complete the dissertation in a timely manner. As it is, it took Jack 9 years from start to finish: time not working at a job, time not on the tenure track, time accruing financial debt, time spent away from family.

Note: In a study that I conducted (Di Pierro, 2014)[1] that includes data from a 10-year period, I found that, on average, most students, especially those in STEM (science, technology, engineering, mathematics) fields, graduated with the first committee. Other fields, such as education, graduated 247 students with an average time-to-degree (TTD) of 6.34 years; of this number, 133 Ph.D. students had configured only one committee with no extensions for a TTD of 5.11 years. Out of the total of 247 graduates, 49 convened two committees with no extensions for a TTD of 5.68 years, and 19 convened one committee but required one extension for a TTD of 8.62 years. In rare instances, students changed committees multiple times and also required multiple extensions.

Each configuration is costly in terms of time and momentum, and so organizing the right committee the first time is critical. Policies that govern reconfiguration of committees vary across institutions, and so understanding the relevant rules and guidelines before assembling a committee is very important. For example, a university

---

1. It is important to note that this research was centered in one institution and results are not generalizable to other institutions of higher education.

may permit committee reconfiguration but also impose a time limit for completion of this reorganization. Delays in locating new members are common, especially during summer months when faculty may not be readily available, and so advisees unable to conform to this guideline may find themselves separated from their programs.

Analysis

Several factors marred the progress of this committee and protracted Jack's degree completion. Let's examine them.

1. *The Impact of Committee Reconfiguration.* The untimely, unforeseeable death of a committee member represents a loss in personal terms and also the resulting loss of balance and momentum that gird committee service. In addition, each member of a committee generally serves as ballast for the various personalities that are brought together. No one knows for certain the extent to which the professor who died would have maintained a solidifying force among the other members, possibly holding in check the ensuing perpetual difficulties or problematic behaviors. These are undecidable factors. Whatever cohesiveness existed among the original committee members certainly could have been splintered by the faculty member's passing, with the psychological and emotional impact upon the committee yet another unknown. However, it is clear that from its inception the committee was characterized by numerous configurations across a span of many years, each distorting the integrity of the whole and creating voids in Jack's progress. It is important for advisors and advisees to be cognizant of the repercussions of committee reconfiguration; it is not benign, even in circumstances when death of a committee member is not a factor. In both instances, whether committee reconfiguration stems from death or member resignation, it is critical to maintain excellent communication and to conduct a transitional or a succession meeting among the various members to ensure continuity of the process.

    Although we cannot prevent the cataclysms spurred by the death of a committee member, it is important for departments to implement mechanisms that lend psychological, emotional, and even technical support to committee members who lose a colleague to death during the dissertation process, and also to do so for committees, like Jack's, that are no longer functioning. We do not know for certain the impact such experiences exert upon committees or their ability to perform. One conjecture is that interventions and aftercare approaches may have prevented the kind of disintegration witnessed in Jack's case. What is clear, however, is that continuous reconfigurations of the committee contributed in some way to a sense of detachment from the student and from the importance of his work and spread to a number of committee members like an inexplicable disorder.

2. *Dedication and Commitment.* Do not agree to serve on a dissertation committee unless you recognize your interest level, the degree to which you are committed, and the time you have available. In this instance, the motif or pattern that characterized the interactions of the group was ennui and boredom with the project. Jack's committee members did not appear to be particularly dedicated to the dissertation or to its completion in a continued, sustainable manner. Sabbaticals, conferences, teaching, and other obligations were used as excuses for failing to fulfill the duties and responsibilities of committee service. These duties can be halted or postponed only at great risk to the advisee. Consider that many professors are not available during the summer sessions; however, this does not mean the student must cease work on the dissertation over the summer months, when, most likely, he or she has time available to devote to the project. Such imposed breaks in dissertation progress are costly to students and to faculty who may all suffer threats to their momentum.

Committee members need to use some "out-of-the-box" approaches. Projections of work to be accomplished over the summer can be delineated by the end of the spring term, but these are contingent upon detailed conversations and planning outlines. In Jack's case, protracted return times for dissertation edits simply enhanced the opportunities for a growing boredom and discontent, along with the notion that Jack was not making progress, a catch-22 at its best. The committee members were frustrated as well. (I'll return to them in a moment.) The summer sessions, which would have been an ideal time frame in which to work, represented lost time. Sadly, Jack's dissertation became an afterthought or, to be more accurate, perhaps it always was.

3. *The Centrality of Regular Committee Meetings.* Would you be surprised to learn that the original committee met only once throughout their five years together and that was to approve the proposal? After that, they never met again. Their style of communication was fragmentary and isolated, reduced to individual interactions with the advisee, but they did not have comprehensive interactions as a committee. From the onset, they did not envision themselves as a team, and therefore *they were not a team.* Nothing held them together, not even Jack, who remained an abstraction with a phantom dissertation. Jack was not only silent, but he was also invisible. It became relatively easy for the committee's more *real* projects to overtake him. In the final analysis, the committee members should have worked in unison, assisting each other and forging relationships among themselves for the common good, lending their expertise to the cultivation of a solid dissertation. With no common investment and no common purpose, no tangible end product or viable outcome, the team broke apart. In reality, however, the signs of fracture were there all along, only no one was diagnosing the problem. They were simply living with their own pathology.

4. *Abnegation of the Advisor's Leadership Role.* The advisor's role is a *hands-on, at-all-times* role. Jack's advisor's style was laissez-faire. It is curious that the dissertation advisor did not monitor the committee's or Jack's progress on a consistent basis. Hovering in the background, he listened to Jack's concerns, but he did not employ his considerable power to unite the committee in the common goal or to intervene when it became apparent that Jack was not receiving the level of attention/frequency of response that should have been accorded him. Moreover, he did not use his authority to help Jack negotiate through contradictory editorial recommendations that Jack received from various members. He should have been monitoring Jack's progress and acting as coordinator; instead, he was a passive bystander.

Further, Jack's advisor did not exert control *from the very beginning* over the constant fluctuation of committee members, both on and off Jack's committee, nor did he attempt to stabilize or ward off the members' commitment to other projects, to sabbaticals, to other students whose needs required attention, or to ancillary projects. Moreover, he did not maintain control over the required committee paperwork or seem particularly interested in managing the graduate faculty status requirement for his own colleague. Without the benefit of a waiver, Professor F would not have met graduate faculty status requirements to serve on Jack's committee, thus compromising *further* an already compromised situation. With the first committee effectively dismissed and a second one in process, risking a *third* reconfiguration, at a time when the student was straddling the request for an extension and trying to defend, would have placed Jack in unparalleled jeopardy. In addition, whether the advisor did this consciously or not, he was unwise and flagrant in relying upon the beneficence of a senior-level administrator to waive the graduate faculty requirement for the newest committee member; a "by-the-book" administrator may have held fast to the rules and not been so accommodating.

Lastly, it was up to the advisor to communicate with the committee and to make the collaborative, informed decision regarding Jack's readiness to defend. It was not up to the committee to tell the major advisor and/or the student when the student should defend. However, in all fairness to the committee, the members may have been compelled to take on the leadership role simply due to the fact that the advisor wasn't leading the team effectively. On certain levels, he had abandoned *them* as well. His seeming disinterest and lack of *hands-on* management may have served as a contagion that signaled an unfortunate and perhaps unintended apathy. If it weren't important for him to get the student through, then it wasn't important for the committee, and they consciously or unconsciously adopted this mindset.

5. *Annual Review Process Incorporated into the Dissertation.* Jack's progress or failure to progress, noted within the draft chapters he submitted as well as in email exchanges with

his committee, was not noted in his annual review report, where it would have served well. Let me draw the use of the word *annual* into question: At the dissertation stage, *annual review* would be most pernicious, the *annual* element not in league with dissertation completion timelines.

Dissertating students' progress *is* actually monitored throughout the entire exchange of chapters, drafting, email, phone conversations, etc. Drafts should improve over time, and the committee should be able to evaluate progress or lack of progress. However, the formal element of the annual review for dissertating students, if conducted during the fall and spring semesters (two times in an academic year), permits for a more cohesive, unified diagnostic. The student's self-assessment also serves as a viable gauge and permits the student, as well as the committee, to enter into a clearer understanding of expectations and needs from both perspectives. The meeting of the annual review committee, as a whole, also reinforces the team concept. The annual review process may not always include dissertation committees, but it should, as these individuals are responsible for the oversight and management of the end stage of the degree process; if a student is going to get into difficulty, it will be here.

Assessment and progress should be managed from the inception of the doctoral degree program and more frequently as the student transitions into the dissertation. The formality of the annual review process, no matter what that form may take, ensures heightened communication and provides the student with guidance and oversight shared by the team, as a unit. Face-to-face meetings offer the opportunity to share ideas or to anticipate difficulties and therefore unite attendees in a common purpose. Communication within this setting is imperative, and the group concept eliminates the propensity for isolated interactions with only the student, where information may be misunderstood or where there is little or no consensus regarding a suggested direction or recommendation.

Although indeed many doctoral programs and departments across many universities and colleges manage annual review in a manner that intersects with dissertation progress, there are many that do not. Thus, the opportunity for delays in progress or the potential for attrition is great because information remains sequestered at the dissertation committee level and does not inform departmental policies or practices. Annual review not only is centered in retention (Di Pierro, 2007), but also is rooted in due process (Weiner & Hustoles, 2004).

6. *Failure to Communicate.* Within the situation described, it is obvious that the entire process was dismantled by lack of communication on multiple levels, as well as by lack of *esprit de corps*. Generally, advisees may be reluctant to voice their concerns with committee members, the power differential being a significant factor. Moreover, some individuals are reticent to admit deficiencies or shortcomings, and in a competitive world, that reluctance may be understandable, but only to a certain degree. In this instance, Jack seemed to enjoy good relations with his advisor and freely expressed his frustrations with the committee within those exchanges, but as we have seen, the advisor did not *close the loop* by bringing these issues to the attention of the committee members. Neither was Jack particularly forthright in communication with the committee. As time passed, this lack of communication exacerbated the situation. The more difficulty that Jack experienced, the less apt he was to address the issues, and so eventually he withdrew and became silent, but as he himself admitted he became "desperate," as well as angry and frustrated.

Silence in these instances is never a good sign, the idea of "no news is good news" aside. *No news* within the dissertation advising circle can be catastrophic; everyone assumes that all is proceeding *fair to well*, until it isn't. In many respects, silence reinforced the committee's lack of accountability, as well as lack of a *take-charge* attitude on Jack's part. Failure to voice an opinion and instead to acquiesce doesn't work in the long run. Think of the committee as you would an athletic team. Football players and baseball players call out the plays to each other in a huddle or create signals that have the same effect; they communicate "next steps," and that's how they win the game. They don't remain quiet, *guessing* or *wishing* that the next plays or moves will be the right ones. They know that stasis and retreat are built-in mechanisms for failure.

Jack's reluctance to communicate with committee members was mirrored, ironically enough, in his advisor's relationship with the department chair or others who could have assisted *before* the situation reached the point of gravitas. Just as Jack's advisor did not communicate effectively with the committee members, Jack also did not seek the counsel of his department chairperson or graduate program advisor/director, both of whom could have offered strategies to resolve the difficulties.

Let's go back to the annual review process for a moment: If the chair and/or program director had been involved in the annual review as annual review committee members, for example, or at least had been provided with an overview of Jack's progress report, they could have entered into a dialogue with Jack's dissertation advisor and collaborated. The problems would have been unmasked and potential resolutions discussed. In addition, use of the annual review report would have provided Jack's dissertation advisor with a formal written narrative that he could have reviewed and then incorporated as a tool to enhance Jack's progress. At this point, the dissertation advisor could have presented the department chair and/or the program advisor/director with the report, if they were not already overtly involved in the annual review process.

In short, we have layer upon layer of instances in which communication either failed or was absent from the process. *What ifs* and *should haves* force us to live in the subjunctive, a point well past what it is possible to resolve.

~ The Take Away ~

1. The essential anodyne to dissertation toxicity is communication.
2. Understand the impact of dissertation committee reconfiguration upon the advisee and committee members.
3. Advisors should not agree to serve on a dissertation commit-

tee unless they recognize their interest level, the degree to which they are dedicated to the process, and their available time.
4. Committees should meet on a regular basis.
5. Recognize that the dissertation chair's role is a leadership role, and leaders are accountable for ethical management of the process.

References

Bennett, W. J., & Wilezole, D. (2013). *Is college worth it?* Nashville, TN: Thomas Nelson.

Di Pierro, M. (2007). Excellence in doctoral education: Defining best practices. *College Student Journal, 41*, 368–375.

Di Pierro, M. (2014). *Western Michigan University profiles of graduated doctoral students for academic years 1992–present.* Unpublished manuscript, Western Michigan University, Kalamazoo.

Weiner, W. R., & Hustoles, C. L. J. (2004). Due process for graduate students. *Journal for Higher Education Strategists, 2*, 87–93.

Chapter 5

Considerations When Forming a Committee: For Advisees

People tell you who they are, even when you don't want to know.
Natalie Rose Furfaro, my mother,
and Catherine Lombardo, my grandmother

Get the Right People for the Right Job

Given Jack's experiences, it is clear that the original committee, in all of its various configurations, sans formal paperwork, was in a state of perpetual degeneration, and right in front of Jack's eyes. In retrospect, Jack admitted that he would have proceeded differently, especially given the serendipitous organization of his second, formally convened committee and its highly functioning capability that stood in sharp contrast to the first committee. If he had not come to the end of his tether and raised an objection but instead chosen to endure further his situation, he would have remained at an impasse and most likely not graduated. Shocked at how fluidly the second committee managed the remainder of the process, Jack said he wished this second configuration could have been in place from the beginning.

The coming together of a dissertation committee should not be serendipitous but rather should result from a clearly defined, cogently thought-out plan. But the plan cannot happen without the right people. Consider this: *If you are a patient who requires surgery, what kind of a medical team would you want? If you are a CEO of a major company, whom would you choose to work for you?* Of course, the answer is simple: you would say, "I want the best." The same holds for the dissertation team: *If you are a student assembling a "dream team," which people would you want on that team?* The same holds for a dissertation advisor or committee member: *What kind of faculty and student would you want to work with, and for a period of years, not just a few months?*

Reasonable "fit" is key. Just as you wouldn't rush off and marry just anyone, you should not rush off to assemble a dissertation committee. That committee is like a marriage. Proceed carefully.

All the members should maintain respect for each other, value the experience of working together, have an interest in the dissertation research topic, and remain committed to seeing the student through to degree completion. If these elements are not present, then you may well be off to a poor start. It is very easy for students to invite faculty members to serve on a committee, but hasty invitations can be exceptionally damaging further along the process when it becomes apparent that the group dynamics are flawed, and members, including the advisee, decide they want "out." We'll come back to this point later.

Telling Details or Motifs

Jack noted the differences between the committees as soon as the second had been configured, and he had a basis for comparison. Let's look more closely at some distinguishing characteristics that set them apart. One of the newly appointed committee members on the second committee attended a group meeting prepared with 70 pages of Jack's dissertation reviewed and edited. He promised that he would hand-deliver the remainder to Jack, who lived in a neighboring city, by that weekend. In addition, when it came to scheduling the defense, not an easy feat given the complexities of the committee members' summer schedules as well as the abrupt configuration of the committee, this faculty member did his best to be available, trying diligently to work around family obligations.

These two examples serve as *telling details* that reveal much about this faculty member and his commitment and dedication. If you didn't know anything else about him, this is all that you would need to know. He is one of those individuals who makes things happen for other people, and when the gears are running smoothly, it's easy to accept the fluidity and forward motion: the disruptions have ended and everything is in place. Such individuals and their efforts are exceptional, but there are times when their efforts and problem-solving skills may not be recognized to the degree they deserve. It's a consensus gentium that when everything works, it's a given. The stuck gears are the ones that draw our attention, ironically enough. Contrast this perspective with the one that characterized the original committee, with its proclivity to relegate Jack's dissertation to low priority status almost from the beginning of its engagement and to reinforce this idea with their words and actions: to paraphrase, *I'm too busy; I have other projects; I have commitments to other students.*

Remember that the seeds of *who* people *really* are, in many instances, are already known to you, only you may not be prepared to *see*. My mother and grandmother used to say, in Italian, of course, "People tell you who they are, even when you don't want to know." This must be a universal saying among wise people. Writer Maya Angelou said similarly, "The first time someone shows you who they are, believe them" (OWN, 2013), or another variant from an unknown source, "When people tell you who they are, listen." In response to Oprah Winfrey, who lamented a failed relationship, Angelou responded, "My dear, why must you be shown 29 times before you can see who they really are? Why can't you get it the first time?" (OWN, 2013). Almost from the beginning, the first committee members, in their various informal configurations, signaled clearly who they were as well as their level of commitment, only Jack did not hear or see the message or did not *want* to hear or see the message. This oversight almost cost him his degree.

Selection of the Committee: Advice for Students

So, you're a student thinking of configuring a committee. You're wondering how to do this, but before you actually begin, consider this: the dissertation is a marriage of sorts. You wouldn't marry someone on the basis of a first date, for example, especially someone that you didn't really know. So, why would you invite someone with whom you have had little association and no real experience to serve as dissertation chair or committee member? The relationship between advisor and advisee is critically important to your future success, as the research indicates. And yet, many students too frequently make this decision without having firsthand knowledge of that person or sufficient information to make an informed, logical choice. The value of exercising caution *beforehand*, rather than attempting to ameliorate a bad choice *after the fact*, cannot be overstated.

Before I begin, let me clarify that if you are in a field of science, the *selection* of an advisor is intricately connected to your shared research interests. Further, in the sciences, research begins very early in a doctoral program, not at the end of the program, as it does in many other fields. If you are in the social sciences, education, health sciences, or humanities, for example, it is not absolutely necessary that the advisor's and advisee's fields of expertise match precisely. So, the idea of a conscious selection process of a particular advisor may not always hold for those students in the sciences; in these instances, it is the focus of the research and the disciplinary expertise that takes precedence. There are, however, certain non-scientific programs that require students to assemble program advisors early on in their doctoral programs, with the intended plan that they intersect into the dissertation phase and become dissertation advisors. I doubt the advisability of this undertaking, especially when many students do not have a concrete research agenda in mind at this point and may not have a shared relationship with their assigned advisor, and so the choice of a dissertation advisor at this stage is premature.

Here are some ideas:

Do Your Research

1. *Attend dissertation defenses.* Students are encouraged to attend dissertation defenses and to familiarize themselves with the working styles of potential dissertation chairs and/or committee members. In this manner, they learn by observing the defense process, its rituals and customs, and the sequence of events that guide the process; in addition, they have the opportunity to observe how faculty interact with each other and with their advisees. This experience provides good insight into the manner in which students can evaluate potentials for committee service. These efforts involve a time commitment: Consider that dissertation defenses are at least two hours in length, but the time spent in witnessing defenses can be invaluable in placing students in closer proximity to faculty within a working context. In terms of training their advisees, faculty can also suggest that students not configure a commit-

tee unless or until they have observed a number of defenses and have educated themselves in this process.

2. *Interview potential advisors and committee members.* Companies and organizations do not hire potential employees without the benefit of reviewing letters of recommendation, resumes, and CVs and interviewing candidates—in essence, vetting the candidates. Before you select an advisor/committee member, it is important to have a conversation so that you can get to know this individual. It is perfectly acceptable to ask the following questions:

How long did it take the potential advisor to complete his or her degree? The advisor's own dissertation experience frequently serves as the model used with his or her advisees. Therefore, the answer to this question corresponds generally to how long it will take *you* to complete.

How many advisees does the potential advisor currently have? The answer to this question equates to the amount of time the advisor is able or willing to give to you. I am aware of instances in which students were on a kind of informal waiting list for a certain advisor who had an excellent reputation for completing students and for being available and dedicated. Many waited patiently, but others had to move on to secure advisors who were more readily available—a trade-off.

How many dissertations has the potential advisor directed? You should not necessarily avoid altogether the potential advisor if, for example, she is an ingénue with little to no experience. However, you need to understand that an individual who has never undertaken this advising process before and is perhaps also a new faculty member, anxious to make an impression on his or her home department and secure tenure, may be more rigid and exacting than is necessary. In the end, this may cost you time.

How long, on average, does it take the potential advisor's advisees to complete their degrees? Again, the answer to this question balances out your awareness regarding your own time-to-degree, which should be a point of major interest to all advisees, unless time, money, and your future career are not your prime considerations.

Is it likely that the advisor and advisee will publish together after the degree is completed or during the process? Who shall be first author? Advisors are generally interested in continuing the advising relationship beyond the duration of the dissertation, and so opening this conversation early on is a good idea. Many advisors acknowledge the importance of the advisee as first author and generally are content with second-author status. Moreover, this partnership opens up possibilities for co-presenting at professional conferences or other venues, and so the steady interaction constructs an important foundation for an ongoing professional relationship.

3. *Conduct preliminary research to secure the right advisor.* The research on doctoral education indicates that the advisor is one of the most important mainstays to doctoral success (see Lovitts, 2001; Bowen & Rudenstine, 1992; and the Council of Graduate Schools Ph.D. Completion Project, 2009). The CGS Ph.D. Completion Project findings indicate that of those students who completed their doctoral programs, 65% posited the importance of doctoral advising and mentoring, sometimes alone and sometimes in conjunction with other factors such as financial support and family support, as a factor that contributed to their success (Council of Graduate Schools, 2009).

4. *Offset strengths and shortcomings.* It is important to balance the potential advisor's strengths and shortcomings with your own strengths and shortcomings. If your potential advisor is a transactional leader, a micromanager who wants to manage every moment of your dissertation, and you are an independent individual who is capable of managing well on your own, this combination may make for a difficult alliance unless you are willing to make the adjustment to the fact that the advisor is going to be involved in every step of the process, dominating all of your activities, step-by-step.

The idea of being micromanaged may seem innocuous from the safe distance of reading this book, but in the *real world* of working together in a professional capacity over a long period of time, being micromanaged can be irritating, fatiguing, and just unpleasant.

Bear in mind that the micromanaging advisor may, in

time, ease up, especially when you prove your mettle by delivering a sterling product. In other words, your daily interactions will prove your capabilities, and he or she may eventually relax and let you fly on your own. Some people, however, simply are micromanagers at heart and cannot deviate from this autocratic style, no matter how capable the advisee. Born-and-bred micromanagers are frequently hardwired for this behavior and have a difficult time unless they are controlling all phases of a process. There is never a payoff for the advisee, and each encounter may as well be the initial one because there is no history that serves as a proving ground. The advisee lives in an eternal Etch-A-Sketch world in which the proving ground is continuously erased.

Conversely, if you are not capable of autonomous work and *need* to be micromanaged, then you will find a match in an advisor who will seize control of the process, *and you*, and keep everything well aligned. In the world of dissertation advising, there is room for many styles, and the key is to find an advisor with a particular style that matches your needs. This means that you find someone whose strengths and shortcomings are offset against your own strengths and shortcomings. Let's go back to the marriage model that I mentioned earlier: paired spouses who are both procrastinators, who both have poor financial skills, or who both have flawed organizational skills are probably going to encounter difficulty somewhere along the way. The similarity in their weaknesses will undermine their ability to be productive or to get ahead.

A micromanaging advisor and advisee will manage themselves into oblivion. By the same token, a laissez-faire advisor and advisee make for a poor combination, as neither is capable of moving a project forward in a sustained manner. The laissez-faire advisor and the independent advisee may also not make for the best match, but in this instance, if the advisee assumes the control and if the advisor is willing to permit the advisee to do so, the situation may still be workable. In this regard, the advisee simply learns how to work *around* the *hands-off* advisor, who may see the big picture but does not necessarily know how to manage the incremental steps of project completion, especially if he or she is burdened with other responsibilities. If, however, such an advisor is not willing to imbue the advisee with this kind of control and, conversely, if the advisor is not willing to assume it, then the dissertation project may stall out or simply falter altogether.

5. *Be aware of your needs if you are a geographically distanced student.* There is one other element to bear in mind when considering a potential advisor. Remember that many dissertating students may not reside in close proximity to their advisors and may live out of state or out of the country, the distance complicating the circumstances for those advisees with the laissez-faire type of advisor. This is the type not prone to responding to email, phone calls, texts, and other means of communication. Also, this may be the type not prone to managing difficult committees and interceding when necessary, as we noted with Jack's advisor. Geographic displacement only exacerbates the fact that the guidance, support, and accessibility the student requires is not happening. In this regard, the advisor is essentially an absentee advisor, not necessarily because of the complexities of geographic displacement, but simply because that is his or her management style. In either case, this fact does not always bode well for dissertation completion.

Here is my story: After my comprehensive examinations were completed, I relocated to Las Vegas, Nevada, from Tampa, Florida, and took an adjunct teaching position at the University of Nevada, Las Vegas (UNLV) while I was writing the dissertation. During the last meeting with my advisor prior to my departure to Nevada, he made the observation that the majority of students who leave the campus proper never finish their dissertations. I hadn't paid too much attention to this statement because, in my view, as long as I had a great library, I could write the dissertation anywhere. *(People tell you who they are, even when you don't want to know.)* Over time, communication with my advisor became more infrequent, and it was clear that he was not responding to my concerns, returning phone calls, or providing timely, useful editorial commentary.

I was dismayed to come to the realization that he had

written me off, especially since he had personally requested that he serve as my chair, displacing another faculty member who had already committed to serving. His admonition that geographically displaced students do not complete their Ph.D.s was becoming a self-fulfilling prophecy brought to the brink of fruition by his laissez-faire attitude. Periodically, the UNLV chair of the Department of English at the time would ask how my research was coming along. One day, I admitted to him that I was not making progress and confided that my advisor had essentially disappeared. His from-the-hip advice was simply, "Get another chair." And, I did.

6. *Understand the combinations of managerial styles.* There are numerous managerial styles, and many of these styles overlap or dovetail into each other so that they remain as *combinations* of styles, not necessarily pure forms. Also, remember that the managerial style may change, and should, depending upon the circumstances of the dissertation experience. An effective advisor will know when it is best to collaborate or consult, to be persuasive or autocratic, and also to be more egalitarian, democratic, or transformational in style.

    Granted, the laissez-faire manager and the micromanager are indeed extremes, existing at opposite ends of the advising spectrum; nevertheless, *proclivities* toward each defined type or style can complicate the process in serious ways. Remember that in successful advising models, advisors may tend to be more regimented in the beginning, and then gradually release their hold as their advisees demonstrate academic sufficiency and autonomy—an ideal. Your goal is to better identify and understand the potential advisor's advising style versus your own working style and establish what you need to be successful. Then, consider whether you can work with this individual or not, based upon the data you gather.

7. *Be certain: Ask your colleagues.* After you engage in a conversation and gather preliminary facts, vet these through your peers and colleagues, those coming through the process or those who have already graduated with a particular advisor at the helm of the advising ship. With clarity of vision, they certainly can look back and provide you with salient

commentary to guide your choice. Do they affirm that the experience was positive and rewarding, or do they tell you that the experience was fraught with difficulty, uncertainty, and continuous problems? Did they have to change advisors, and, if so, at what point in the dissertation process? One advisor I know has a long history for directing dissertations, but only up until the proposal has been finalized, at which time advisees are serendipitously dropped, prior to operationalizing the research. The advisor has brought to completion only two advisees, as of this writing. Yet, this fact, well known in the department, is ignored frequently by unwary students who think the situation will be different for *them*. Drawn to the advisor's professional credentials, the publications, and the accoutrements of a successful career, they discover at the most vulnerable point in the process that they have entered into a Venus flytrap, and the cost of extrication is going to be exacting. I will return to this later in the book.

8. *Remember: You are the rule, not the exception.* Remember that survivors of the process are some of the best arbiters of your potential success, and in listening, remember that *you* are not the exception. If other students have endured difficulties, most likely you will, too. Human nature being what it is, it is easy, if not flattering, to consider ourselves as exceptional or different from others; however, if you hear a chorus of voices joined in the same sad refrain, you owe it to yourself to listen to the dissonance of a cautionary tale.

9. *Read the potential advisor's dissertation: What does it look like? How is it organized?* You can learn a great deal about someone from his or her writing. Writing styles emerge, as well as linguistic proclivities, organizational patterns, logic, modes of discourse, reasoning ability, attention to detail, skill in debate, and research acumen, among others. The manner in which your potential advisor's monograph is organized, written, and delivered can reveal important clues regarding that individual's expectations of you.

10. *Remember the Rules of Engagement: What are your expectations of your advisor?* Make certain that you fully understand the advisor's role. What can you anticipate from this individual? What is the extent of his or her involvement with you?

Is there mutual respect? Is the advisor sincerely interested in your dissertation topic? Is this individual a leader who will shepherd you through the process at every phase, guiding, mentoring, and advising, or is this an individual who anticipates that you need little encouragement or involvement and are self-reliant, independent, and self-sufficient? Has the advisor arranged a regular meeting schedule with you and with the committee members? Some of this information can be gleaned via knowledge of the potential advisor's managerial style, but only in part. The remainder will stem from clear conversations regarding your interactions with this individual and clear delineation of expectations from both sides.

Remember that almost no one will ever say to you, "You can expect that I'll respond to you infrequently" or "I never answer email during the summer," or "I never clear the messages from my voice mail," or "It will be months before I return edited chapters of your dissertation to you." However, the *emergence* of these tendencies, especially as you listen to your colleagues' experiences, represents fair warning that difficulty may lie ahead. *Ask: What is the turn-around time for returning drafts? What editorial approach will the advisor use: track changes, hard copy, Microsoft SharePoint? What is the best way to contact the advisor or committee members?* Hearing directly from them is the best way to avoid getting tangled up in a grapevine game.

When I was a doctoral student, an administrative assistant provided me with a professor's home phone number, encouraging me to contact him so that he could respond to an important issue that had developed. When I hesitated, she reaffirmed that calling him would be perfectly fine. It wasn't. He was not at all pleased to receive a business call at his residence, only this fact was not known to me nor had it ever been discussed with me. Had I been forewarned, I would not have ended up creating a faux pas that resulted in a stinging reprimand, which, at the time, wielded more magnitude than now, with the distance of many years.

11. *Remember the Rules of Engagement: What are the advisor's expectations of the advisee?* What does the advisor expect in terms of implementing editorial commentary? Should you

highlight your edits so that he or she can readily identify those areas that you have addressed and not have to resort to painful crosswalks between drafts? Has the advisor discussed the timetable for submitting edited chapters? Has the advisor indicated how you should work with him or her, how you will interact with the committee members, or how those committee members will work with each other and with the advisor? There are multiple layers of individuals with whom you will interact, communicate, and essentially *live with* for a long period of time. Understanding the process is critical.

A dissertation committee represents a wide network of individuals who all should work with each other in defined ways, with their roles clearly delineated so that they understand how to work with the advisee, with each other, and with the advisor, across a continuum of actions that move toward completion of the dissertation and graduation. Yet, it is clear that too frequently many committees do not engage in conversations of this sort prior to working with each other and with their advisees.

12. *Be aware of the difference between capability and expertise versus niceness.* Select an advisor based on his or her expertise and capability, not necessarily on the variables of *niceness* or *kindness.* Of course, we all would want the best of both worlds. In his book *Unaccountable: What Hospitals Won't Tell You and How Transparency Can Revolutionize Health Care,* Dr. Marty Makary (2012), a surgeon at Johns Hopkins Hospital and associate professor of health policy at Johns Hopkins School of Public Health, writes about two doctors, Dr. HODAD (Hands of Death and Destruction) and the Raptor. Dr. HODAD was essentially an inept surgeon but had a wonderful bedside manner, and his patients loved him; the Raptor was exceptionally skilled as a surgeon but had no social skills and was rude, apathetic, and condescending. Patients interested in an excellent surgical outcome would have made the better choice in Raptor, rather than HODAD, but examining only the surface qualities in either individual would have eclipsed the stark realities that niceness could not possibly trump expertise. A potential patient would have to drill down far deeper than the superficial elements of a

starched lab coat and a bright smile versus a growling countenance in order to make the best choice of a surgeon. So too a doctoral student seeking a dissertation advisor. Do not be beguiled by niceness/kindness versus expertise and skill. But, if you can garner both, do it.

13. *Avoid transgressing boundaries.* You and your advisor should maintain a healthy and safe distance from each other, for a variety of reasons. This is a professional relationship, not a friendship. Once that line is crossed it is exceptionally difficult, if not impossible, to restore distance, which is necessary to this process of producing a dissertation, for both advisor and advisee.

    Years ago, at a dissertation retreat, I encountered a doctoral student who lamented the fact that she and her advisor had moved their professional relationship into a casual friendship. Jogging together in the mornings, they commiserated about being young mothers and contending with professional responsibilities, one just beginning her career as tenure-track faculty, and the other enmeshed in the rigor of writing the dissertation. The equality they enjoyed as friends tipped precariously when it became necessary to step out of their friendship roles into the advisor–advisee relationship, in which there was no longer an egalitarian balance, but more of a power differential.

    This fact disrupted both elements of their relationship, the friendship part and the advising part, and required a great effort on the part of the advisee to maintain the balance necessary to complete the degree. According to the advisee, the advisor appeared unaware of the dilemma, perhaps because for the advisor the power differential remained in place: she was in control, whereas for her advisee, that differential fell along blurred lines.

    Yet another example of an advisor–advisee relationship that crossed boundaries makes the point. An advisor decided to migrate regular office meetings with the student to a bar that was frequented by college students and faculty. The original idea of having a drink while discussing the dissertation became transmuted into a weekly command performance that made the student uncomfortable. When the student attempted to reestablish a more professional relationship and revert to meetings within the office setting, the advisor objected to the sudden reversal in what had become a casual friendship that he valued. Boundaries play a critical role in the interactions between advisor and advisee, and it is critical not to blur them. Your advisor is your advisor, not your friend.

~ The Take Away ~

1. Remember: In most instances, you are the *rule*, not the exception.
2. Listen to your colleagues' views and experiences.
3. Learn the art of negotiation and compromise: Can you work with this individual(s) and, if so, what are the best, most effective ways? What are the least effective ways?
4. What are the advantages of working with the potential advisor/committee members?
5. What are the disadvantages of working with the potential advisor/committee members?
6. How many advisees has the potential advisor *graduated*?
7. What resources do you need in order to be successful in the dissertation process?
8. Are you and the potential advisor/committee members a good match for each other?
9. The advisor is your advisor, not your friend.

References

Bowen, W. G., & Rudenstine, N. L. (1992). *In pursuit of the Ph.D.* Princeton, NJ: Princeton University Press.

Council of Graduate Schools. (2009). *Ph.D. completion and attrition: Findings from exit surveys of Ph.D. completers.* Retrieved September 2, 2014, from https://cgsnet.org/phd-completion-and-attrition-findings-exit-surveys-phd-completers-0

Lovitts, B. E. (2001). *Leaving the ivory tower: The causes and consequences of departure from doctoral study.* Lanham, MD: Rowman & Littlefield.

Makary, M. (2012). *Unaccountable: What hospitals won't tell you and how transparency can revolutionize health care.* New York, NY: Bloomsbury Press.

OWN. (2013). Oprah's life lesson from Maya Angelou: 'When people show you who they are, believe them.' Retrieved May 23, 2014, from HuffPost website: http://www.huffingtonpost.com/2013/03/14/oprah-life-lesson-maya-angelou_n_2869235.html

Chapter 6

Selection of the Advisee: For Faculty

Considerations for Advisors When Working with Advisees

The process for potential advisors is decidedly more abstruse because there are fewer experiences upon which to base a good fit. A faculty member may have taught a student in a course or two, but other than that does not have more complex information that ensures the student is a good match for him or her as advisor. Advisors may also acquire information from other faculty members, but in passing only. However, rather than succumb to flattery when asked to serve on a committee, it is always best to use the same approach that I advocate for students when selecting an advisor. The interview approach is an excellent tool to implement in the process of determining whether to invest your time and energy in dissertation advising with a particular advisee.

Commitment and Capability

Determine how the potential advisee has performed within the context of a course you have taught. A hardworking, capable, diligent, dedicated student frequently maintains the attributes and skills necessary to withstand the complexities of the dissertation. Is the potential advisee committed to the dissertation process, as well as capable of delivering the final product? Is the student capable of exercising logic and reason, capable of excellent oral and written communication skills? Students may be in a graduate program that has placed little demand upon research and professional writing; therefore, the student may not have a solid background to withstand the demands of the dissertation process. Many students come to the dissertation with scant research experience. Students in science, technology, engineering, and mathematics (STEM) are the rare exceptions. However, many of these students may excel at the bench but still lack writing experience. In lieu of writing-centric courses, other indices are necessary from which to determine the student's potential to meet these challenges.

What strengths or shortcomings do you, as potential advisor, observe in your potential advisee, and are you willing to invest sufficient time in your schedule to accommodate those needs and provide the resources necessary to a successful outcome? A student who has difficulty writing will require hours of editorial expertise, patience, and commitment on the part of the advisor. How do you feel about surrendering some or all of your own writing/publication time to help an advisee who requires extensive intervention? If your schedule does not rest in accord with an advisee's needs, you may not be well suited to working with this particular individual throughout the dissertation phase—a period of years, in many instances.

Ability to Take Direction

Is the potential advisee an individual who will be open to constructive criticism and willing to take direction? This is a critical question because the student who is resistant to receiving instructions or recommendations, or simply unable, will prove to be burdensome in the long run. A student may have a vision of the dissertation that is not solid, does not have sufficient strength or power to carry the monograph, or is not substantiated by a review of the literature; yet, the student insists upon his or her perspective, despite an advisor's admonitions. Such a student who chooses to personalize the warnings, rather than see the value in a divergent perspective, is not going to be an easy partner in this process.

In such cases, the advisor will have to contend with a difficult process as well as an uncooperative advisee, and so will have a dual burden. This is not necessarily the kiss of death, however, and there are strategies for success that can be implemented. For example, adding another committee member with whom the student has a viable rapport but who can also echo the advisor's recommendations frequently serves well to overcome obstacles. Ironically, the advice is generally the same, only spoken by another voice that somehow resonates with the student. This is precisely what happened when one of my colleagues, almost at his wit's end with a non-compliant advisee, asked me to step in and lend assistance. In the final analysis, I was simply reinforcing my colleague's recommendations, but, for some reason, when those words came from *my* mouth, the student heard them differently. He was suddenly receptive, a fact that changed the problematic dynamic almost immediately, helped to restore the advisor's equanimity, and made the remainder of our experiences together as a committee enjoyable and productive.

Writing Acumen

Some advisees are simply unable to conceptualize ideas or topics, or write and edit drafts of chapters. One advisor in particular found fault with an advisee whom he claimed was incapable of implementing global edits into the document and weaving ideas into an integrated whole. For example, a latent change in the methodology section of the first chapter necessarily involved changes in the remaining sections of that and other chapters, but the advisee remained oblivious to the global ramifications prompted by that methodological change.

In addition, the advisor expressed concern regarding the advisee's quick turn-around periods of a day or two for resubmitting edited chapters. In the advisor's view, the advisee was rushing and not paying proper attention to the document, hurrying along and not finessing the language or the conceptual framework in a scholarly manner. Thus, the two remained at a frustrating impasse for a long period of time, each endeavoring to hit the mark, but each not clearly communicating expectations, procedures, and outcomes. In this instance, the student was challenged not only by the demands of the writing/conceptualization process, but also by the inability/unwillingness to follow directions or to apply the advisor's recommendations and suggestions in a thoughtful, studied manner.

This was best noted when, in reviewing drafts, I noticed that the student placed editorial bubbles in the margins of the draft, in which curt, impatient responses or ruffled retorts to the advisor appeared, but no attempt to address the crux of the advisor's editing concerns was reflected in the narrative text. In essence, the advisee was *arguing in the margins*, within the safe but soundless confines of her editorial bubbles, which she deleted upon completion of some revisions she chose to implement. In the end, the advisee was simply acquiescing and no longer giving credence to the advisor's commentary. Note the advisor's frustration when he observed that few editorial suggestions had been addressed in the "revised" drafts he received. In his view, the advisee was simply wasting his time. And he was right.

Students' ability to write well in a course you have taught will be an important tool in determining whether you should serve as advisor or even as a committee member. While it is true that almost every good writer has an exceptional editor, every Hemingway has a Gertrude Stein, as the saying goes, a dissertating student must *always* have an exceptional conceptual editor, and that means that both individuals are highly invested in the process: to read, edit, make recommendations, implement, refine, rewrite, proofread, and integrate throughout the document to ensure uniformity and coherence. And this is a process, which means that it is done over and over again.

An advisee who is essentially recalcitrant and argumentative, or worse yet, passive aggressive, or who displays tendencies toward these behavioral patterns will be an obstacle. An advisee who cannot carefully employ reason, is unable to intersect ideas in a cogent manner, has to be led continuously to conclusions or observations, or cannot analyze or synthesize is going to represent a formidable challenge to the advisor and to the committee. An advisee who cannot employ elements in a literature review to create a justification for his or her study and who cannot employ the discourse modes of exposition, argumentation, and persuasion in a studied manner signals an essential departure in those qualities and skills necessary to completion of the doctorate. Glimmers of these sorts of behaviors frequently appear through our engagement with students in the classroom and in the papers they write for us, especially when students are provided with opportunities to rewrite and resubmit. *These are critical signposts through which the editing process or lack of it can be witnessed closely. Pay attention.*

You Told Me What to Do, Now Tell Me How to Do It!

One trend of which I have become aware is the need to meet with certain students and explain in person the editorial commentary previously sent. This means that each and every suggested revision in a draft must be reviewed and explained in a face-to-face meeting or via phone, using a facilitated review format. I have learned that the use of track changes placed into the text, as well as my engagement in a written narrative dialogue, are not always sufficient tools in the editing process. I have had to interpret the dissertation advisor's comments as well, because advisees were struggling with the technical implementation and/or did not understand what the advisor actually meant, even though the ideas and recommendations were clear to me.

Liken this observation to what happens when we ask a trusted friend to accompany us to a medical appointment. When we are the patient, we may not always hear or want to hear the doctor's pronouncements; however, the friend is the logical, rational listener, the conveyer of information, who translates, records, and communicates with us, reinforcing the doctor's advice. We should leave that office with an objective view that captures reliable information. The doctor told us what to do, and why. Did we understand? Can we follow those directions? Remember that simply providing students with your edits is not necessarily the alpha and the omega of the writing/editing process; you may also have to dedicate yourself to a series of objective *clarification meeting*s, or *facilitated reviews*, as we discussed earlier, and all of this requires substantial time on your part.

Writing Challenges and Committee Reconfiguration

The difficulties addressed above sometimes result in committee reconfiguration because the working relationship has become hopelessly impaired, either by growing ill will or insufficient time to contend with the ongoing demands of the advisee's writing and editing challenges.

Reconfiguration of a dissertation committee is not a benign event, as we have seen, and it can carry with it serious challenges to degree completion due to political and economic ramifications. In addition, ongoing or continuous friction between advisor and advisee may account for a number of students who attrite at the end stages of their programs and remain ABD (all but dissertation). Such losses impact the individual student and the institution at large. As of this writing, I am not aware of any studies that actually track the economic losses of doctoral attritions in various fields, such as the humanities, social sciences, or the STEM fields, which would make an excellent research project for an enterprising student.

Perhaps if an actual financial cost were attached to each individual attrition in each of these disciplinary categories, institutions of higher learning would become more serious about implementing retention initiatives, such as better admissions processes/standards, training for dissertation advisors, and leadership training. Moreover, they would not only more fiercely guard the financial investment in associateships and assistantships, but also consider the uncalculated losses in faculty time, advising, teaching, publishing, and researching that occur when faculty invest in students who do not complete. What is the value in time *not* spent on these activities? Concomitantly, they would consider the value of the loss of a Ph.D. to their institutions, the value of lost research, the price of students' emotional and financial loss, as well as loss of career potential. A dollar figure for such losses would resonate clearly with institutions of higher learning, which would invest more carefully in retention initiatives critical to the doctoral educational process. Tracking non-completers and conducting exit interviews of those who leave their programs, instead of focusing on mere enrollment numbers, represents a viable strategy in averting losses.

Research Experience

Advisors may want to consider inquiring about the level or kind of research experience, if any, a potential advisee has amassed. As indicated previously, many students are unprepared for the research experience (see Golde & Dorr, 2001; Lovitts, 2005), and they actually learn the art of research during the process of writing the dissertation. I will expand upon this point in a subsequent chapter. However, even brief experience can be a boon: working with a faculty member on a proposal, a grant, a conference project; engagement in bench or other research; development of an article; activities related to the scholarship of teaching and learning; or students' experience as teaching assistants, service assistants, or research assistants. All of these experiences will stand students in good stead when they embark upon formal research. If you have been impressed with a potential advisee's scholastic performance in a course or writing a research paper, volunteering at a conference, publishing, or working with you as your DA (doctoral assistant) or GA (graduate assistant), then you will have a fairly sound idea regarding the manner in which this individual applies critical thinking skills, employs reason and logic, and is able to create sustained arguments.

Level of Autonomy

Is the potential advisee capable of working independently to a certain degree, or will this individual require constant monitoring and vigilance? If the latter, the level of interaction on the part of the advisor is considerably heightened. The advisee should grow more independent over time, as this tendency is a natural progression for any graduate student, but a student who must be managed excessively or who cannot maintain a semblance of independence may never make the smooth transition from what Barbara Lovitts (2005) identifies as the "course taker" phase to the "researcher" phase. We will revisit this point later in the book.

Reasons for Earning the Ph.D.

It is important that potential advisors understand a student's rationale for embarking upon the Ph.D. The modeling of the student's professional experience throughout the curriculum, as well as the selection of the dissertation topic itself, should rest in accord with the student's motivations in seeking the degree to begin with. A student interested in a tenure-track position as a researcher should be exposed to the world of publications, research, and teaching, three critical columns upon which tenure is based. This preparation does not begin *after* the student graduates but rather is an integral part of the student's entire training, and it is part of the advising process for the dissertation as well. The advisor's role here is to cultivate those professional experiences that will dovetail into the student's overall objective in earning a Ph.D. and that will coalesce eventually in the chosen career field. The rationale for electing to undertake the Ph.D. may be as varied as the individuals who enter into such programs. However, an understanding of how a potential advisee estimates this important decision will better inform the advisor regarding the kind of advising strategies and overall objectives that are most appropriate to that particular individual in his or her quest for the degree. An advisee may not necessarily intend to secure a tenure-track position and, in this instance, must be guided through alternative career pathways.

Advisor's Commitment to the Process

In contemplating whether you are a potential fit with an advisee, consider the time that you have available to invest in this *particular* student. Remember that if you asked and answered the questions or points addressed in the list of topics discussed above, you will have garnered *sufficient* information (but not comprehensive) to better understand this student's capabilities within the dissertation process.

The question now revolves around a self-evaluation: your level of commitment, your schedule, your capability, and your interest in serving as advisor. Doctoral advisees deserve the best opportunities for success. Commitment to the process, dedication to the student, and sustained mentorship, guidance, and advising are requisite if indeed the student is to reach the other side of the dissertation in a timely manner. Unless you can commit to the process, avoid signing on. There is nothing wrong in an honest refusal: "I'm delighted that you asked me, but my schedule is such that I cannot accept the invitation at this time."

~ The Take Away ~

1. Is the potential advisee committed to the process of earning a Ph.D. and is he or she capable?
2. Can the potential advisee follow directions?
3. Does the potential advisee have writing skills that will sustain the dissertation?
4. Does the potential advisee have research experience?
5. Is the potential advisee capable of working autonomously?
6. What are the potential advisee's motivations in seeking the Ph.D.?
7. Are you, as potential advisor, capable of investing your time in this process?
8. Ask for a potential advisee's writing sample; a previous research paper or master's thesis provides excellent insight.

References

Golde, C. M., & Dore, T. M. (2001). *At cross purposes: What the experiences of doctoral students reveal about doctoral education* (www.phd-survey.org). Philadelphia, PA: A report prepared for the Pew Charitable Trusts.

Lovitts, B. (2005). Being a good course taker is not enough: A theoretical perspective on the transition into independent research. *Studies in Higher Education, 30*(2), 137–154.

Chapter 7

Other Considerations for the Advisor as Leader

Building the Dissertation Team

Let's say that you have agreed to serve as a dissertation advisor. A matter to consider now is the best configuration of the committee. It is up to the advisor, in collaboration with the advisee, to structure the committee in a balanced manner, one that accounts for the diverse needs of the advisee, as well as the delivery of the research, including the linguistic frame through which the research is delivered. Advisees may not necessarily be aware of faculty expertise or of professors' working relationships, and so it is important that the advisor lead carefully in order to ensure the appropriate configuration.

Graduate catalogues generally include information regarding committee configuration for the various degree levels and should be consulted before configuring the dissertation team. Generally, a committee consists of a dissertation chair and a faculty member from the student's department, as well as a committee member external to the student's department. The following roles can be filled by committee members qualified in the following areas of expertise and/or also can be filled by other individuals who lend these skills to the advising circle but are not necessarily committee members. Here are some examples of these functions that are critical to the dissertation process:

Content Expert(s): The dissertation advisor does not necessarily have to be the content expert. As stated previously, STEM fields (science, technology, engineering, mathematics) are generally one exception. An individual(s) who is an expert in the field, though, is requisite. In many instances, this individual can serve as an external committee member by being granted graduate faculty status with the advisee's university or college. The choice of a content expert is important because the level of expertise relates to the value of the study and its contributions to the field. The more prestigious this individual's reputation, the more prestige is showered upon the advisee and the research and, of course, the institution. Given the advent of increasingly diverse disciplines and areas of interdisciplinary intersection, it may be common in the future for faculty external to an institution to serve as dissertation advisors/co-chairs, especially when the management of the dissertation and the management of the research intersect.

Methodologist/Statistician: An individual who is skilled in quantitative/qualitative methodology, for both the design of the research study as well as the statistical/quantitative/qualitative methods through which data will be collected and analyzed, ensures the integrity of the research. Not every faculty member is a methodologist or a statistician, and it is not feasible to assume they all possess these skills. However, there is accountability for ensuring that these skills are at least available to the committee and to the student, if not actually represented on the committee by a member with these skills.

Conceptual Editor/Writing Expert: An individual who is a skilled conceptual editor is an important member of the dissertation team. Many faculty members are published and understand the rigor necessary to produce a solid dissertation; however, a committee member who will oversee the consistent and sustained development of the monograph and who is capable of serving as an editorial liaison between the advisee and the committee represents an unparalleled resource. This individual will be able to resolve any contradictory editorial commentary provided to students, the kind of commentary that frequently results in a sort of literary paralysis because students do not know how to negotiate around editorial paradoxes that may arise or simply do not possess the scholarly writing skills necessary to the dissertation.

Other Support Resources

Professional Formatters: Post dissertation defense, advisees should consider contracting for professional editorial/formatting services. Professional editors and formatters are skilled in citation management and in ensuring that the final document adheres to the standard formatting styles of their respective disciplines and graduate schools/colleges. If hired, they will generally be the last set of eyes to review the monograph, unless the committee or the advisor requests to see the text again in final form if revisions are required post-defense. This critical service is well worth the financial investment, but advisees do not always know that such services are available through their respective universities or privately. It is a sound idea to inform advisees of these services and to widen the circle of resources available.

Statistical Consultation: Students should also be aware of their own need for statistical support, regardless of whether they have a statistician on their respective committees. Students need to think beyond the scope of their committees, and availing themselves of the expertise of statistical consultation is very important. The statistician serving on the committee may not necessarily want to or intend to be involved in the application of each and every statistical method but will review the data after the student and the statistical consultant work together. At my university, the Graduate Center for Research and Retention, at the time of my auspices as director, offered ongoing, sustained statistical support throughout the entire dissertation process, sent in-depth reports to the student and the advisor after each consultation, and even prepared the student for the dissertation defense by reviewing the methods selected as well as the results. Moreover, it disseminated satisfaction surveys to each faculty member and to each student following every statistical consultation in an effort to ensure the quality of this resource. In this manner, there was continual interaction between and among the student, the advisor, and the statistician. Our model required that students learn to do the analyses themselves, with the guidance and oversight of the statistical consultant. Although it is true that some students will actually hire an independent statistician to run the analyses for them, at the end of the day it is the student who will have to defend the selection of methods, as well as the results of the analyses. My philosophy is that the more hands-on experience a student has, the better, but it is not a given that students must or will undertake the statistics process themselves. They simply must know how to articulate the rationale for methods selection, as well as understand and defend results.

~ The Take Away ~

1. Build a solid dissertation team: consult the graduate catalogue to determine configuration requirements at your institution.
2. Configure the team: chair/advisor, faculty member, external committee member, content expert(s), methodologist, statistician, conceptual editor, and/or writing expert.
3. Determine the need for other support: professional editor/formatter.

Chapter 8

Vetting the Committee

Once the committee has been configured, it is important to sign the appropriate paperwork that formally appoints the individual members to the committee. This action moves through channels of approval that will vary from institution to institution and that will take place at different points in the process. However, these processes must be examined and evaluated for their efficiency. It is never a sound idea to vet committee members after the dissertation proposal has already been developed and approved.

I am aware of several instances in which committee members, including an advisor, served on committees without knowing they were not qualified to serve and had not been granted *graduate faculty status*. How did this happen? Most likely, lack of good communication within the department or program is one culprit. Lack of process management constitutes yet another. The process was not front-ended, but rather back-ended, the vetting occurring at the end of the process, when the discovery of faculty ineligibility was late. In two instances, the committees had to be reconfigured, and at the end stage. End-stage reconfiguration may pose risks: new members may magnanimously accept the proposal, without implementing changes; or alternatively, they may wish to exercise their authority to initiate changes, an occurrence that may impact the integrity of the proposal and result in delays. In both instances to which I refer, the proposal remained intact, but that is not always the case. All in all, it is the student who will suffer the consequences when the vetting process is not observed *at all* or when it is conducted at the wrong time, *late in the process*.

The advisor to whom I refer above was removed after serving as dissertation chair for a period of two years, during which he incorporated the advisee into his research and moved the dissertation forward from that vantage point. The advisor was in a STEM field (science, technology, engineering, mathematics), and so a new advisor taking over would not necessarily have the same research focus, thereby necessitating a reconceptualization of the advisee's proposal.

Consider the loss of faculty time and energy when someone serves on a committee, develops the proposal's concept, oversees the editing, cultivates the research, spends countless hours mentoring the advisee, and then is not permitted to see the process through to its conclusion or gain credit for committee service, which may be integrally connected to the bid for tenure. Consider the loss of the student's momentum, as well as an aborted research agenda, in addition to the time lost in reconfiguring a new committee, especially one that elects for a reconceptualization of the topic.

It is clear that emergent problems signal to us whether or not a process is effective, and in most instances, these dilemmas prompt us to seek resolutions. At my university, before the above problem was resolved (as a result of my intercession), dissertation proposal approval and committee approval had been part and parcel of the same document; hence, a group of individuals (quasi-committee) that was working together for a period of time could conceivably approve proposals, even though the committee itself had not received graduate faculty status, thereby jeopardizing potentially the student's proposal.

~ The Take Away ~

1. Vet potential committee members for graduate faculty status at the *beginning* of the process, as soon as the decision to appoint them to a dissertation committee is made.
2. Be on the alert for university practices that synchronize the dissertation proposal approval process with the appointment to a committee process. These should be two distinct processes, with the faculty vetting process in place prior to the proposal approval process. Ensuring that policies align logically is just good common sense.

Chapter 9

Discovering the Dissertation Topic

The Preliminary Literature Review: Unmasking the Gap

Generally, there are two kinds or types of literature reviews relevant to the dissertating student. The first is conducted to discover the general academic trends, thoughts, ideas, and research in given areas, in an effort to establish the student's research interests and to inform students about the critical studies relevant to potential topics. By examining various studies, students learn about research gaps or new directions upon which to frame their work, with authors frequently leading them to new areas for continued research or those places in extant research that require further investigation. The discussion chapters (final chapters) of completed dissertations often lead to these pathways, and so they too should be considered an invaluable resource for students to explore and determine academic as well as personal interest. This type of investigation represents more of a perusal in general directions, a kind of culling through or examination of information to locate research trends and to generate student interest.

Years ago, in one of my English undergraduate classes, the professor claimed that the dictionary was a "palace of saltatory heuristics," and he asked us to explain what that meant. Of course, we had to go to the dictionary to find out. We discovered the following: quite simply, when we consult the dictionary, we learn the meaning of words as well as gain knowledge by jumping/skipping around from word to word. The initial literature review resembles this jumping/skipping process because when it is first undertaken, there is a great deal of information that must be explored. Just as one word leads to yet another when we consult the dictionary, one article in an initial literature review will lead to others. Also, the focus is not yet clearly defined, and so advisees may find themselves on a somewhat erratic learning pathway, until they discover a viable direction. Consider them as being on a quest: searching, exploring, playing with ideas.

The Problem, as *Problem*

The literature review unmasks an academic problem, as *problem*. The dissertation itself represents an opportunity to problem solve. It is project management brought to an elevated level that requires skill and expertise in researching, writing, investigating, synthesizing, and analyzing, and that reflects dexterity in decision making. Inherent in the idea of decision making is the idea of making *conscious* decisions about next steps in the process, with each step building sequentially upon the previous. Randomness does not hold sway here, as not everything discovered in a literature review is relevant. This is frequently the problem for students who may discover they are overwhelmed by the vastness of the literature and struggle with separating relevant from irrelevant literature. Remember, not everything in the review of literature is applicable; advisees may come across information that is interesting, but in an ancillary manner.

Resources

The best support can be gained through the student's university library, working with a reference/research librarian to locate scholarly journal articles, books, dissertations, theses, as well as proceedings from conference presentations—in short, the compendium of information on a topic of potential research value. A perusal of these works enables a student to view a primary work or a major work through a network of critical secondary sources and, thus, to establish a framework through which a research gap emerges. This gap represents a place that may serve as the focal point for a new study that leads in new directions. The major work should never be sacrificed in favor of reading secondary sources only, but should serve as the driving force around which the secondary sources are assembled. Primary works and then secondary critical sources create the lens through which various contextual relationships emerge, constructing academic perspectives, theories, and ideas that foster continued research. Intensive investigations provide a platform or background to gather information and to structure arguments that advance the scholarship in new dimensions. These efforts serve as heuristics that demonstrate the interconnectedness or departures in those paradigmatic relationships that shape ideas. Exciting intellectual endeavors emerge through this academic kaleidoscope that holds the potential for differing shapes and colors of nuanced ideas to emerge.

Many students endeavor to discover a topic, but not necessarily through studied activities such as the ones described here. Instead, they may try to connect to a topic they are generally interested in, thinking that their interest alone is sufficient to launch themselves into a certain research area. However, they may not necessarily have enough solid information to guide their choice, and that fact results in a topic that may not be of real interest to the academic community and therefore will not support the requirements of a dissertation in the effort to at least aim for, if not produce, an "original and significant contribution" (Berelson, 1960). In other words, they have not used the literature review as a tool to discover an appropriate focus and to create a rational justification for the study. Further, they may not always appreciate the manner in which the literature review figures logically within the scope of their research or know how to gather these resources beyond their efforts to simply *hack the stacks*. Research librarians hold the key to amassing information critical to dissertation research, the reason why their work is regarded as a science. Research librarians generally are keen listeners and adept communicators, able to visualize a topic from multilayered perspectives, filter down into critical areas of investigative inquiry, and locate corresponding resources. They are an invaluable asset to all researchers and should be included as members of the dissertation committee team.

Literature Review as Tool

A topic that is too thin and that cannot support substantive investigation can send a student along an endless pathway that leads nowhere. Generally, it is necessary that students combine their intellectual interests and passions along with what scholars in the field are calling for as a necessary continued step in the research. A student can be interested in a topic that no one else finds particularly important, simply because the idea has little, if any, scholarly merit.

A former professor of mine once discussed coming upon an obscure poem, written by a famous poet. As an up-and-coming graduate student at the time, he concluded that this poem would make for a marvelous thesis for his master's degree because he could not find any studies whatsoever about it. He was certain that he had made an amazing discovery by resurrecting this relic from its darkened catacomb. Later, he learned that the obscure poem had remained obscure because it was not a significant work, but rather an example of the poet's early efforts to write, a perhaps disconcerting exercise that the poet himself may have wanted to relegate to a tomb.

Other critics were focusing on the truly great works of the famous poet, but not on the one, sole disappointing production that the student had stumbled upon and regarded as a lost treasure. Advisees must remember that *obscurity does not necessarily equate to greatness.* By the same token, a dearth of scholarship may be the result of the fact that the subject is just not of academic interest or concern. Further, consider that a limited topic may actually limit the career potential of a candidate because the areas of expertise are constricted and may not necessarily stretch into more general position descriptions.

The point is for advisees to conduct their research before they begin researching. Consider the following: Is this a topic that the academy is calling for? Is this a topic worthy of a dissertation in terms of rigor? Will the outcomes of the research be significant or at least of value to the academic community or to entities in the real world? Is there a likely opportunity that this research will find value at professional conferences and in publications in peer-reviewed journals? Can a potential career/area of expertise be linked to this particular research?

The preliminary or general literature review is an important pedagogical tool through which advisees explore the academic landscape to determine the gap in the research that may lead to the dissertation topic and to the subsequent formulation of the research questions. Advisees in the fields of science, technology, engineering, and mathematics (STEM) may not experience the intensity of the searching initiatives as do their counterparts in the humanities, social sciences, education, and other fields. STEM students generally, but not always, dovetail their research into that of their faculty advisors, as I have stated previously, and so the steady continuation of research is born out of a predetermined platform. It is not that STEM students skate by because they do not have to discover a topic; the issue is centered in the fact that their advising model accounts for and encourages a steady progression of research, advisor-to-student, and so on, unlike many other fields in which students generally do not continue an advisor's research but rather discover their own unique research agendas. This fact may account for the shorter time-to-degree (TTD) of STEM students, compared with those in other fields. For example, in my own study on TTD at Western Michigan University, the average doctoral TTD for the entire university during the 10-year span of the study was 5.78 years with a standard deviation of 2.47, but for STEM students, it was 5.18 years, with a standard deviation of 1.98 (Di Pierro, 2014).

Preliminary Literature Review to Research Questions

Research questions are frequently generated from the preliminary literature review. Again, the literature will shape the new directions that students can consider as viable options for the dissertation topic. What questions did extant research answer, and what kinds of questions do scholars put forward as issues still to be addressed? Usually, the last chapter of a dissertation (Discussion) represents a treasure trove of research potentialities offered up to the next generation of dissertating students. In essence, the researcher is saying, "If my research were boundless and I didn't need to get finished, I would have done X, Y, and Z."

Naturally, all studies have parameters, and in order to finish, students and advisors need to clearly establish those boundaries or risk researching ad infinitum. Advisees must be encouraged to invest in this investigative process and to spend the time necessary to self-educate. Advisors certainly must cultivate a sense of autonomy in their advisees but, at the same time, consider that students at this stage require hands-on guidance, especially as they are contending with vast library resources that must be organized and coded into decipherable modules of information. Precision in defining the research questions is critical. Students should understand the necessity of constructing questions that encompass *precisely* what they intend to research and then answer. The outcomes of the research must dovetail into those questions, and when research questions are murky or abstruse, it is a foregone conclusion that the student will be off to a complicated, if not improbable, start. *Advisees need a synchronized connection from preliminary literature review to research questions, as a beginning point.*

~ The Take Away ~

1. Advisees should understand the concept of the preliminary literature review: discovery of the dissertation topic and the gap in the research that *their* research will fill.
2. Advisors and advisees should continue to discuss ideas relevant to the discovery of a particular topic and keep the lines of communication open as concepts are being framed.
3. Advisors should be accessible to their advisees because the perusal of literature can quickly resemble a trek through the desert without signposts along the way to indicate that an oasis is forthcoming.
4. Advisors should remember that most students are not library scientists and are essentially untrained in bibliography and library research. Encourage advisees to seek out the expertise of research librarians to assist them in amassing the most critical library resources necessary to fulfill the objectives of the dissertation.

Secondary Literature Review: Dual Roles

Professor vs. Attorney

The secondary literature review is born out of the research questions. Advisors should clarify the differences between the preliminary literature review—to discover a topic/to discern the gap in the research, versus the secondary literature review—to establish the background surrounding an academic inquiry in an effort to indicate the scholarship, to reveal current arguments, and to create a justification for the research. Successful academic writers understand that the secondary literature review actually represents a sustained argument or justification, and that its rhetorical discourse modes are exposition (professor's role) and persuasion/argumentation (attorney's role). In the hands of knowledgeable writers, this kind of review serves as a powerful tool that reinforces theories, concepts, and ideas, and that creates a solid backdrop against which the research is framed and its value projected as a viable potential under construction.

To consider the secondary literature review as a series of independent critical studies that are under review only for the sake of conducting a review is to miss the point entirely. Advisees need to be aware of recurring patterns, motifs, variances, and connections that can be utilized to sustain the logical development of this critical backdrop. The use of headings interspersed throughout the narrative of the literature review unites the writer and the reader in a synchronized momentum that establishes points and provides justifications; further, these distinct but related headings actually lend to a kind of coding scheme punctuated by white spaces or areas within the text that permit for the reader to adjust easily to the next piece of information. The element of exposition demonstrates the advisee's capability to deal with concepts and to integrate them in a cogent manner: to explain/analyze/interpret them in a way that makes sense to intelligent readers and that convinces them of the academic merit, not only of the project, but of the writer as well.

A Fool's Errand

Sending an advisee off to write the literature review chapter before the research questions have been approved by the advisor and the committee is to send him or her off on a fool's errand. There is absolutely no purpose in such an endeavor except to generate frustration, for in the final analysis there is no nucleus around which to structure any sort of analysis. What results is a kind of floating of ideas, untethered to a concrete concept and its logical offshoots. Similarly, advisees who wish to *surprise* the advisor by writing the literature review chapter on their own, without the advisor's guidance and direct involvement, will discover the same unpleasant end: their time will most likely have been wasted, and so will the advisor's in reading useless information.

~ The Take Away ~

1. Advisors and advisees should conserve their time and energy. Both should ensure a shared understanding of the appropriate frame for the secondary literature review and that its purpose is clear: to provide a critical backdrop that frames the research questions and that supports the study under construction.
2. Advisors and advisees should discuss the organization of the secondary literature review and its logic. The manner in which it is organized and delivered also reflects a particular logic that should be discussed with the advisee. The incorporation of distinct headings throughout the narrative not only aids the writer in the organizational process, but guides readers through especially long narrative structures by creating white spaces. This approach should be used during this investigatory stage, for certainly it will emerge during the actual crafting of the concept paper, as well as in the literature review chapter of the dissertation. It is a skill best cultivated sooner, rather than later.

Integrating the Research Questions with the Literature Review

Research questions and corresponding literature review components must be well aligned and correlated. The integration of the two provides the foundational backdrop for the literature review chapter. The following two examples indicate the interconnectedness of the research questions to their respective literature review components and reflect the selection of specific components that are correlated and aligned. Thus, the foundation for writing the actual literature review chapter is established.

Integrated Research Questions and Literature Review Components: Example from Evaluation, Measurement and Research Discipline

Research Questions
1. What are typical policies, guidelines, and requirements for program evaluation and evaluation reports, posed by international donors for health interventions agencies?
2. What are the common types of research designs used to evaluate international health interventions? a. Do evaluators determine attribution of effects to the program/intervention (i.e., determining causation?) b. What are possible threats to internal and external validity evaluations of international health interventions given the study design?
3. What are common components and contents of reports from evaluations of international health interventions? a. What is the relative completeness of reports from evaluations of international health interventions? b. Do the evaluation reports contain sufficient details about design, methods, data sources, and limitations?
4. What is the level of rigor of those designs used to evaluate international health interventions?
Corresponding Literature Review Components
Background and Theoretical Framework: Context of the Study: International Health Organizations;
Major International Organizations Promoting Health;
Evaluation Design in International Health Interventions;
Distinctions and Similarities between Research vs. Evaluation: Defining Evaluation/Defining Research in a Social Context/Fundamental Differences Between Research and Evaluation;
Classifications of Evaluation Designs: Commonly Used Research Designs/Quasi-experimental Designs for Social Interventions/Non-Experimental Designs;
Determining Causation and Impact: Experimental Approach/Non-Experimental Approach/ Causal Inference: The Debate;
Assessing Evaluation Adequacy;
Fundamental Threats to Quantitative Design Elements: Statistical Conclusions/Internal Validity/Construct Validity/External Validity
Fundamental Threats to Qualitative Design Elements: Assessment of Credibility/Transferability Assessment/Establishing Dependability/Establishing Confirmability

The author acknowledges the dissertation of Dr. Julien Kouame: Evaluation, Measurement, and Research, Western Michigan University.

Integrated Research Questions and Literature Review Components: Example from Public Affairs and Administration Discipline

Research Questions
1. What are civil engineers' perceptions regarding mandatory continuing education?
2. What reassessment method(s) do licensed civil engineers prefer in meeting their continuing competency requirements?
3. What is the relationship between demographic and professional variables (age, years of experience, level of education, field of practice, level of responsibility) and civil engineers' attitude toward mandatory continuing education?
4. What is the relationship between the number of competency/negligence events in those instances where mandatory continuing education requirements are enacted vs. the numbers of events in states where no mandatory requirement exists?
Corresponding Literature Review Components
Critical studies in the following areas:
"Regulation issues" for various professions that have "public safety" or "well-being" as a common variable (medicine, law, etc.).
An "approach by approach" overview of continuing education for each of these professions. What does the recertification process look like for these professions? (This serves as a platform or "set up" for the way in which the engineering paradigm for continuing education/recertification unfolds—and also serves as a point of contrast.)
The impact of continuing education on the efficacy of health care professionals in the field, as well as on the welfare, health, and well-being of the public.
Development and evolution of national standards for these professions. How are national standards affected by continuing education requirements OR what is the relationship between continuing education requirements and the ongoing development of national standards?
Perceptions of individuals in the health care professions/law who are required to engage in continuing education practices or who voluntarily engage in them. (This serves as a point of contrast with the research to be conducted on civil engineers.)

The author acknowledges the dissertation of Dr. Alee Sleymann: Public Affairs and Administration, Western Michigan University.

Mosaics and Modular Patterns

Modules consist of smaller units that I will refer to as mosaics, each of which lends to the emerging representation of the dissertation, in much the same manner that the beautiful mosaic tiles in Ravenna, Italy, were configured to create astounding designs that grace cathedral walls and ceilings. Individual mosaics cannot themselves tell the story, but in the collective, they lend to the majesty of an artistic rendering, just as individual modules lend to the portrait of the dissertation. Notice that the *mosaic* organizational patterns in both examples permit for (1) ease in research, and (2) ease in writing, both key factors in working through vast literature review materials. In addition, this organizational pattern permits for advisees to work in a modular style that allows them to pare down this task into multiple but more doable pieces of information into which they can write. Consider the demanding lifestyles of busy professionals and those who are also working within domestic circles who must learn to take advantage of free moments whenever available. You may not have the luxury of an entire day to write, but definitely available are smaller chunks of time that can be accommodated into busy schedules. Even writing for 20 minutes a day is better than not writing at all.

The modular approach encourages the completion of smaller series of tasks, *mosaics*, that when organized together in one unit, complete the literature review in an integrated and professional manner. During the actual weaving together of the individual sections, grammatical connections between ideas or modules (and between mosaics) will have to be developed, but at this stage, it is fundamentally critical to create a platform for the ideas under construction, and the modular approach serves exceptionally well.

Further, by using this method, it is relatively simple to gauge the need for additional information/other critical studies to be placed into each module. As new research is uncovered or revealed, it can be included wherever it makes sense within each modular frame. The idea here is that a *mosaic* approach, a modular approach, ensures that the difficult task of writing an entire dissertation is reduced into smaller tasks, each of which has a definite beginning, middle, and end. It's far easier for a student to say, "I'm going to write 2 modules of my literature review this month," than to say, "I'm going to write my entire literature review."

The same is a consideration for advisors directing students through the literature review process, or really through any element of the dissertation; more manageable tasks are less threatening and, when completed, provide the student with a sense of accomplishment and movement, rather than the dissatisfaction of remaining stagnant, with little progress to spur continued effort. The psychological benefit of making progress is necessary for both advisee and advisor, and this approach ensures a continued action plan with an end goal in sight. This approach is useful at any time when many dissertating students may be working and caring for children and others in their domestic circles.

~ The Take Away ~

For Advisees: When writing the actual literature review chapter, make certain to:
1. Begin the review with a *set up* or overview of the statement of the problem and the significance of the research, as a prelude to the literature review. This approach serves as a justification for the research.
2. Delineate the *component sections* or the *narrative plan* for the literature review chapter. Such an approach represents the organizational logic for this chapter. In other words, it signals that "This is what I am going to do" or "This is what you can expect out of this chapter," and prevents readers from getting lost in the narrative text. The overview accounts for each of the component elements, each of the groupings of the critical studies, and represents a series of signposts for the reader, a directional "heads up" that guides readers from point to point.
3. Sustain the logic and narrative flow between each of the modules so that they connect to each other in terms of argument, point, and relevance.
4. Ensure that your references are not dated, particularly in fields such as science, technology, engineering, and mathematics, where information quickly becomes outmoded and replaced by new and emerging technologies. The general rule of 3 years is an acceptable range for critical studies in these fields. Naturally, the exception to this general rule may be seminal studies that, regardless of the time frame in which they were written, are considered disciplinary cornerstones. Advisors/content experts should be consulted for their particular perspectives in this regard.
5. Include an appropriate conclusion to the Literature Review chapter that summarizes the most salient points that you want to reinforce for readers' benefit.
6. Ensure that you are appropriately incorporating the rhetorical modes of discourse—exposition and argument/persuasion, as important tools necessary in writing the review.

7. Use *headings* and *white space* as a means of directing readers through the entire literature review. This is accomplished via language usage, as well as spacing. An argument that continues page after page, without the benefit of a heading or white space, eventually wears away on readers' interest and is distracting, whereas the use of white space lets the eye rest somewhat, as headings signal the content of a particular section.

Advisors should reinforce these approaches.

References

Berelson, B. (1960). *Graduate education in the United States.* New York, NY: McGraw.

Di Pierro, M. (2014). *Western Michigan University profiles of graduated doctoral students for academic years 1992–present.* Unpublished manuscript, Western Michigan University, Kalamazoo.

Chapter 10

The Concept Paper and the Quality Circle Review

The First Committee Meeting: Preliminary Matters

Let us assume that the advisor and advisee pair is in place, the committee configured and vetted, the preliminary/secondary literature review begun, and the Rules of Engagement discussed during the initial formal meeting of the committee. The matter of proposal development is exceptionally important, and it is necessary to discuss the means by which the proposal will be delivered. Yet, there are times when the student is sent off to write up the proposal, generally three chapters, but without the use of a preliminary document upon which the proposal should be framed. This expectation often enough results in endless hours spent in futile efforts because many doctoral students do not have the degree of experience necessary to deliver the proposal on their own. Moreover, the committee's time may also be wasted in attempting to resolve logical or conceptual issues *at the proposal level*, which is not a good place to determine major flaws.

The appropriate place to vet the design and the unity of the dissertation concept is at the concept paper level, not at the proposal development stage. In many instances, dissertation committees utilize the proposal as if it were a concept paper, but a concept paper of 100 or more pages is a difficult if not impossible place to vet the integrity of the future monograph. Countless hours needlessly devoted to restructuring an entire proposal is not an efficient use of either the committee's or the advisee's time.

Length will not improve an idea that is out of kilter. A concept that is not apparent in approximately 5 or 6 pages is also not going to be apparent in 100 pages or 150 pages. You get the point. I'm more than certain that on at least a few occasions educators have chased a student through an entire paper in quest of an elusive thesis that the student is convinced is present. The same frequently holds true for the dissertation proposal. The emotional and technical difficulty, frustration, and stress endured by the student during an endless "back and forth" of crafting impossible possibilities will eventually take their toll. With time at a premium, students need a more hands-on, collaborative approach that guides them through the complex process of conceptualizing their dissertations. Advisors and committee members would do well to uncover efficient, more streamlined methods for proposal development and invest in these processes in clearly articulated ways that spell out their relationship as dissertation project partners.

The use of the concept paper and the quality circle review are two important tools that the advisee and the committee will find critical to the efficient and effective development of the dissertation proposal. Further, the implementation of these tools can safeguard the timely trajectory to the Ph.D., help to staunch end-stage attrition, and place the student into a closer proximity with the actual demands of the dissertation.

End Stage Attrition

Although much of doctoral attrition occurs during the first two years after matriculation, a significant proportion of students (15–25%) experience *end-stage attrition,* occurring after candidacy (Di Pierro, 2007, p. 373; Lovitts, 2005, p. 138). At this stage, students appear to have mastered obvious hurdles: demanding coursework and grueling comprehensive or qualifying examinations. However, students often underestimate the difficulty of writing the scholarly monograph and sometimes unwittingly refer to the dissertation as nothing more than the final task in a long checklist. Such attritions represent a tremendous institutional and personal loss, as Barbara Lovitts' (2001) seminal study on departure illustrates.

Non-completers are not less intelligent or less motivated than their colleagues who complete (Lovitts, 2001). They are, however, overcome by a series of barriers, one of these being the inability to fully conceptualize and deliver a completed dissertation. Too often, students are unable to produce a book-length study without consistent guidance and assistance. Moreover, dissertation advisors and committee members often assume, incorrectly, that students possess requisite skills.

Findings from the Council of Graduate Schools (2009) indicated that 298 out of 1,856 doctoral students (16%) who participated in the Ph.D. Completion Project at 18 institutions had neither completed their programs of study nor withdrawn (p. 1). Like many of their colleagues, these students remained "on the fence," unwilling or unable to make the important decision to leave or stay. Thus, they remain at a difficult impasse.

Underestimating the Dissertation Challenge

Many doctoral students underestimate the challenge of conducting dissertation research and find themselves unprepared. Compounding this dilemma of unpreparedness for the task of the dissertation is the fact that students are too frequently left to their own devices to assemble a research agenda and return to advisors with a prospectus, an introductory chapter, or, worse yet, a completed three-chapter proposal, as my experience with them has borne out. Many of the students with whom I currently work fall into this category and find themselves at a standstill; they do not have the knowledge or expertise to contend with the writing task, and many of them have completely underestimated the project's scope. Lovitts (2005) indicates that the research and writing of the dissertation, including the selection of the major advisor on the dissertation committee, are "often vague and alien concepts" to students (p. 140). The approach of leaving students to their own devices in these matters creates a formula for potential disaster because it pushes students' limitations, not lessens them (Di Pierro, 2011). Yet, there are many advisors who use this model of the *scholar in isolation*, instead of more collaborative models that conjoin them with their advisees in productive partnerships that explicate the dissertation process. Students have *notions* regarding the elements that comprise a dissertation, but frequently do not understand its structure or how it functions. It becomes clear, then, that it is necessary to break the monograph down into "doable" elements in the form of a concept paper and provide students with an organizational edge in their favor.

Another dilemma for doctoral students is that many underestimate the proximity of the dissertation within the time frame of their programs. For many doctoral students in education, the social sciences, and the humanities, the dissertation resides in the distant future. Unlike many of their counterparts in the fields of science, technology, engineering, and mathematics (STEM), their research is often not connected to their advisors' research. They must *discover* a topic, an intimidating activity. The science advising model has been recognized as an efficient model that not only advances the advisors' research and continues the academic conversation, but also spares students from potentially long, infertile periods of topic formulation. This model is not generally used by non-STEM disciplines, but adoption of this model across all disciplines is worthy of consideration.

Bowen and Rudenstine (1992) suggested that this discovery process represents an "unusually vulnerable" period (p. 14) that may require students "to spend one and two years searching for the 'right' topic and preparing a dissertation prospectus" (p. 254). Students generally enter into this stage after completion of the comprehensive examinations, and thus enter into a kind of dead zone, where they may dwell for long periods, searching. The price of this ongoing and sometimes fruitless search may be protracted time-to-degree or attrition. Therefore, it is necessary for advisors to bridge this artificial gap by first recognizing it, and then by implementing interventions so that students avoid entering into a labyrinth. Engaging students about their research *earlier* in their educational process, through the use of a concept paper, could serve as a catalyst to the research process and could aid them in overcoming what Lovitts (2005) describes as the "critical transition," the pathway from course taker to researcher (p. 138). In this manner, the doctoral educational process moves logically into the dissertation and is not interrupted by the void that occurs between the completion of comprehensive exams and the development of the prospectus/proposal.

The complexity of the process in creating and writing dissertations may not be as apparent to students as advisors might surmise. Students frequently discover that the skills that ushered them through coursework are not necessarily transferable to the demands of the dissertation. Lovitts (2005) writes that students are admitted into doctoral programs because they have been "good course takers" at the undergraduate or master's level. Doctoral level work, however, requires "independent research" and the creation of an "original contribution" to the field (p. 138). These elements do not necessarily emerge out of the course-taking period in students' trajectory to the Ph.D., and students' discovery of this inability to produce a viable framework for the dissertation is disconcerting. Moreover, *doctoral students are often reticent to communicate this inadequacy* to advisors and committee members. Students do not always reach for support mechanisms in a timely manner, nor do they often announce difficulty. They discover that they have not adequately planned for (or, more accurately, been prepared for) the research project, and it is the lack of an approved plan for the dissertation that undermines confidence and thwarts progress.

Advisors can overcome some of these impediments to degree completion by actively exposing students to research initiatives and having them conceptualize research agendas as part of doctoral practice, early on in their educational programs. Moreover, they should ensure that academic/scholarly writing within the framework of graduate-level courses becomes a mainstay throughout the graduate education process. Unless students cultivate writing acumen as a learned skill sustained throughout the entirety of their educations, they are bound to discover vast deficiencies at the dissertation stage, when and where they can least afford them. I will return to this point later in the book.

Implementation

A streamlined, efficient approach is required. Conceptual conversations, as a way to generate ideas necessary to the development of the concept paper, make sense. I think of, and use, the concept paper in this manner: The concept paper is actually a predecessor to the prospectus or initial form of the dissertation proposal and serves as an innovative tool for both students and advisors throughout the discovery process, that tension-filled time of locating, exploring, and uncovering the idea to be developed. The conceptual conversation drives this process, which then translates from verbal expression to a written format, where it can be examined further, discussed, and refined until it meets with the advisor's approval to develop it along the *next* level: the prospectus (for certain disciplines, political science or history, for example) or the three-chapter proposal (the standard for most disciplines.)

Thus, students in this discovery stage are not asked to produce a *prospectus* of 40 or more pages; they are asked to produce a preliminary document, a concept paper of approximately 6 pages, which serves as a scaffold for the prospectus/proposal. Research ideas that are congruent, as well as those that are not, are immediately observable in the streamlined elegance of the concept paper. The construction of the concept paper itself may well demonstrate how students need to structure and design their research agendas and the manner in which they need to think about (conceptualize) their ideas. Thus, through the use of concept papers, advisors and students may *begin* to bridge the gap between the initial coursework stage of doctoral programs and the actual research phase.

Framing the Prospectus

Advisors who require students to begin with the prospectus, rather than a concept paper, may notice their advisees struggling interminably before eventually locating a viable idea for presentation in the prospectus format. The prospectus is often not a benign document in terms of its expansiveness, its depth and scope, the expectations of the advisor, or the student's understanding of how it is constructed. Students can easily misinterpret its configuration or the purpose it serves and remain inextricably confined within its elusive structure.

The description of a prospectus for one program at a Tier I institution slowly transfigures the prospectus from an initial 10 to 20 pages, including a bibliography and a chapter outline, to a document that suddenly finds expression in the *dissertation* and the future *book* it will birth, all swaddled together. In essence, the student is required to construct a prospectus, but with an eye that also envisions it as dissertation and, eventually, a book.

In many descriptions of the prospectus, the precise organization of the information to be placed into it is not delineated in a clear fashion, and students are encouraged to confer with their advisors and committee members and to write drafts until final approval is authorized. Since the organization of the prospectus is somewhat amorphous, it may vary in format across different dissertation committee members in the same department, which means that precise modeling may not be possible. In addition, a *global perspective* of the work to be accomplished, often a feature of these descriptions/requirements, may not serve students in the initial stage of discovery, where the arrangement of more specific categories of information may take them to that more expansive perspective anyway, but through a different, modularized route.

In other instances, the prospectus is a document isolated from the dissertation proper and is considered a "working document subject to alteration." It is the place wherein students discuss, draw out, and design the dissertation concept, but in many cases, the prospectus does not translate directly into the logical segments/chapters of the dissertation. This begs the question regarding why the prospectus is not a more standardized document that dovetails logically into the monograph for respective disciplines. Other prospectus models require a bibliography with primary and secondary sources, a timetable for completing the research and writing the dissertation, chapter outlines, as well as charts and tables.

All of this would be fine and well with the proviso that all proceeds smoothly in the development of the prospectus. However, experience teaches us that this frequently is not the case; a student can spend an inordinate amount of time developing a complete prospectus, including a detailed bibliography, only to learn that the committee does not approve the topic, something that should have been discovered prior to the crafting of the prospectus document, which the student was told to present to the committee to begin their conversations. In this regard, the conceptual conversations occur after the student writes the prospectus, not before, where perhaps some obvious difficulties could have been detected up front. Some prospectus models indicate that certain prospectus requirements, such as chapter outlines, for example, have limited value, and then the models go on to dismantle the idea that these outlines will find placement in the final version of the dissertation. Students sometimes learn, up front, that their efforts in crafting the prospectus satisfy only the specific end of establishing consensus among committee members regarding the direction of the dissertation, a consensus that perhaps could be gained through less time-consuming approaches. It would seem that time spent in more productive aspects of developing a dissertation plan is necessary.

The concept paper, through its economy of form as well as its innovative placement as a precursor to the prospectus, streamlines the development and writing processes by helping advisors to see into the intricacies of the proposed research, without wasting time. In addition, the design of the prospectus should be reconsidered to make it more compatible with the philosophical and theoretical objectives, expressed pragmatically in the final monograph. If not, then it serves as a kind of unfortunate gatekeeper to completion of the Ph.D.

The Conceptual Conversation

Successful writing requires several important elements, among them an interesting and valued idea and a skilled editor. Consciously incorporating some form of conceptual framework may significantly benefit advisors and committee members as they assist students in developing clear goals for research and writing.

To begin with the obvious, advisors should talk with their advisees about potential interesting and valued ideas that could serve as a foundation for the dissertation. I always ask students to tell me what they want to research. Sometimes their responses are straightforward, but some students struggle in verbalizing thoughts; the dissertation topic remains slippery, vague, and ill-defined. Complicating this is the fact that doctoral students who intend to write a dissertation of quality are expected to make an "original and significant contribution" (Berelson, 1960, p. 173) to the academic conversation in their respective fields. This mindset is critical to crafting the monograph so that it becomes, as Olson and Drew (1998) write, "the first major project that a scholar completes as a 'professional,'" instead of the "last major project a scholar completes as a 'student'" (p. 59).

Time spent up front in discussion is a critical part of the advising and writing relationship between advisor and advisee. The "any port in a storm" approach to dissertation writing, a certain sign of the directionless writer, does not bode well for scholarly success. Some students just want to be done, the topic itself of little concern. In these cases, the dissertation is only as important as any other assignment or task that must be completed. Such students are not energized by the project and do not regard it highly, and so it remains unpleasant. It is not difficult to see how and why a project that does not engage its writer can be set aside, the momentum lost entirely.

The effort to unmask ideas that allow the doctoral researcher, and ultimately the dissertation, to enter into the academic conversation is worth the investment in dialogue. Sonia Foss and William Waters (2007) describe the inherent value of "articulating the pieces [students] want in [their] dissertation out loud through conversation," as an act that makes these pieces "evident" and allows students to explore ideas in more deliberate ways (p. 26). Foss and Waters employ Nelle Morton's label "hearing to speech" to describe the process by which the articulation of thoughts and ideas with the advisor brings those ideas into the writer's consciousness (pp. 26–27). Sage guidance and interaction with advisors attuned to the dimensions of crafting a professional product, original and significant, maintain high standards for the dissertation. In addition, setting the bar this way benefits advisees. They will carry with them a standard of excellence to apply to their own advisees and extend this recursive process well beyond the scholarly monograph.

Students need time and space in which to talk about their ideas, determine the feasibility of a project, and assess their level of interest and comfort in meeting project requirements in a timely manner. When do they want to complete the dissertation and graduate? Students often do not consider this question or contemplate the logistical, intellectual, psychological, and personal demands of the dissertation within a *lived* context.

Most students do not have unlimited resources and need to formulate a plan of action that takes them to degree completion. Is their proposed project doable? This is a critical question. If a project is too expansive, it will not get done and students risk non-completion, despite the resources that may be available. A project that is too thin marginalizes the entire purpose of the dissertation and may jeopardize career opportunities. The acts of talking, discussing, stating, and framing ideas orally put students in a teaching position. In this manner, they rely upon exposition and argument as modes of discourse that bring ideas into being. Initial ideas or concepts that exist in the mind as possibilities are brought forth orally and analyzed for suitability to the project. Socratic dialogue with an advisor unleashes a host of variables that figure in the development of the concept under construction. At the heart of this dialogue is the emergence of a problem-solving heuristic through which the advisor–advisee team strategizes for all elements of the final outcome.

The atmosphere for these conversations between advisor and advisee should be conducive to comfortable engagement. Through careful listening, prompting, guiding, and sage interaction, advisors initiate conversations that raise levels of awareness and provide a sense of direction and focus. During this time, advisors should take notes and record salient elements of the conversation. By asking questions and writing down responses, advisors produce a written document that aligns the objectives for the project with the necessary logistics. The dissertation is project management raised to an entirely new level.

The Concept Paper

The veracity of ideas generated in this conceptual conversation can be tested by framing them into a concept paper. The concept paper is a simple, five- or six-page document, invaluable in helping doctoral students conceptualize ideas. It is applicable to any major writing project: a research grant proposal, an article for publication, or a dissertation, for example. The concept paper permits students and advisors to visualize the arrangement of ideas, like integrated pieces of a puzzle that reveal a picture. The picture represents the framework for the writing and reflects the viability and integrity of the project. In short, it displays the array of ideas that supports the project through an integrated and logical sequence.

The beauty of applying the concept paper to the dissertation process is its streamlined efficacy. Ideas that are incongruent become apparent and signal the need for continued conceptual conversations, refocused research questions, refined methods, and the implementation of revised ideas into a new concept paper. In the absence of this approach, advisors who send their advisees off to produce a chapter-length prospectus of 40 to 50 pages may risk wasting precious time and energy, sifting through a document that goes nowhere. Advisors and advisees both would benefit from a seamless transition that transports them from concept paper, to proposal/prospectus, to dissertation.

Elements of the Concept Paper

The concept paper structure I use consists of the following: (1) statement of the problem, (2) significance of the research, (3) research question(s), (4) literature review components, (5) method, (6) theoretical framework, (7) results and analysis, and (8) discussion. It is important to note that the concept paper contains all of the elements applicable to a complete dissertation, but it is meant to be a work in progress. The concept paper will not have any results to report because the research has not been completed, nor will it have a discussion section at this time. Therefore, these sections in the concept paper may be listed as "under construction."

Subsequent and completed components of this "master" framework document, however, will be placed into the respective chapters to which they correspond in the traditional five-chapter dissertation:

Chapter 1: Introduction. The introduction reflects all items in the concept paper; list items 7 and 8 as "under construction."

Chapter 2: Literature Review. Each of these literature review categories is developed into a comprehensive narrative.

Chapter 3: Method. The method for data collection and data analysis is specified. Students may include a review of the literature that pertains to this specific method(s).

Chapter 4: Results and Analysis.

Chapter 5: Discussion.

1. *Statement of the Problem.* The statement of the problem is a rational and reasoned argument that posits the problem as a problem and indicates the necessity for the research. Critical studies or elements of the literature review that provide supporting information for the gap or intersection in the current research that the student's own research will fill should be addressed in this segment of the text. Students should understand and articulate the need for their research. This articulation appears to be self-evident, but students often struggle to determine the problem or the gap within the context of the literature. Thus, they do not provide the necessary justifications for their work.

An inability to discuss the problem or articulate the importance for the research will affect the viability of the project. For example, Simone, a doctoral student writing a dissertation in the field of education, could not articulate clear reasons for centering her research on the failure or success of school uniform policies to improve school attendance and behavior. She originally intended to replicate a previous study and change only the venue to a different school grade level, but nothing more. In choosing a "safe" project, but certainly not an original or significant study, she began to derail her dissertation. Her committee's sustained conceptual conversations with her revealed that experts in the field were calling for additional research into the identification of variables that accompanied the implementation of uniform policies and that could account for changes in attendance, behavior outcomes, or academic achievement. By widening the circle of thought to research these additional factors, Simone conducted a meta-analysis of critical studies that accounted for both the success and failure of uniform policies. She examined other variables/factors that could potentially account for the outcomes noted in those studies. Thus, in changing the way she perceived and stated the "problem," she was able to create an intersection into numbers of inconclusive studies and, therefore, contribute to the scholarship by focusing upon the element of conflict resolution, a factor not previously appreciated in other studies.

2. *Significance of the Research.* The student identifies the various stakeholders in the future research and cites the beneficiaries of its outcomes. Far-reaching implications of the project findings should be included. Simone's research intersects with stakeholders on all levels: students; schools that may consider the implementation of uniforms; principals, administrators, and parents; policy makers; alternative schools; inner-city schools grappling with gangs and street crime; and future researchers who need to be informed about new research approaches.

3. *Research Question(s).* The research questions embody the thesis and should be clearly phrased in a precise manner that captures the exact research initiative. Students are often enmeshed in the research process on intuitive levels, rather than by a series of clearly crafted questions that guide the direction of the project. Once the research question(s) is written out and is clearly before them, they can move toward the objective. Something in the act of verbalizing the questions and then writing them down makes the target more concrete and promotes a straightforward approach. Simone asked this overarching question: What does a meta-analysis of critical studies regarding the success/failure of high school uniform policies indicate about the identification of variables that correlate with changes in the attendance, behavior, and academic achievement of students?

4. *Literature Review.* The components for the literature review are generated from the research questions and listed in the order to be used in writing the dissertation. When designing the literature review, students consider key terms in the research questions from which to structure the review. In addition, students should bear in mind what others reading their dissertation need to know about this research enterprise so that the research is framed against the review, which provides a backdrop of sorts. This organizational arrangement also facilitates library research.

5. *Method.* The method for data collection and analysis that best complements the research questions and fits the project is described in this section. When developed completely, this section becomes Chapter III of the standard dissertation. It is advisable to use a process analysis mode of discourse to structure this piece. If the research involves human subjects or substances that require review by an institutional review board, information about the appropriate protocol should be included in this section. (Advisors and students should always consult with their institution's research compliance officer before conducting any kind of research to ensure that the appropriate protocols are in place, if those are necessary.) Simone incorporated document analysis and meta-analysis in her study.

6. *Theoretical Framework.* The theoretical framework of any study is correlated with main ideas or concepts that are present in the research questions, against which data are analyzed. As the concept paper represents a frame or a blueprint for the dissertation, a theoretical framework is also a blueprint of sorts that presents an established theory (a concept or a perspective, if you like) that correlates to the research and provides a lens through which the implications of the entire project are explained. This framework legitimizes the dissertation research and grounds it in established ways of *seeing* a particular situation, circumstance, problem, or event, and it connects to these ideas logically. Another student, Zala, chose human capital theory as the framework for her study regarding the effectiveness of legislative educational policies in post-apartheid South Africa to increase accessibility to education and employment among white and black South African women.

7. *Results and Analysis.* Once data are amassed, they are reported and analyzed. This section becomes Chapter IV in the traditional dissertation format.

8. *Discussion.* This section includes an overview of the most salient research findings, limitations of the study, and recommendations for future study. Students should keep track of the recommendations for future study as they move through the process of research and writing so that information, ideas, and insights remain fresh and relevant. The discussion section becomes Chapter V in the traditional dissertation format.

In spite of its page limitation, a concept paper represents a comprehensive document that encapsulates the research project. Conceptual conversations with the dissertation advisor or committee members are necessary to enhance and refine the concept paper, which is the road map for the dissertation. Ideally, negotiations and reaching consensus with advisors should occur at this point.

Disciplinary requirements for the dissertation vary, as will respective dissertation formats. However, concept papers can be adjusted to account for variations. The point of a concept paper is to produce a working document for the student and the advisor to efficiently and effectively strategize toward the dissertation. They accomplish this via the conceptual conversation and the concept paper, the document in which those ideas are written and observed and which permits the template for the writing project to emerge. Guidance, oversight, and one-on-one interactions with the advisor, dissertation committee members, or a dissertation coach solidify the writing relationship with the student and foster success through mentorship.

Versatility in Design

The use of the concept paper addresses the needs of doctoral students in almost all disciplines, but where it does not match precisely, it can easily be modified. The value of the document is its flexibility and economy; it preserves the time of advisors and committee members. As they review drafts, they refer to key elements of the plan and direct wandering students back to main points. Writers benefit equally because the concept paper provides signposts for the journey and permits for a kind of modular writing: students can focus upon elements of chapters, rather than struggle with writing entire chapters.

Currently, at my institution, the concept paper is used almost exclusively in one Ph.D. program, the Interdisciplinary Ph.D. in

Health Sciences, where it constitutes the foundation for the comprehensive examination process, as well as for the dissertation, and appears in the program handbook. During my tenure as Graduate Center director, I incorporated it, and still do, into my work with graduate students writing a dissertation or a master's thesis in fields such as public affairs and administration, science education, educational leadership, counseling education, counseling psychology, engineering, music, health sciences, geography, and sociology, among others. I have used this model with over 100 graduated doctoral students, and at the time of the first edition of this book, with over 150 master's level students, as well. This involvement extended to their respective advisors, as well as to those with whom I currently collaborate on dissertation committees.

Ideally, students will work with advisors to shape the research concept. However, that is not always the case and students frequently referred themselves to my office for assistance. They sought a quiet, confidential setting to discuss their work at length, and they left my office with notes from our conversation that included possibilities for their research. These notes were structured into concept papers for presentation to advisors as a kind of groundwork or initial frame for the dissertation, after students worked with me to hone and shape the document. Sometimes, advisors directly referred their advisees to my office and encouraged them to begin the conversation with me, develop the concept, and submit the concept paper back to them for final conceptual development. Either way, I admonished students and also assured advisors that the advisor is the ultimate authority regarding the direction of the dissertation and has the final word. I did not then, and do not now, make an assumption that my work with the student represents the final foundation for the dissertation. In many instances, I consulted at that time as an ad hoc member of students' dissertation committees, helping to explicate the directions of the advisor and committee members and keeping the student focused and on track in developing/shaping the concept paper and implementing it into the three-chapter proposal. Advisors were always kept in the informational loop and students were always referred back to the advisor for input, thus sealing gaps in communication.

Certainly, the concept paper is not used by the entire university, and I would not lay claim to such a statement. I can say, however, that its utility is valued and appreciated by those who have been exposed to it in the real-life experience of advising students through a complex writing process. In addition, the value of having an in-house dissertation coach to reinforce or to explicate the advisor's directions benefitted many students and faculty during my tenure as center director.

The Quality Circle Review

The feedback that dissertation committee members provide, as well as editorial suggestions and recommendations for enhancement of the monograph, identifies and tracks the advisee's position within the real time of dissertation writing. Feedback must be provided in a timely manner to ensure relevance. Also, students should implement revisions consistently and carefully, returning new drafts to the advisor as soon as possible. Without sustained and frequent interaction, both advisors and advisees easily lose momentum, and the intricacies of the project fall prey to deadly inertia, as we saw with Jack's committee.

There are times, however, when navigational signals in the editing process are compromised and writers, like drivers on a highway, must take alternate routes. This does not mean that the destination is no longer in sight; writers must recalculate and get back on course by reviewing their concept and ensuring they meet its objectives through the writing process. This is true also of editing, which is recursive by nature and draws back upon itself as it continues toward the final product. Good writers usually have good editors to guide their journey, and committee members serve in this capacity by providing a holistic perspective.

However, a tool called *quality circle review* also can be employed to provide writers with an instrument that compensates for discrepancies between a writer's familiarity with the subject matter and a reader's understanding. Thus, the quality circle review can serve as a navigational system that helps writers fine-tune their route.

Quality Circle Review Defined

Quality circles are a tool of total quality management, derived from the work of W. Edwards Deming with Japanese manufacturers in the 1960s (Blair, Cohen, & Hurwitz, 1982). These circles are "organizational interventions that seek to improve an organization's productivity and the quality of its products through direct employee participation" (Blair et al., 1982, p. 9). Quality circles are thought to yield recommendations for "improving work methods and quality control" and to "increase employee commitment to implement these changes" (Blair et al., 1982, p. 9). Also, they are thought to generate cost savings, reduce defects, and enhance efficiency (Blair et al., 1982, p. 10). Currently implemented across a wide spectrum of disciplines, from health care to manufacturing, they are an integral element of continuous process improvement. They are also used in the grant-writing world in mock review sessions that replicate the review process used when the final proposal is submitted. Participation in quality circle reviews for faculty writing research grants served as my initiation into the possibility that this tool could be important in helping students to hone their dissertations.

An invaluable resource for writers, quality circle reviews offer dissertation writers an opportunity to enhance the quality of the monograph, save valuable time, and improve writing and research efficiency. The process we adopted is similar to the one used by reviewers of research grant proposals; in some respects, it resembles the configuration of the dissertation committee. David Bauer (1999) writes that the benefits of the quality circle review are contingent upon how closely the mock review process scenario replicates the actual review process used within the dimensions of the grants world (p. 150). This relates also to the world of dissertations.

These review circles, just like dissertation committees, are often comprised of specialists, internal to the writer's field of expertise, and generalists, external to the writer's field of expertise. As readers of the dissertation chapter or research grant proposal, both groups have distinct advantages and serve the writer. They offer opportunities to clarify and strengthen the writing, ensuring that the linguistic framework of the document comports with the conceptual plan of development.

Specialists in the writer's field of expertise are familiar with the language and current scholarly conversations relevant to a particular discipline, so they read the work with an accepted understanding of the terms, practices, or issues. However, when writing for a generalist population, writers must step outside of their field of expertise and clearly respond to those places in the text where readers' understanding is not a given. Generalist readers, whether they are readers of dissertations or grant proposals, offer a rich context of ideas to receptive writers. Their questions, concerns, and insights provide authors with an excellent opportunity to improve the quality of the final document.

The quality circle review lends critical objectivity to the writing process that is not always present when we review our own writing. Writers know what they intend to say. Whether or not they've truly said it is the issue, and the reason for submitting work for a review. Generally, reviews are focused upon one dissertation chapter that either the dissertation advisor or the student thinks may be problematic or simply wishes to enhance. The chapter undergoing review is always accompanied by the first chapter, the introductory chapter, which includes the framework for the entire monograph. If the chapter undergoing review is the first chapter, the writer is asked to submit the chapter, along with a concept paper. Reviews typically last several hours, depending upon the issues to be addressed.

The quality circle itself is actually a doctoral conceptual editing team, facilitated by a dissertation coach, and focused upon one student's work. It controls for a balanced number of participants, both internal and external to the writer's discipline, and provides the writer with "real time" interactions in a face-to-face environment. Further, the quality circle team conducts a detailed crosswalk between the introductory chapter of the dissertation and the chapter under construction to ensure that all objectives delineated in that first chapter find expression within the given chapter under review; thus, it has oversight of the conceptual development of the project and ensures that the writer is indeed delivering those specific outcomes. In the instance of a first chapter under review, the crosswalk is conducted against the writer's concept paper. Standard peer review groups, including virtual groups, frequently do not go to these lengths, nor are they always facilitated and directed by a seasoned dissertation coach. In addition, standard peer writing groups share time equally among members of the group and do not typically focus upon the work of one individual per session. A conceptual editing team differs from a peer writing group in dimension, goal, and outcome.

Quality circle review offers the opportunity for superlative review of the dissertation, although admittedly it is time-intensive for participants, as well as for the writer whose work is undergoing review. Collapsing the editorial suggestions of the team may prove difficult for some writers; however, anecdotal evidence from both students and advisors is positive regarding their perceptions of the value of the experience in enhancing the quality of the dissertation. In the past, we conducted several quality circle reviews per year, mostly in the wide expanse of educational fields and the social sciences, but the demand, over time, increased and students were driving the process by requesting this intervention as well as by incorporating it into their schedules and planning ahead to allow sufficient time for the review process.

Quality Circle Review Participants

Ideally, quality circle review teams include five participants but also can be convened with fewer than five. Typically, two doctoral candidates internal to the writer's field of expertise and two doctoral candidates external to the writer's field of expertise serve. (Doctoral candidates are the ideal reviewers, but doctoral students 1 to 2 years into the process may also serve.) At my institution, I served as the fifth reader and group facilitator. Students who request a review should identify appropriate colleagues within their same field of expertise. Members of the review team receive materials to review at least 2 weeks, and preferably 3, prior to the team meeting.

The Quality Circle Review Process

The following is a description of the process that I used during my tenure as director: The writer whose chapter is being reviewed signs a Confidential Disclosure Agreement, which safeguards the confidentiality of, and restricts access to, that individual's research. Writers also submit a signed copy of their dissertation proposal approval form prior to the review. We also ask them to tell us the positive and negative characteristics of the chapter, and we invite advisors to comment as well.

The process: Readers are seated at a conference table with a copy of the dissertation chapter they have previously reviewed that reflects their annotations. Close textual reading allows questions or comments regarding the logical/linguistic frame of the argument to emerge. The facilitator moves the review team through the chapter, section by section, and asks for comments about each section. Particular attention is paid to conceptual development, logic of argument, exposition, and organization. If necessary, the team alerts the writer to the need to restructure sentences and to address grammatical and mechanical problems. The writer receives constructive criticism, suggestions, and recommendations to strengthen the quality of the chapter, as well as an assessment that the chapter functions, meets its linguistic and pragmatic obligation, and is well executed.

The writer is actively engaged in the process, but more as a listener than a speaker. However, on occasion, the writer may be called upon to explain or clarify certain points that reviewers think problematic or warrant further explanation. The writer takes notes on his or her copy of the dissertation chapter and annotates reviewers' comments. The act of writing down this commentary sustains the writer's engagement with the team and solidifies the new direction.

At the conclusion, all information (i.e., all dissertation chapters) is returned to the student, as outlined in the Confidential Disclosure Agreement. Students reserve the right to implement those changes that best complement their work; they are not coerced into adopting reviewers' recommendations. The facilitator provides a detailed report to the dissertation advisor, who should remain closely connected to the quality circle review process.

Quality circle review sessions are conducted in a positive atmosphere of respect and support. The team's main objective is to enhance the quality of their colleague's dissertation chapter. Dedication and commitment to the project are necessary to a successful review experience.

Reviewer Benefits

The commitment to review is substantial. Doctoral students are busy people who need to focus upon their own research. However, the process of lending a critical eye to their colleagues' work helps them to understand the dissertation writing process and avoid potential pitfalls in crafting their *own* monographs. Moreover, the invaluable opportunity to review successful and not-so-successful examples reinforces their learning about the dissertation process. Since these reviewers typically have never reviewed dissertation drafts, strategies that illuminate the writing/editorial pathway represent a "win-win" for all participants. Participation in peer review of writing provides students with a learning experience through which evaluation/assessment of writing, via collaboration, becomes a mechanism for improvement of the document (Topping, 1998).

Of great importance to future faculty is that exposure to the quality circle review within the framework of their own dissertation experience prepares them to implement this tool with their advisees. The experience steadies them to meet the formidable challenges of dissertation advising and represents a "Preparing Future Faculty" component in the process. Advisors who use this tool not only help their own advisees but also train future dissertation writers, those serving as peer reviewers in the review process. New faculty also benefit from the training experience and are taught to work within a viable process that intersects logically with continuous process improvement.

In Retrospect

For the 17 years of my tenure as director, the Graduate Center was configured as an institutionalized unit responsible for students' safe trajectory to the Ph.D. through its services, seminars, programs, and expertise. It brought to campus renowned experts in their respective disciplines, as well as in the field of graduate education, and created positive change in the practice of doctoral education at my university. Retention and graduation rates increased, and attrition decreased. Such positive inroads can reasonably be attributed to participation in national research projects in graduate education, internal research, the heightened accountability and dedication of faculty to their advisees, and, most importantly, implementation of best practices in graduate education. The use of the concept paper and the quality circle review are two examples.

~ The Take Away ~

1. We know that when students and advisors embark upon the dissertation journey, they do not want to guess or suppose that they will arrive. Interventions such as concept papers and quality circle reviews are critically important as prescriptive measures that enhance opportunities for degree completion and graduation. Getting lost along the way should not be an option.

References

Bauer, D. (1999). *The "how to" grants manual: Successful grantseeking techniques for obtaining public and private grants* (4th ed.). Phoenix, AZ: The Oryx Press.

Berelson, B. (1960). *Graduate education in the United States.* New York, NY: McGraw.

Blair, J. D., Cohen, S. L., & Hurwitz, J. V. (1982). Quality circles: Practical considerations for public managers. *Public Productivity Review, 6*(1/2). Retrieved June 2008, from https://www.jstor.org/stable/3380398?seq=1

Bowen, W. G., & Rudenstine, N. L. (1992). *In pursuit of the Ph.D.* Princeton, NJ: Princeton University Press.

Council of Graduate Schools. (2009). Ph.D. Completion Project: Findings from the exit surveys of Ph.D. completers. *The Communicator, 42*(4), 1–8.

Di Pierro, M. (2007). Excellence in doctoral education: Defining best practices. *College Student Journal, 2*, 368–375.

Di Pierro, M. (2011). Disambiguation: Through the looking glass—From debriefing to process improvement. *Journal for Quality and Participation. Making a Difference, 40*(4).

Foss, S., & Waters, W. (2007). *Destination dissertation: A traveler's guide to a done dissertation.* Lanham, MD: Rowman & Littlefield.

Lovitts, B. E. (2001). *Leaving the ivory tower: The causes and consequences of departure from doctoral study.* Lanham, MD: Rowman & Littlefield.

Lovitts, B. E. (2005). Being a good course taker is not enough: A theoretical perspective on the transition to independent research. *Studies in Higher Education, 30*(2), 137–154.

Olson, G. A., & Drew, J. (1998). (Re) Reenvisioning the dissertation in English studies. *College English, 61*(1), 56–66.

Topping, K. (1998). Peer assessment between students in colleges and universities. *Review of Educational Research, 68*, 249–276.

Chapter 11

Implementation of Editorial Commentary and Technology

As I said earlier, one of the most difficult processes to manage during the dissertation is the editing phase. The fact is that most people do not enjoy editing, either doing it or receiving it. The presence of red marks and track changes on a document can drain the life out of even the most stalwart of advisees, and depending upon the number of committee members, there will be that exact number of editorial drafts to be incorporated into a single document. The sheer management of this process alone can be daunting; however, the implementation of some simple measures can assist.

Line-by-Line vs. Conceptual Editing

First, it is critical that the dissertation advisor take control of the editing process by reverting back to the Rules of Engagement and delineating additional rules that guide the editing process, as I stated earlier. It is important *not* to assume that students understand your editing style, and so explaining *how* and *why* you edit as you do is important. Some advisors prefer to use track changes in Microsoft Word, while others prefer to edit on hard copy. Some prefer to use a *sentence-by-sentence* editing style combined with a conceptual editing approach, and others will not use the line-by-line approach but will stay focused on conceptual development only, leaving the grammar and mechanics to a professional editor who manages only the external elements, not content. Brent's story (Chapter 3) illustrates the point that failure to articulate editing procedures and expectations can easily forestall the progression of the draft into a finalized product.

In my work, I use both styles simultaneously and also use the text as a place to establish a dialogue with the student. In this manner, the editing style assumes the characteristics of a *conversation* and engages the student in a more critical interchange during which I make comments, suggestions, and recommendations, but also ask questions. The point here is to actively engage the student in the entire editing enterprise and to prompt responses to the text that move it toward finalization.

Editing concerns far more than just the mere implementation of correct punctuation marks or word usage, but involves intensive connections to the literature and to matters of logic, analysis, and synthesis of ideas. Students have to think actively and critically about what they are doing, and why. When their writing elicits challenging questions in the minds of readers, students need to think and reason from the perspective of those readers, not to stay blindly manacled to their own opinions or perspectives. This idea of casting themselves as *readers* of the text, not simply as *writers* of the text, is fundamentally important. In many respects, good writers cast themselves in the dual role of writer/editor and continue to hold themselves up to the task of self-evaluation or self-assessment at all turns. If their writing prompts a question or poses a doubt, then *that* is the place that generally draws their critical attention. Progress can be enhanced if advisees are taught to anticipate readers' counterargument to the written document. A place in the narrative text that generates a reader's question or objection or a need for further information or clarity is the precise place that should draw the writer's attention.

Knowing When It Isn't Working: For Advisors

So, the advisee has submitted a first draft of a chapter and the advisor has returned it with editorial commentary for implementation and is now reviewing that particular revised draft. It is up to the advisor to instruct the advisee about accepted procedures for the implementation of the committee's editorial suggestions and also to point out inherent difficulties so that the student is conscious of them. In many ways, it's a learn-as-you-go approach, with students held accountable for successful management of the critiques. The following are some signs of difficulty that should be noted immedi-

ately, as in many instances they can become compounded over time and threaten successful completion of the dissertation:
1. *Lack of Authorial Control.* The student lacks scholarly authority over the text and is not comfortable with the critical dimensions of the argument or with contending with the literature. When pushed to respond to or to change the narrative, the student lacks the capability to implement changes because he or she simply does not have a firm grasp on the material. Information appears to be inserted into the text without cognizance of purpose or rhetorical function. Quotes appear to be dropped into place, but without relevance to the ideas under construction; in other words, these are citations for the sake of creating citations, not for the purpose of constructing points in an intellectual argument.
2. *Cut and Paste Issues.* The advisee does not take the time to clearly address the advisor's editorial changes within the text, but resorts to "cutting and pasting" information from various sections of the first draft into the "saved as" or second draft; the advisee continues this pattern, but without consistency or uniformity, without understanding the purpose of a change or how the implementation of a series of those changes actually alters the text, permitting it to develop and grow into a scholarly document. The cut-and-paste approach is superficial in nature, permitting the student to get the editing job *over and done with,* rather than to create a document of substance.
3. *Excision of the Text vs. Addressing Change.* An advisor may call for substantive changes or explanations that the advisee contends with by simply excising or omitting those particular parts from the narrative. There are many places in the multiple drafts of a dissertation that will require change or clarification, and if the advisee resorts to eliminating them, rather than addressing them, there won't be much of a dissertation left. A great deal of this response to the committee's editorial commentary is a result of the fact that the writer does not know how to address the requested change. Therefore, the writer resorts to swift elimination of the pesky problems.
4. *Ignoring Editorial Commentary.* The advisor/committee

members have taken great pains to edit the document, only to find that the advisee has decided to ignore completely the recommendations and has left the document unaltered. Nothing elicits more frustration for advisors than an advisee who ignores commentary critical to the dissertation's continued refinement.

5. *Lack of Conclusions.* The writer is not able to *pull the thread through* the argument and leaves the reader without concluding ideas or without a logical conclusion to a statement or series of statements. In these instances, the "So what" or "This means" part of the writing is missing, either because the writer writes from his or her own perspective and *knows* the conclusions but fails to communicate them, or he or she has simply not considered that the outcomes/conclusions may not be obvious to the reader or, worse yet, hasn't considered outcomes or conclusions at all.

6. *Lack of Organization.* The elements of the narrative are not unified and are not arranged in a meaningful way that takes the reader from point to point. Inexperienced writers often do not understand the value of *white space* or of using a series of *headings* to take readers from point to point. Refer to commentary in Chapter 9.

7. *Writing Around the Topic, or Planning vs. Writing.* This characteristic can be likened to a kind of prewriting stage during which writers attempt to plan out the writing task or discover a new direction in their writing. However, it is more of an internal dialogue, rather than a true writing of the text, because there is no central plan of action to anchor it. Advisees who tend to dabble in this manner actually don't know what they truly want to say, and so they tend to *write around* an idea, rather than directly approach it. It is always best for them to consider the value of a writing plan of action, rather than simply begin a writing journey without the benefit of a compass. If, however, they want to indulge in prewriting, there is nothing wrong with this approach as long as the prewriting is not presented to the committee as a chapter-in-progress. It is an idea-in-process only and should have preceded the writing of a chapter.

8. *Grammatical and Mechanical Errors.* The presence of gram-

matical and mechanical errors in dissertation drafts is unacceptable. From the advisor's point of view, the document appears assembled in haste and looks sloppy and unprofessional. The external appearance may reflect negatively on the committee's impression of the internal construction of the document. In other words, the committee could easily conclude that academic solidity may be flawed and, therefore, doubt is cast upon the integrity of the whole. In addition, shifts in verb tense and person also signal that the advisee is not in control of the text. (Dissertations, unless they are creative works of art, are generally not to be written in first person. Certainly, qualitative dissertations would reflect first-person attributions from research participants.) Further, the use of run-on sentences and sentence fragments mar readability and therefore meaning. Incorrect word usage, typographical errors, and flaws in punctuation significantly dismantle the sense of the writer-as-scholar. The fact that the advisee is writing a draft does not excuse him or her from producing a document that is professional on all levels, and so, yes, appearance and content matter. Refer to item 12 for additional commentary.
9. *Repetition.* The writer reinforces the point, not strategically within the body of the text, but rather at too frequent intervals. This tendency results in a circular type of writing, which hammers the point continuously and doesn't let up on it; three or four sentences in a row that all make the same point are not productive from a content or an organizational perspective. Generally, the repetition is a sign of not knowing how to advance to the next step in the writing process, and so circularity provides a grounding, albeit it a nebulous one.
10. *Lack of Awareness of Audience and Purpose.* Advisees who begin the writing process but who are not aware of the audience (*Who are the readers?*) or the purpose of the writing, whatever that purpose may be, are off to a poor start. These perspectives are part of the tactical plan of action and are necessary to a successful dissertation outcome or any writing outcome, for that matter. Even texts, email, and instant messages through social media, despite their seeming infor-

mality, should be written with considerations of audience and purpose.
11. *Parataxis.* Dissertating students frequently have difficulty in coordinating elements of the monograph into flowing sections that are congruent, synchronized, and harmonious, moving readers from point to point, logically. Therefore, ideas seem to be dropped into place, without the benefit of coordinating them together. Thus, what results is a kind of disconnection that poisons the entirety of the document. The writer may not see the holistic argument or the integrated sense of logic that must be present in the writing, or he or she experiences difficulty in the narrative presentation of ideas. Both of these are not mutually exclusive. A student may be able to shine as an orator, but not be so stellar when it comes to presenting those ideas in a narrative. Sudden starts, stops, U-turns, and backtracking in a document are signs of parataxis.
12. *Lack of an Appropriate Bibliography/Reference Style.* The majority of academic readers will generally begin perusing a document from the back cover, in other words, from the works cited pages or references. Failure of students to use a substantial bibliography can negatively impact readers' perceptions of the text, which appears inadequate to the task at hand. The lack of seminal studies or the works of established scholars in the field contribute to the unfortunate impression that the student has not prepared appropriately. Refer to commentary in Chapter 9 regarding consultation with research librarians.

    Students should get into the habit of submitting an individual bibliography with each separate dissertation chapter, since separate chapters are generally reviewed, one at a time. In this manner, students continuously signal their professionalism to the committee. At the point of dissertation proposal defense, submission of a single bibliography for the entire three chapters is acceptable. Moreover, in this day and age of the internet, the use of online references and material from blogs may raise concerns, and it is always best to consult with advisees regarding the viability of incorporating such sources into the bibliography and also to review with them the extent to which such references are appropriate to specific disciplines. Drafts should always be written with the reference style appropriate to the respective discipline: MLA, APA, Chicago, etc.

13. *Lack of Consistency/Sloppy Editing.* Advisees will implement changes, but inconsistently, providing no rationale for addressing certain changes or failing entirely to address other changes. This haphazard approach to the editing task protracts progress and also frustrates committee members who find themselves in the position of having to re-edit the same sections of the text that they had previously addressed in order to bring the document to the next level. In essence, the committee ends up chasing the advisee through a morass of red ink.

14. *Argumentative or Confrontational Behavior.* Students who are experiencing difficulty in writing/editing the dissertation sometimes lapse into a confrontational stance with their advisor or committee members regarding editorial/conceptual recommendations. Whether this becomes a temporary situation or a permanent one is something that advisors/committee members need to be wary of. Occasional issues can generally be resolved, but a solidification of poor attitudes into habitually negative, consistent behaviors can undermine the committee's efforts to bring the dissertation to completion. Lack of cooperation and willingness to work with the team may result in the withdrawal of committee members, including the advisor. Long-term manifestations of poor attitudes cannot and should not be tolerated.

15. *Implementation of Non-Recommended Changes.* The tendency to change sections of a chapter when such changes were not recommended poses a serious difficulty to the advisor and the committee members, as well as to the advisee. As mentioned previously, the result is a series of "first drafts" only, without the benefit of advancing the work to the next level. This means that the time spent in editing a previous chapter has essentially been wasted because the advisee has ignored those edits and decided to create a new chapter that the advisor has not seen before. A pernicious dimension of this difficulty concerns students who implement changes

to an approved methodology, without the benefit of vetting such substitutions with the chair or the committee. This issue became the *proverbial straw* for a committee that I served on: Of her own volition, and without cognizance of the implications, the student altered the method as well as the corresponding data collection process, substituting new procedures for those the committee had already approved to fulfill the research agenda. These discrepancies were discovered serendipitously, emerging during the finalization of the proposal and resulting in an agreement by all parties to dissolve the committee, which had surpassed its tolerance level. It is important to note that (1) a series of difficulties such as the ones described in this chapter had already occurred during the working relationship with the student and undermined the trust and confidence that girds the advisor–advisee relationship; (2) the substituted method/data collection procedures would never have aligned with the research objective, and according to the student "just sounded better"; (3) the committee members were broadsided by the student's actions and determined that future engagement had been hopelessly compromised.

Knowing When It Isn't Working: For Advisees

If you are an advisee who resorts to any of the 15 characteristics just outlined here, then the process of effective editing and working with your committee is not in place. A critical examination of your own style in both receiving and responding to the advisor's editorial commentary will be necessary in establishing your level of skill and commitment to the editing task. Just as writing is a skill, so too is editing for both the advisor and the advisee, and it is a cumulative skill. The more you do it, the better you become at doing it. Balk at doing it, and you are hindering your own progress in completing the dissertation and getting done.

In Chapter 3, we saw that it was apparent the editorial exchanges between Brent and the advisor were not efficient. Advisors need to be clear in their editing directives, but advisees need to be dedicated to understanding the advisor's editing style. They need to communicate their difficulty and ask for assistance or clarification. However, they should at least make the attempt on their own and endeavor to learn the advisor's editing style. If this proves not to be effective, then arranging for face-to-face meetings to clarify editing issues, as I described previously, is a good idea. From that point forward, a combination of both approaches may be necessary. What is clear, however, is that advisees must learn to work independently. The ultimate goal of the doctoral degree is the ability to conduct research autonomously, and the dissertation is the springboard into that goal. Are you up to the task?

Signs of further difficulty occur when:
- it becomes obvious to you that the advisor's commentary remains difficult, unclear, or just confusing, and there are no indications that this trend will change anytime soon. Think of Brent's advisor's penchant for using exclamation points or question marks, without an editorial narrative that explained those punctuation marks.
- several committee members provide contradictory editorial commentary and you are at a loss to resolve their suggestions.
- you do not understand the goals or objectives of each dissertation chapter and are therefore not adequately fulfilling them.
- your writing is not unified, coherent, or organized appropriately.
- your writing wanders without meaningful direction or logical purpose.
- there is no nucleus or guiding principle that reflects a viable concept or frame for the dissertation, or when the objectives shift, and when randomness and contingency become the hallmarks of your work.
- you use erudite, convoluted, abstruse sentences to impress the committee, instead of using plain English, and when your word choices are entirely off the mark and ill chosen.

These, as well as the 15 variables listed above, are all indications that the editing and writing processes are off kilter and are not coalescing in a final product.

At this point, it's time to stop and rethink other writing/advising strategies that will be more productive. It may simply be that you do not understand what the advisor or committee members are looking for, or if you do, you may lack the editing and writing skills to deliver those recommendations. The inexperience of a novice writer may account for some of these issues, as many students have not encountered previously the type of rigor that surrounds the writing of the dissertation. Remember that writing is a skill acquired through continuous and studied practice, not through some gift dropped down miraculously from the skies.

If any of these signs emerge, it is time to engage in a *diagnostic conversation* that helps you and the advisor or committee members to understand the expectations. Remember that the purpose of writing is to communicate, and unless your writing communicates clearly and succinctly, you are not achieving the end goal.

~ The Take Away ~

1. Advisors and advisees both need to understand the telltale signs that indicate the process is drifting off course. Self-reflection is an important first step; it is likely that communication may be faltering. Has the advisor clearly articulated instructions? Is it that the advisee does not comprehend these instructions or agree with them, or does not understand how to logistically implement editorial commentary and direction into the narrative? Has the advisee placed himself/herself in a position of authority that presides over the authority of the committee and taken the reins without forethought or awareness regarding the repercussions of such choices? In all instances, once trust and confidence are undermined, the prospects for a viable working relationship between advisor and advisee may be eclipsed.

Chapter 12

Naming Conventions for Maintaining Draft Files

Failsafe Practices

The manner in which advisees and committee members keep track of their respective documents concerns the use of naming conventions for their files. These must always be consistent, as well as accurate, in terms of date. If you are using an electronic format, one technique is to rename the file document with the current date of the editorial commentary. Consider the case of one advisee who continued to label her quite numerous files with the label "FINAL" with no date or further identifying information. Searches to access the *true*, *last* final copy were nightmarish escapades, excruciatingly painful, and a complete waste of valuable time that she could have spent in other activities.

Committee members should agree to the same naming convention practices so that all documents for those individual members follow the same procedure. However, not all members will edit at the same time, making the consistent use of a synchronized naming convention unwieldy, if not impossible. One way to address this issue is for advisees to create separate folders on their laptops and maintain individual files for individual committee members. For example: *Chapter I: Mary Smith, October 4, 2020.* (The date provided equates to the date that Dr. Smith completed her editorial commentary and submitted the document back to her advisee.) Inside the document itself, the advisee should make a note on the actual document that explains that he or she is implementing Dr. Smith's edits and indicates the date: *Chapter I: Implementation of Smith's October 4, 2020 edits, completed on October 27, 2020.* In this manner, there is a traceable history of all submissions, edits, and resubmissions for each committee member. This is a huge undertaking, considering the fact that there can be at least three members on a committee, and possibly at least double that number, in some disciplines.

Advisees can also use separate memory drives for individual committee members and maintain control over the editing process in this highly structured manner. They can use the same naming conventions as illustrated above, but a separate memory drive would be assigned to each committee member. Committee members who prefer to edit in hard copy can scan their edited document into a PDF file, thereby permitting the advisee to save the document electronically and label accordingly.

Lost Data: Imagine the Unimaginable

The key in all of this is to establish efficient tracking systems for all editorial reviews among advisor, student, and committee members. In addition, it is critical to create multiple electronic back-up systems for all work on the dissertation: the research, the writing, as well as data collection, each stored in different locations. I became aware of one doctoral student in a STEM field (science, technology, engineering, mathematics) who lost all of his collected data due to corruption of his files. Devastated and depressed, he spent 8 months lamenting his lost work and vowed to walk away from his degree. His advisor persuaded him to collect the data again and to rebuild his research, which he slowly recaptured, only to lose the data a second time due to the same issue: corrupted files and no back up. It is true that lightning can indeed strike twice, as this case bears out. The student did not complete the Ph.D.

Lost data take many forms, not just via corruption of files due to viruses. We have all heard tragic accounts of lost or stolen computers that house the *only* copy of a student's dissertation. We have listened to doctoral students' heartrending entreaties to thieves to keep the computers, just return their dissertations, no questions asked, no charges pressed. At such points, retrieval is doubtful, and loss of the research and the degree are very likely. Jessica Osuna, a doctoral candidate at the University of California, Berkeley, was meticulous about safeguarding her intellectual property and had several seemingly failsafe methods in place (see Troop, 2011). However, when someone burgled her home and took her laptop, as well as broke open her safe where she kept an additional hard drive, she realized the fragility of her efforts to ensure the safety of her data. "I wish I would have backed up just one CD of the processed final data, and then just e-mailed myself a copy of the manuscript every time I left it.... Those two things would have saved my butt."

Unlike Osuna's experience, Anjali Adukia's is characterized by humor. Adukia, a Harvard University doctoral candidate in the field of education, traveled to India to secure data for her dissertation research. In a celebratory moment, walking down a pathway with a copy of her data on a DVD in one hand and a banana in the other, Adukia was surprised when a monkey jumped suddenly from the bushes, grabbed the DVD from her hands, and sprinted off. Adukia, shocked at the unexpected theft, tossed the banana at the monkey, causing it to let go of the DVD and instead opt for the treat. In the online video reenactment of this event, Adukia jokes that through the act of tossing the banana she realized she had "defended" her dissertation (Harvard Graduate School of Education, 2011).

Note that in this case it is only the fortunate outcome that permits for an appreciation of ironic humor. The point here is to *imagine the unimaginable* when it comes to protecting your research data; viruses, thieves, or monkeys aside, lost data can spell disaster for researchers.

"Failsafe" Technology

The emphasis should be on prevention, rather than recovery and compensation, and this will require some disciplined practices. Maintaining and backing up multiple memory drives with current changes and/or storing information on hard drives or on secure servers is one way. Storing them appropriately is yet another: in fireproof boxes, safety deposit boxes, in relatives' homes, or, better yet, "into the cloud," as Don Troop (2011) suggests in his *Chronicle of Higher Education* article, or even by sending files to yourself in email attachments. It is important to note, however, that some engineers would disagree with Troop's idea of cloud safety as the *be all and end all* of data storage, as I noted during one of my presentations when I extolled the merits of cloud storage to a group of students, and several Ph.D. engineering students overruled guarantees of data safety in the cloud, or anywhere for that matter. It is perhaps best to integrate these strategies across a spectrum of techniques rather than select just one method. All of this requires continual monitoring, and none of these procedures is without investment of time and consistent management. Acknowledging that memory drives can indeed become corrupted with viruses and other content-altering programs, and that cloud systems can indeed be hacked, dismantles the illusion that technology is failsafe.

Anti-virus software should be running on your computers all the time. Avoiding the placement of your memory drives into others' computers or prohibiting individuals from placing memory drives into your computer may appear to be hypervigilant or just plain unfriendly, but in the end, these practices may save you from untold harm. One of my students placed a memory drive that contained academic materials and several photos into the photo-processing computer at a nearby chain store and was horrified to discover days later that the drive had become corrupted. Information on the drive was completely inaccessible, and the cost of data retrieval from a professional company was prohibitive. In the end, she had to resort to recapturing information via email attachments that she had sent to committee members and other faculty and restoring lost files as best she could in this manner. As she herself stated, "My life was on that drive," but she was just fortunate enough that her dissertation research was not also on that drive.

The system described above is used frequently by both advisors and their advisees, but as the advantages of technology emerge, a shift in dissertation management is on the horizon, and it makes great sense to explore it. IT professionals and engineers, experts in data management who understand the threats to security, offer a wellspring of guidance and should be consulted to provide knowledge about heightened, state-of-the-art protections.

Global Editing Architectures: Microsoft SharePoint

Years ago, Van Andel Institute in Grand Rapids, Michigan, constructed a new building via a collaborative effort among key players who spanned the United States. The tool used to unite architects, draftsmen, supervisors, and construction managers was Microsoft SharePoint. The idea is this: "If you can build an entire building with this software, then why can't dissertation committee members use it as they build dissertations?"

If you are an out-of-the-box thinker, unafraid of technology, you may prefer to use an electronic system for the collaboration and management of electronic documents. Microsoft SharePoint may provide a more user-friendly, efficient way for dissertation committees and their advisees to confer on the dissertation project. In addition, it can track various edited versions of the dissertation, especially as they undergo evolutionary changes over time, as did the Van Andel architectural project.

Content can be modified, edited, and altered within the collaborative environment of the dissertation committee. Moreover, instead of the advisee managing three, four, five, or even six sets of edits, each corresponding to various committee members and for each specific dissertation chapter, SharePoint allows multiple editors to access a document and to share in the editing process in a collaborative manner that engages each of the members with the advisee. It permits for a "check-in"/"check-out" feature that lets a member of the committee complete his or her editing and signals the completion of that particular editorial task, thereby allowing other editors (committee members) to enter into the process and avoid duplicating each other's efforts (Rockinson-Szapkiw, Dunn, & Holder, n.d.). This approach simplifies the process and unites the committee in the focused or "shared" interchanges of creating editorial feedback. The advisee simply examines the last file's updates and then implements changes accordingly.

Dr. Amanda Rockinson-Szapkiw, former chair of the research division in the School of Education at Liberty University, and her co-authors, Randall Dunn and David Holder (n.d.), advocate this software for online graduate programs with non-traditional students, but it is nevertheless an invaluable approach for traditional students as well.

~ The Take Away ~

1. Use failsafe practices, technologies, and procedures to ensure safe trajectory of the dissertation from draft to completed document.
2. Committee members should use the same naming conven-

tion practices to ensure continuity and consistency of labeling.
3. Advisees can use separate memory drives for each committee member in order to maintain control over the editing process.
4. Emphasize *prevention*, rather than *recovery*; consult with IT and engineer experts.
5. Consider the value of using Microsoft SharePoint or similar software in the dissertation editing process.

References

Harvard Graduate School of Education. (2011, January 13). *Hey! Hey! It's a Monkey!* (with Anjali Adukia) [Video]. YouTube. https://www.youtube.com/watch?v=J6HtRWyiL98&t=17s

Rockinson-Szapkiw, A. J., Dunn, R., & Holder, D. (n.d.). *SharePoint collaboration: Streamlining the dissertation process for online students*. Retrieved October 7, 2013, from http://digitalcommons.liberty.edu/cgi/viewcontent.cgi?article=1173&context=educ_fac_pubs

Troop, D. (2011, March 13). Keep the laptop, give back the dissertation. *Chronicle of Higher Education*.

Chapter 13

Working Against the Grain: For Advisors

The "No Asshole Rule" for Advisors

Let's return to Robert Sutton's (2010) book, *The No Asshole Rule,* for a moment and understand the value of being able to recognize the "asshole" in others, as well as in Self. An important distinction that Sutton makes is that we all hold the propensity for being assholes from *time to time,* or *perpetually.* As he tells us, we can be forgiven momentary lapses, but continued, sustained asshole behaviors can destroy the emotional, psychological, and ethical landscape in which advisors, advisees, and others dwell. Worse yet, such behaviors destroy self-esteem and confidence and may forestall the ability of a student to overcome the distinct challenges of writing the dissertation, which hinge on being able to deliver the final product. This delivery cannot take place in a hostile setting. However, my first rule is this: "Do not abandon the ship" at the *first* sign of difficulty because this is not a wise move, and for a variety of reasons that we will explore. *Sustained* untoward behaviors, however, are another matter entirely.

Renee's story is a good example of how the advisor–advisee relationship degenerates and, moreover, when it does, how this collapse may dismantle working relationships within the department.

Renee's Experience

Renee was a doctoral student at the dissertation proposal stage when she contacted me in the early summer several years ago, explaining that the situation with her advisor had "escalated." She did not know how to resolve the problem and sought my assistance. She and the advisor had worked together in a *fairly* satisfactory manner, but the real difficulty arose when the advisor would not provide Renee with editorial commentary on a Human Subjects Institutional

Review Board (HSIRB) protocol, a document necessary because Renee was conducting research with human subjects. Further, the advisor prohibited Renee from seeking assistance from the research compliance office in an effort to write the protocol according to HSIRB specifications so that she could return the document to the advisor for final editing and approval. Renee's dissertation proposal had been approved 8 months previously, and so filing an HSIRB protocol should not have posed delays since the component sections of the proposal would have addressed the elements necessary to the protocol. A committee-approved dissertation proposal meant that everything was in order from a conceptual standpoint. The next step was to file the HSIRB protocol, and so an 8-month delay on the advisor's part appeared unnecessary.

You're Fired!

Renee indicated that the situation was untenable from her perspective: she had lost a great deal of time and for no reason. Once her HSIRB approval was finally in place, she remained firm in her decision to find a new dissertation chair and feared that her doctoral program was in jeopardy and that the current advisor would not get her through to completion. Their relationship had been problematic for some time and had already resulted in the loss of one year from the time of the comprehensive examinations to the proposal phase, but it limped along until it reached this point of no return. Her confidence undermined, Renee had already decided to terminate the advising relationship when she came to see me, and she could not be persuaded to think otherwise. *Preserve and Repair* is always my first tack. Dismantling of an advising relationship and reconfiguring a new committee are serious matters, but Renee did not agree that the issue could be resolved. However, she did agree to take my advice and contact the advisor to arrange a meeting during which Renee would discuss the issue. The advisor failed to respond to several requests to meet, this silence only solidifying Renee's view that the relationship could not be salvaged.

Departure Etiquette

Renee decided to move forward in terminating the relationship. At my suggestion, she contacted her department chair to inform him of her decision and to propose that her second committee member now become the dissertation chair. The department chair agreed, but with the proviso that Renee attempt to contact the first advisor and have a conversation about ending their association. Previously, even before speaking with me, Renee had made the attempt to meet with this advisor and try to work out the relationship. The intent at that time was to salvage it, not terminate it. But the advisor never responded to that initial request.

The department chair thought it imprudent to proceed without a conversation, and he was right. Protocol and human decency require at least some form of communication and civility. Renee complied and again placed several phone calls and also sent email to the advisor, requesting a meeting to discuss the precarious state of their relationship and the advisability of mutually agreeing to dissolve the relationship. But after waiting for 10 days, without a response, Renee determined that the situation was in stasis. The conclusion playing out was that Renee could have a new chair, contingent upon a meeting with the first chair; however, such a meeting was unlikely because the advisor would not answer email or return phone calls so that arrangements for the meeting could ensue. The only recourse was to take a "wait-and-see" approach.

Power Dynamics

Note that delays such as this one frustrate an already complicated situation, and it is clear that the dynamics of a power struggle were in full throttle: a student with little power versus a powerful advisor. Note also the difficulty for the department chair in the unenviable position of attempting to negotiate a complicated situation and do the right thing for all parties concerned. I am certain his hopes were that the advisor and the advisee would work out their difficulties on their own, either reconcile or terminate, without his direct intervention, thereby avoiding potentially messy political issues for the department.

The advisor eventually responded to Renee with an email to say that she (the advisor) had initiated contact with the department chair and that she and another department professor would meet and that "someone" would contact Renee "in the near future." No date was specified and no agenda set. Renee was understandably worried by this email, especially since a meeting date had not been set. Also disconcerting was the fact that from the language in the email it appeared that she (Renee) was not to be included in this meeting and could not present her perspective.

Stasis continued well into late summer, at which time certain of these key players were on hiatus and not available. The department chair reiterated that he could not replace the first advisor unless Renee had engaged in a conversation with her, and it was clear that that was not going to happen. In Renee's words in an email to me, "I am trying to stay optimistic about my chances of finishing my dissertation and earning my Ph.D., but that is getting harder and harder as all these obstacles continue to pile up against me."

Diversions

Then, out of the blue, Renee received an email from the advisor requesting certain research data be sent to her by the close of business the next day. However, certain facets of Renee's data collection method did not permit her to send the data in an email as attachments; she responded to the advisor that she would gladly come to her office and display the data on a computer. In an email to Renee, the advisor ignored Renee's suggestion to bring the data to her, but reiterated that the department chair, another department professor, and she would meet after the summer hiatus to decide a course of action. In addition, she instructed Renee to continue to prepare the data materials and to send those to her as soon as they were finalized, again ignoring the fact that the data could not be sent via email and that a meeting would be necessary to display them. The point of all of this remained unclear. It begged the question why an advisor on the way out the door would be interested suddenly in reviewing a soon-to-be former advisee's data or, further, why she would refuse a meeting to finalize the separation.

Saying Goodbye: Academic Divorce

At this point, I thought it prudent for Renee to send a formal notification to the advisor. The following is an edited version of Renee's parting letter, which she also sent to the department chair:

> Dear Dr. X,
>
> I would like to start by saying that I find it regrettable and disappointing what has happened with our relationship. I had hoped we would be able to meet, in person and in private, to discuss our advis-

ing relationship. I wanted to hear from you regarding what precisely you needed from me in going forward and how I could best work with you to make this relationship a successful one as I work toward graduation and my career. I had also hoped to speak with you about my perspective and what I need to be successful as a student. I was also advised ... [of this] ... as a first step toward resolution of any difficulties we may have jointly experienced. I contacted you several times requesting this meeting; unfortunately, this did not happen ... [and] my requests for a meeting were not acknowledged.

I understand you have forwarded my concerns as you heard them from [the department chair] to [the other department professor]. I want to make this perfectly clear that I would have welcomed the opportunity to speak with you first directly about these concerns before others entered into the conversation. I was hoping to resolve any negativity that may have arisen or any miscommunication issues between the two of us.

I learned ... that you and [the other department professor] are planning a September meeting, and that I will be notified when scheduling occurs.... I am requesting that you coordinate schedules with and include [the department chair] in this meeting so he can continue to be aware of the situation and help in the process of changing advisors and moving forward toward completion of my degree.

Your most recent email indicates that you will do this, and so we both agree that his presence is warranted. Moreover, I am requesting that I be present in the meeting so as to communicate directly with all of you about the issues, rather than occupy a passive role and remain without a voice in procedures that impact my future.

I would like to honor your request to receive my data, though I am confused about the purpose of sending you my materials, given the state of our relationship and the uncertainty that it will continue....[*Renee suggests again that she is unable to transmit the data via email.*] ... However, I would arrange a meeting with you in which I bring in my computer and show you my work, if this still remains your preference. Again, the purpose of this review of data appears moot at this point given the instability of our relationship, but certainly you are welcome to see these data, if you prefer, and I will provide you with them. Kindly advise.

Thank you for your efforts to coordinate the meeting with ... [the department chair and other department professor] in a timely manner. If there are any materials or information required for this meeting, please let me know, and I will prepare them.

Sincerely,

Renee

Tripping Over Elephants

Renee's difficulty spanned from early summer until the very end of October, when the issues were finally resolved and a new chair was in place. She had lost a total of two years in her doctoral program in resolving her substantial issues with the advisor, but she did complete her degree.

It is clear that the advising relationship was flawed, and perhaps from early on in the advising relationship, a time when it is difficult for any student to believe that the elephant standing in front of them really is the elephant standing in front of them. It is often difficult to pinpoint the exact moment when a relationship tips off course, but, generally, the signs are there.

Only in retrospect did Renee come to recognize an ongoing series of complexities surrounding her relationship with the advisor: repeatedly missed or canceled appointments without warning, failure to respond to phone calls and email, imagined infractions. When Renee attempted to coordinate a committee meeting, the advisor claimed Renee had undermined her authority as chair, viewing this as an *ethical* transgression, and subsequently reported her to a departmental committee without informing Renee that she was doing so. Ironically enough, this action was its own ethical transgression because it defied the policies and procedures outlined in the program handbook.

Elements such as these serve as warning signs that need to be read for what they are: danger signals. (*People tell you who they are, even when you don't want to know.*) It is true that only in hindsight do we have 20/20 vision; when we are compromised by difficult situations or are in the midst of them, it is difficult to gauge the true measure of the circumstances. (*Is what I'm seeing for real?*) And for doctoral students, paradoxically *uncertain* individuals heavily invested in the doctoral process, it is even doubly so. The majority of students that I have known over the years will do almost everything within their power to preserve the advising relationship and keep it intact, and they will absorb the complexities until they reach that moment of awareness that confirms their suspicions of a "going nowhere" and perhaps even hostile relationship.

Collateral Damage

What is clear, however, is that collateral damage is a reality, and what would have been lost in this instance is not only Renee's Ph.D. as well as her research, but also the damage to other students and faculty, all wary observers in an untoward process, witnesses to a game without rules. Such situations signal a kind of terror, distrust, and uncertainty among students; in short, students worry about what *might happen to them* as they journey toward degree completion, especially so late in the process when loss of the degree threatens. Advisors, too, face consequences, and they are concerned about blights on their reputations when they get entangled in brouhahas with their advisees.

At play also are departmental politics at their best. Which faculty member is willing to take on someone else's advisee, especially at the risk of insulting a colleague? Department chairs themselves are vulnerable to political liabilities and often enough do not want to enter into precarious situations that hold the potential for alienation. Frequently, they prefer to let the advisor and advisee work out the issue on their own, without getting directly involved at the onset, as we saw in Renee's situation. It cannot, however, be regarded as a noble idea, and, in fact, can be likened to watching a beloved pet with a terminal illness: we pray for it to go peacefully in its sleep, but that seldom happens. In the end, involvement in the sad task is required.

In this case, the matter was not resolved in a spirit of cooperation and respect between two individuals coming together to recognize that their advising relationship was not productive or rewarding for either of them, and thus allow it to die with dignity. The protracted delay in resolving the issue falls to the department chair: in Renee's case, notions of etiquette and perhaps even departmental protocol and politics held sway, and the chair failed to exert his authority and end the situation, especially when it became apparent that the advisor had become difficult, uncooperative, and punitive, and when the advisee clearly stated her decision to dissolve the relationship.

Revenge for terminating an advising relationship, however, can play out in damaging ways.

The Academic Divorce: Aunt Tillie's Tea Kettle

Failed advising relationships are not uncommon, and often it is the personality combination of the two individuals, advisor and advisee, that destroys the balance. However, the points of departure can be dangerous and uncertain places for the student, as well as disappointing and embarrassing places for advisors. No one likes to hear "This isn't working for me. We're done." But this is a system that does not frequently allow for guided interventions before they escalate into compromising situations. Further, it clings to idealisms regarding conflict resolution and does not consciously examine why such conflicts arise or understand how they can be resolved in pragmatic, diplomatic ways. It is clear then that students and faculty alike are frequently left adrift to figure things out on their own. Without formal advisor–advisee conflict resolution training, it is easy to understand how a difficulty can degenerate into a complete relationship failure, especially when individuals are left to their own devices and when common decency does not prevail. And yet, there is little in the way of formal training for both students and faculty advisors in this area. Dissertation seminars may be one place to address this issue, but generally conflict resolution is not a primary focus of such seminars; involvement of the ombudsman or equity office signals an inability on the advisor–advisee level to rectify a worsening situation and indicates the need for professional intervention when all else fails.

Michigan State University sponsors an online conflict resolution program that features various video snippets showcasing a compendium of ethical situations in which students and faculty may encounter each other. At Western Michigan University, Dr. Michael Pritchard, professor of philosophy, years ago created similar videos, which were played for audiences of faculty and students, and then in an open discussion forum were examined from a multiplicity of perspectives. These are rich tools through which students and faculty can engage in productive, informed conversations that can potentially avert complicated issues.

Wasn't This in Our Prenup? We Had One, Right?

I once heard a divorce attorney refer to the phenomenon of Aunt Tillie's tea kettle. We all have an "Aunt Tillie's tea kettle" in our homes, and most of us simply ignore it as it just blends into our domestic environments. It was handed down, bequeathed, or given to us as a gift. It's simply there in our midst. It isn't until a divorce that Aunt Tillie or her tea kettle assumes grave importance, at least in the minds of feuding spouses who each insist that the kettle really belongs to him or her. Up until that point, tea brewed peacefully and no one considered ownership—that is, until the divorce. Now, that kettle is up for desperate retaliatory grabs.

In like manner, some advisors may retaliate when the advising relationship fails by withholding the rights to a dissertation proposal they developed with the advisee; this is a slippery slope in many instances. In one case, an advisor withheld the use of an instrument that she had designed and originally granted permission to the advisee to adapt to her own research, but that was *before* their relationship had ended. When the relationship became confrontational and the student wanted to part ways after unsuccessful attempts to balance it, permission to use the instrument was withdrawn. Moreover, the faculty member viewed the proposal as *her* intellectual property, because she had shaped it conceptually and contributed to its evolution. Again, this is another slippery slope for faculty and students to consider as they court each other for the advisor–advisee role. A professor, highly invested in the dissertation process, will most likely experience some difficulty simply withdrawing when the going gets tough and a separation from the advisee appears imminent. Understandably, there is a great deal of ownership invested in the dissertation process, no doubt, but in the idealism of a new evolving advisor–advisee relationship, the complexity of parting ways is most likely not part of the conversation. But perhaps it should be.

In yet another instance, a failed advising relationship ended with a faculty member extending his rights over the advisee's data, since his name appeared on the HSIRB protocol as principal investigator. Initially, he refused to allow the student to have access to the data, thereby compromising her ability to complete the dissertation, but also raising questions regarding a faculty member's ability to block an advisee's access to this information, especially when that faculty member served as principal investigator on the protocol. Later, he recanted but insisted on being credited in the dissertation with the results. This demand only exacerbated the difficulties he and the advisee were experiencing because it appeared punitive to her, a last ditch effort to establish control and also to punish her for the failed relationship.

The Price

Such actions indeed penalize students, not only emotionally and psychologically, but also through threatened degree completion by removing them from their focus, by consuming their valuable time, by destroying their concentration, and by usurping their energy and motivation to complete the dissertation. Moreover, the threat to the integrity of the department and the assault upon collegial relations may be a high price to pay for a poor attitude and a wounded ego. As educators, can we afford to pay this price?

It is wise to consider that the advising relationship, just like marriages, can well fail and at any point in time. In many instances, students come through the process successfully. However, this is not always the case for everyone, and a failed advising relationship can spell disaster for the student, especially as difficulties manifest at the conclusion of the proposal stage, as the cases just addressed demonstrate.

Rather than fight over tea kettles, it is wise to assume an attitude of diplomacy and reach for the higher ground: first, agree to meet, talk through differences, and seek resolution. Resolution does not always mean that people stay together, whether in marriages or in the advising relationship. Resolution may simply mean that the parties agree, in as amiable a way as possible, to part ways. In the end, our actions teach students how to behave in the real world, and advisors who grouse and threaten may yield similar progeny who, ironically enough, may perpetuate these behaviors in their own advising relationships, even unwittingly.

What If It Doesn't Work Out?

I am almost certain that this is a question seldom, *if ever,* asked at the onset of the advising relationship. But the "what if" or prenup agreement should really be on the table for discussion early in the process. Naturally, it is best to proceed from the perspective of optimism and joyful engagement in this most important stage in the doctoral educational process. Over time, faculty members and their advisees develop important and rewarding relationships with each other and should come to value their joint efforts. However, it is a smart idea to consider the possibility that a rupture, one that cannot be overcome, may arise. If that should happen, discussing options ahead of time might be an anodyne to a bitter departure, or, even in some instances, prevent one from happening.

Let's revert back to the Rules of Engagement for a moment: How can the advising relationship be sustained over time so that it remains viable and productive? This involves more than just the technical dimensions of working together. Difficulties that become cumulative, rather than incidental, signal that the relationship is veering off course. All of those broken appointments, missed meetings, failure to return chapter edits, perpetual complaints about being too busy with other obligations, for example, undermine students' confidence in the advisor to lead them successfully to degree completion. Unaddressed, these issues simply fester and deepen the gap in the advising relationship. A few rescheduled appointments or a late chapter return is not going to dismantle the relationship, but a steady diet of excuses wears out even the most tolerant students, who interpret all of this as a series of barriers. When advisors' actions threaten or dismantle, when they elicit fear and distrust, when they foster resentment and anger, it is time to reconsider the value of maintaining the status quo. Stasis is not the safe ground.

Academic Divorce Protocol

If a *divorce* becomes imminent, I suggest that the advisee send a formal, respectful letter to the advisor that announces the termination of the advising relationship, such as this example:

Dear Dr. X,

> After our last conversation two weeks ago, I am experiencing lingering and serious reservations about continuing our professional relationship as dissertation chair and advisee, and these remain unabated. Consequently, after much careful deliberation and self-reflection, I have decided to reconfigure entirely the current dissertation committee and begin again. This is not a decision that I arrived at easily, but given the circumstances, I have concluded that it is within my best interests to proceed in this manner and to ensure a fresh start.
>
> I acknowledge your considerable investment in my dissertation, and I thank you for your contributions during our association. Certainly, I will make mention of your efforts in the acknowledgment

section of the dissertation and where appropriate within the dissertation proper.

Thank you for your time and for your gracious acceptance of this decision.

Sincerely,

Student's Name

Advisors should also consider sending a very brief letter to their former advisee:

Dear Mary,

It is with regret that we have agreed to terminate our advising relationship. I am writing to wish you well in your future endeavors.

Sincerely,

Dr. X

~ The Take Away ~

1. *Don't be an asshole advisor to your advisee.* If the relationship is not working, address the issue as soon as a problem appears. Maybe you just don't like working with this person; maybe your life has changed and you no longer have time to dedicate to this individual; maybe there are complicated family issues confronting you; maybe you are sick and tired of endlessly editing dissertation chapters that seem to be going nowhere. The reason is less important than *what* you intend to do about it, and *how* you do it. Don't put your head in the sand. If you can't resolve the issues between you, find someone at your institution who will mediate. Generally, the department chair and the ombudsman are two resources. A seasoned faculty member with dissertation advising experience is yet another, and this individual does not necessarily have to be from your department. Avoid retaliation and stay focused on the issue at hand; generally, issues can be resolved as long as everyone remains respectful and is motivated toward a successful resolution: *reconciliation* or *ter-*

mination. Avoid contributing to the department scuttlebutt by gossiping about the advisee. People's *actions* generally announce who they are, and so if the advisee proves to be something of an asshole, there is no need for you to be the town hall crier.
2. *Define your expectations.* Be explicit about the working relationship and how it can succeed, as well as how it could fail if these expectations are not met. Advisees do not have clairvoyance and so it is imperative to carefully delineate the Rules of Engagement. If you observe a potential problem, seize the moment up front to explain the difficulty to the advisee so that your complaint or concern is understood and potential solutions discussed together.
3. *Make yourself available.* Answer your phone. Return email within 24 hours of receipt. Clear your voicemail. Keep your appointments. Don't make students chase you down. Anything less is not professional, let alone civilized behavior. Students panic when they attempt to contact advisors who have successfully sealed themselves off from the standard forms of communication. Moreover, students standing interminably outside of your office door for an appointment that you missed or forgot about signals apathy on your part.
4. *Maintain civility.* If resolution is not possible, then agree to part ways in a positive, respectful manner that does not taint reputations or force colleagues, students, and faculty to take sides. Agree to part in ways that do not harm the other individual. Generally, the advisor–advisee relationship begins in a positive spirit with both parties respectful of each other and eager to benefit the other. Try to remember this as the relationship is terminated.
5. *Be accountable/avoid internalizing failure.* Failed relationships are a fact of life and often are the result of the wrong combination of individuals, not the individuals themselves. Agree to move on, but before you do, ask yourself, "What is my role in this failure?" and "If I had to do this over again, what would I do differently to ensure a better outcome?" Then, apply these revelations to your next advising relationship.
6. *Ask for conflict resolution training.* Departments should train faculty and students in the art of conflict resolution, either by

offering workshops or seminars or including this training in dissertation seminars. If you are a seasoned advisor, guide your faculty colleagues and share your expertise. Seek the expertise of the ombudsman as a professional who explores options and facilitates resolutions.
7. *Write a formal letter*. Write a respectful, formal farewell letter to your advisee, with a "cc" to the department chair. This should not be a letter that details each and every discordant fact, but should express the decision to terminate the advising relationship.

Reference

Sutton, R. I. (2010). *The no asshole rule: Building a civilized workplace and surviving one that isn't*. New York, NY: Business Plus, Hatchette Book Group.

Chapter 14

Working Against the Grain: For Advisees

The pendulum swings both ways, and experiences with advisees can frustrate and tax the good will of advisors beyond what can be imagined. Such individuals can also harm the reputations of colleges and universities. Let's take a look.

Marcia's Story

Marcia was a doctoral student whose interactions and relationships with faculty, administrators, and others were characterized by what I will describe as extreme complexity. Ill-tempered, impatient, and unwilling to do the hard work required of the dissertation, she remained combative and argumentative, failing to comply with the direction and guidance of five dissertation committees, chaired by three different faculty, and comprised of no fewer than eight faculty members and one administrator. Her dissertation was focused on the political fallout that had ravaged her native country. Having escaped and taken refuge in the United States, she was nonetheless protective of her homeland and wanted to tell the story—her way.

My Way or the Highway

The concerns of all five committees were centered in *how* she should tell the story, *not* that the story should not be told. Concerned with the integrity of the research, the committees sought to direct the project accordingly: committee after committee observed major design flaws that had to be addressed. However, Marcia was convinced that she must maintain authority to write her dissertation as she saw fit, and she translated the committees' recommendations and suggestions into an assault upon her academic freedom. In her view, she understood how to conduct the research and she wanted no part of their involvement in a project that she clearly felt she owned.

Her steadfast resistance to committee directives compromised her ability to complete acceptable work, and this resistance manifested with the very first committee that had been convened. It remained an unalterable feature of her relationships with the host of committee members that followed the demise of the first committee, and all the subsequent committees.

None of the committees could be described as unreasonable or difficult. Marcia objected to any and all suggested changes to the dissertation and viewed these as personal effronteries. One recommendation from the first committee concerned editing down the literature review chapter, which had mushroomed to over 120 pages. Marcia refused to revise the chapter, indicating that without that vast information, no one would appreciate the political, economic, and social ramifications of the event that served as the basis of the dissertation. Additional revisions and editorial suggestions were summarily dismissed, including one regarding the validity and reliability of her survey instrument.

Marcia's response to the faculty's grappling with her linguistic issues, narrative disconnects, and design flaws was to threaten to disband the entire committee and send everyone packing. The first committee had had quite enough and resigned of its own volition, en masse, after Marcia sent an email to them admonishing them that if they were uncomfortable serving on her committee, she would excuse them. (*Translate "uncomfortable" this way: "I'm doing what I want, regardless of what you think, say, or do. If you don't like it, you can go."*) Over a period of time, the en masse exit of the first committee was followed by a series of other individual faculty resignations across the five committees. These professors all agreed that the study was thin and predictable in terms of outcomes, and they attempted to implement methodological approaches to make it a more robust study. Each time, Marcia refused.

And this is the reason why: Marcia insisted that the committees' editorial and conceptual suggestions violated her rights, and she cited ethnic indifference, discrimination, compromised academic freedom, and a host of related complaints. Like harpies, these complaints flew into the far-reaching corners of her university, from the president's office to the office of equity and into any hallway that seemed to proffer an ear for her sad tale. In between, Marcia pummeled committee members with vitriolic email blasts, while she sent formal letters to several individuals in the hierarchy of her university, protesting her unfair treatment.

In retrospect, it is not possible to restrict these disputes to individual professors who just did not get along with their advisee, as that was not the case. The sheer number of committees convened stands as testimony to the faculty's good will and their efforts to assist the student, and each other, in what had become a Herculean effort to get the student through. It is not that Marcia was abandoned on any level whatsoever, as her university expended generous resources in an effort to assist her, a remarkable fact. However, she remained undeterred in her refusal or her inability to take direction that would result in an acceptable dissertation, as determined by the committee and the department.

A Question of Grades

Marcia could be described as a *fair* student in terms of ability. Had her department conducted annual reviews on a regular basis, and especially more frequently at the dissertation stage, an assessment of her performance would have revealed that she lacked the intellectual acumen and skills to complete her degree, and she should have been counseled out of her program, in my view. This, however, did not happen, and failure to initiate the annual review gave the department little room to negotiate a dismissal. She was a student with compromised capability, and yet she had been admitted into a Ph.D. program. Armed with the idea that admission equates to guaranteed graduation, she concluded in numerous meetings that I attended that it was her right to graduate.

Mounting Difficulty

When trouble with the dissertation arose, Marcia grew sullen and angry, believing that whatever committee was working with her at the time was intentionally thwarting her goal. She did not view these intercessions as ways to improve her dissertation, nor did she understand that a dissertation evolves over time and that drafting is part of the process. She cited her 4.0 overall GPA as evidence of success, and yet the glaring gaps in terms of oral and written communication and conceptualization observed in her speech and in the dissertation narrative drew that GPA into sharp question. The student's 4.0 GPA seemed incongruous with her sudden inability to perform at a high academic level. She consistently demonstrated that she was incapable of good clear academic writing; lacked organizational, grammatical, and mechanical skills; and had forgotten how to spell, think, reason, or understand research methodology.

As noted previously, researchers in doctoral education, such as Barbara Lovitts (2005) and others, recognize the proclivity among some doctoral students to fail to navigate the "critical transition" from coursework to the dissertation. In these instances, the act of writing the dissertation becomes the ground work or the frame from which research skills are acquired and the dissertation completed. However, it was apparent in Marcia's case that she was operating from the standpoint of a major deficiency that could not be overcome readily. Lack of requisite skills, as well as her bellicose attitude, compromised the entire process.

Hedging the Bet

Now, providing a student with the opportunity to overcome academic insufficiency through guided assistance and departmental commitment is not necessarily a bad thing. The department must have recognized that Marcia's academic record, as evidenced through a graduate degree from another institution, was not sterling, but perhaps (in the vernacular that has crept into doctoral education to an extent) *good enough*; the department rolled the dice and took a chance on someone who might be able to turn academic liabilities into successful outcomes. As long as that commitment is honored, as long as the student works in concert with the faculty and the department to meet those goals, and as long as there is documented evidence of progress, then a compromised situation may turn into a potential win-win all around.

This did not happen in Marcia's case. She was generally incapable of taking direction, a fact that must certainly have been apparent during the coursework phase of her program. It should have become clear that her writing, in fact, her ability to conceptualize, analyze, and synthesize, was seriously challenged. Yet, her grades did not reflect these problems, and so, in her view, she was a superlative student who should have sailed through the remainder of her program. She had a 4.0, didn't she?

A number of variables may have accounted for her high GPA, one of which was lack of writing-centric courses through which serious writing/language issues would have emerged along the pathway. If writing problems had emerged, did faculty refer Marcia to a writing center or a tutor, or offer to assist her personally? Did Marcia argue loudly over grades, and did professors simply give in, awarding her a good grade just to get rid of her? When we think of graduate programs, we think of the necessity to structure them so that writing becomes a skill cultivated throughout the process, not just tacked onto a capstone, a thesis, or a dissertation. Marcia's writing problems, emerging as they did at the onset of the dissertation or perhaps earlier in her courses, created a formidable obstacle to her success. But her questionable attitude also played a major role.

The Disconnect

From my perspective, the quandary arose because Marcia had been permitted to stay in her program for too long and actually should have been counseled out far earlier in the program, before her expectation of graduation gelled into a vitriolic demand. Her skills were not commensurate with the grades she had been awarded, and she had come to equate those grades with a sense of herself as an accomplished individual.

No Annual Review

Most importantly, she had never undergone an annual review and, hence, there had been no discussion of shortcomings or challenges to the successful completion of her degree within the formal venue of annual review. Program dismissal was one option under the annual review policy, but because a review had not ever been conducted, the department had no leg to stand on when problems with her various committees emerged. If we look at due process, it is clear that students cannot simply be dismissed without cause, without warning, without a historical account of circumstances that warrant dismissal without appropriate strategies for amelioration. Further, there had been no cohesive historical account of the numerous committee configurations or any documentation of the confounding events that moved faculty onto and off the committee, that is, until the configuration of the last committee. In a certain sense, the failure of the department to conduct an annual review undercut its ability to deal with Marcia. So, it had become effectively muzzled.

We Gotta Get Out of This Place, Don't We?

Yet, throughout all of this, it is quite interesting that faculty even agreed to join the ranks and serve in the first place. Perhaps they thought *they* would be the ones to usher her through to success and were up for the challenge. *Remember, "You are the rule, not the exception."* However, her problematic history could not have been concealed entirely, for word of her difficult nature certainly had to leach out through the revolving door of faculty replacements that she seemed to spin with veritable ease. *"People tell you who they are, even when you don't want to know."*

Coming to the Finish Line

The penultimate committee was configured, although we didn't know that at the time. I refer to it as Committee 5. The dissertation chair discussed the history of the student and reviewed the past problems, as well as projected the difficulties ahead. A new tenure-track faculty member agreed to serve, but later, realizing that future problems were very likely in this case, decided to withdraw and avoid potentially jeopardizing the tenure bid. And who can lay blame, really? A final configuration occurred when another member joined, who also, at this point, was understandably reluctant, but fortunate enough to be tenured and therefore protected. It was at this point that a formal annual review was written and the entire historical account of this case was established, but mostly as an insurance policy if Marcia did not succeed. As part of the annual review process, she was presented with the fact that if she did not cooperate, work with the committee in a respectful manner, and show progress, she would not graduate.

Leopards do not change their spots. Marcia may have restrained herself enough to work successfully with the committee and to secure approval of her work. She had to realize, even unconsciously, that she had reached an impasse or simply had exhausted the faculty ranks, or perhaps even herself. However, even at the end, her confrontational, combative behavior reared itself during her work with the individual hired to edit and format the dissertation and resulted in untold stress and problems for a person whose goal was to finalize the project so that Marcia could graduate.

Catch-22

The fact that the last committee did not walk away from her is more a testimony to them, as committed professionals, rather than to the effectiveness of Marcia's threatening, abusive behavior. The problem for the committee concerned the jarring contradiction that enmeshed its members in a daunting ethical situation. Both the student and the institution had been done a disservice: (1) Marcia had been left in place too long and did not have the skills necessary to complete the dissertation. Her performance had not been assessed via annual review, a policy that permits for dismissal if amelioration does not take place; (2) Institutions of higher learning are in jeopardy when they award Ph.D.s to students whose performance is highly questionable and who appear incapable as well as opposed to delivering even a marginal product. Let me clarify: it would be one thing if a student with fair skills worked earnestly to improve those skills and to acquire mastery over the dissertation research. Lovitts (2005) writes about the centrality of creativity to the doctoral experience and indicates that creativity "inheres in the relationship the individual has with the domain and its gatekeepers" (p. 142). Further, "in order to make a significant contribution to a domain, the individual has to know the domain well enough to know what is and is not important in the domain" (p. 142); however, this knowing "requires specialized training" (p. 142). The years of both undergraduate and graduate study equate approximately to the 10 years that are required to "master a discipline" (p. 142). Lovitts concludes that an individual's creative capabilities could possibly be enhanced via "interactions with the domain and the field," since it is within these relationships that creativity inheres (p. 142).

It is these investments that Marcia was not able or willing to make and that prevented her from moving into a more creative, scholarly, or refined approach to her work. It is important to state that many students rise to the occasion and deliver a good product by reaching for their own excellence, establishing it, and delivering a respectable study. They are cooperative, earnest, and sincere. There *is* nobility in such efforts. But this was not the case with Marcia.

What factors made the last committee a success when all the others failed, I cannot say for certain. In the end, Marcia seemed to understand that *this* committee represented her last opportunity.

She successfully defended and graduated. Again, the committee approached the defense and the graduation with a sense of *dis-ease*, a disquieting flood of contradictions catching them up on the prongs of a Morton's Fork: If Marcia graduated, they lost and also won, and if she were dismissed, they also would have lost and won. The perceived necessity to award the Ph.D. to a student whose skills were not at all commensurate with the degree stood in direct opposition to late-stage program dismissal.

Admittedly, this is an extreme case, and extreme cases have their price.

Anne's Story

Several years ago, Anne was sent to me to provide her with assistance in completing the dissertation. Here is her story.

Anne was in a Ph.D. program and had a dissertation chair who retired from Anne's university. She had worked with her professor for a period of years prior to the professor's retirement and had developed a substantial portion of a dissertation. The problem occurred when the professor retired, relegating his advisor duties to another professor who would serve as the new chair, with the retired professor installed as a quasi co-chair. However, there had been no discussion of how this arrangement was to actually function: a big mistake. The actual division of authority between the two had not been established, and this left Anne struggling between two professors with vastly different managerial styles. To add to an already complicated situation, the new advisor did not approve of the quality of the work that Anne had produced under the direction of the first advisor. He indicated that it was not structured or focused and found the language unclear and the conceptual framework marred.

Before too long, trouble began to brew. Anne wanted to continue working with her first advisor, who liked her proposal, rather than work with the new advisor. But a university policy prevented retired professors from chairing dissertation committees. It appeared to Anne that she was suddenly handed off to the new advisor, and she found herself caught between these two powerful forces. The relationship with the new advisor chilled because Anne refused to believe that her proposal was really all that bad. Her objections to his managerial style mounted, and so did her refusal to implement the editorial changes that he recommended. Eventually, there was a complete rupture and the new advisor withdrew from the committee.

Remember that a specific *hand off* or transition of the student from the major professor to a new advisor had not transpired, and so the acceptability of the proposal and its legitimacy had not been established, nor had the chair/co-chair arrangement and what that meant exactly when one of these parties had retired.

It's Complicated

Anne refused to accept the fact that the work done thus far was not acceptable. She had amassed a tremendous amount of material and information that she would not relinquish. Further, she could not tolerate any additional threats to the completion of the manuscript. Translate *threats* to mean editorial revision or revamping of ideas or reconceptualization, those very ideas suggested by the new advisor who had observed the proposal's failings.

While Anne could not understand why her work was no longer acceptable, neither could the new advisor understand why Anne could not understand this point. Both were pretty much done with being jangled around. The new advisor perceived he had been dealt a bad hand in getting stuck with a going-nowhere dissertation that needed to be delivered to the ash heaps, not to his desk; the student had been led to believe by her first advisor that her dissertation was moving along swimmingly, incredulous to learn that her work was not credible in the estimation of the new advisor. I was asked to provide an independent evaluation of the proposal, the historical details of the situation kept confidential to avoid potential bias. A crosswalk between my work and the work of the new advisor indicated that our analyses aligned, and Anne was presented with our findings. Her tack was to hold onto the life raft of a sinking dissertation, despite many hours I spent working with her to demonstrate how the dissertation could be restructured, including efforts to locate a new advisor.

Misalignment

Despite the assistance offered to help her revise the proposal, Anne still had difficulty letting go of her work and moving on to develop a viable topic. This disappointment and lack of trust sometimes led her to engage in heated conversations, veiled threats really, about securing legal arbitration through which she surmised her proposal would be accepted as it had been designed under the auspices of the first advisor, and the degree awarded. She considered holding her university responsible for what she considered its faculty's failings but never actually carried the idea forward. Still, such discussions were disconcerting and, to a certain degree, alarming. In many instances, mediation and interventions solve many of these problems, but once people begin to talk about *lawyering up,* they tend to dig in their heels and remain entrenched in their own perspectives, failing to compromise and operationalize the extended offers of assistance. Recognize also that such conversations about lawyers and lawsuits undermine the confidence of those serving on/chairing committees or even considering such service. No one wants to work under conditions in which even the potential for legal involvement constitutes the backdrop for a working relationship that is already problematic. In Anne's case, such circumstances complicated an already complicated situation and fostered a sense of hesitancy among potential committee members.

Epilogue

For a period of time, it seemed unlikely that Anne would graduate. In the intervening months after Anne showed up at my office, we exchanged many emails and phone calls; academic and financial interventions to lend assistance to her were arranged, as well as hours spent in deliberations with potential dissertation chairs and committee members to secure their services. Despite these efforts, Anne continued to threaten legal action but eventually settled down with a new advisor/committee. She registered for dissertation credit hours, as required, and secured a program extension so that she was legitimately protected in her program as an enrolled student. For an expanded period of time, she was not able to produce the preliminary proposal required by the newest advisor, still haunted by the ghost of the previous document that the first advisor had approved but which she still struggled to surrender. Anne remained mired in her commitment to the former first advisor and the so-called veracity of the document they produced together but came to understand the need to modify and revamp the study under the direction of the newest advisor. Over time, she gradually, painfully perhaps, became aware of the need to separate herself from the past and move on to complete her degree, which she did. The point is this: Students who resist helpful outreach will seal their own fates, one way or another. Their actions severely protract degree completion, poison the academic landscape, and leave departments, programs, faculty, and their student colleagues with the taste of *ashes in the mouth*. Students need to examine the reasons why they won't or can't produce, and then overcome those obstacles. Here is the lesson: When the universe *rights* itself, you should be moving right along with it.

~ The Take Away ~

1. *Avoid tantrums.* Combative, argumentative, abusive, and childish behavior *may* win the day on some days and under some circumstances, but don't count on it winning all the time. Marcia's example serves as an anomaly in many ways, and the majority of students would never make it to first base if they behaved similarly. In Marcia's case, a series of procedural glitches served to protect a student who, in my opinion, did not deserve such protectionisms. Anne personalized her second advisor's findings that her proposal was substandard and rejected attempts to reorganize it and bring it into conformity with the program's standards. Both students refused to understand or accept that their proposals, as written/designed, did not reflect credit upon themselves as budding researchers, or their departments.

2. *Cooperate and graduate.* Like any demanding educational process, the Ph.D. consists of a series of benchmarks, expectations, and requirements that must be met. Can you imagine medical students refusing to follow a checklist for treating patients in cardiac distress just because they didn't want to? How about deviating from a standard surgical procedure without securing the patient's consent because they felt like trying something new and doing it *their* way? How about refusing to take direction from senior medical personnel? We would call that being careless, foolhardy, and outrageous, and we would be right.

   In like manner, advisees do not have the right to refuse continuously to implement committee members' editorial recommendations, without regard for the rationale that guides those recommendations and suggestions: to deliver a quality dissertation that is produced ethically. This is not to say that advisees cannot debate a point of contention or offer an alternate perspective that may change the committee's view. To *defend* a point is a solid move; to *insist* on a point, without the benefit of justification, is not a credible approach. And much of that justification should be based squarely on the literature, empirical evidence.

Consider that it is the genesis of alternate views that has spawned some of the most amazing innovations in science, medicine, and technology that we enjoy today. However, the right to dispute is earned out of a steadfast commitment to the discipline, out of hard work, and out of a pioneering spirit that yearns for new discoveries, not one that seeks to rebel for the sake of rebellion. Such academic conversations that consider alternate perspectives should take place in an atmosphere of respect, dignity, and intellectual engagement. Moreover, such academic conversations should be framed within the context of the literature, within the parameters of credible research. Both Marcia and Anne refused to acknowledge the fact that their proposals were flawed and required reconceptualization. Students may not be in a position to determine the feasibility or the viability of their proposals, which is why they have committees to oversee the process in the first place. Marcia resorted to aggression and retaliation as her means of protesting that oversight, and Anne resorted to a passive-aggressive stance, by hinting at lawsuits.

3. *Stop escalating the issues.* The idea of *talking* about hiring lawyers and filing allegations of discrimination and violations of academic freedom may sound impressive, but it is a highly questionable tack. If you've reached this point, you most likely are not effectively communicating with anyone on your committee anymore. Why? Because you've conveyed the *impression* that you already have a lawyer who is doing all the talking. This means that you have effectively closed off the opportunity to reach a congenial outcome, because even the *conversations* about securing an attorney signal an inflammatory stance. Do you really want to venture

down this pathway? Is this a productive activity that inspires confidence?

4. *Don't break olive branches.* Avoid beating people over the head with their own olive branches. When assistance is offered, graciously accept it and move on. Try to see the bigger picture, the one beyond the ego. When the universe tries to right itself, get on board with the new direction and accept the extended hand. Avoid remaining mired in the past: what happened in the past should stay in the past. If you continue to resurrect it, you effectively seal yourself off from positive and purposeful change. Continue complaining about all of your hardships, lack of support from previous faculty, and wrongdoings suffered and you effectively turn a blind eye to those who are currently aligned with you and who want to be part of your success. If you're hell-bent on payback, you're walking down the wrong pathway. This is a game you may well lose. Eventually, universities and professors will run out of resources and leave you to your own devices.

5. *Let go of your baggage.* The adage that sow's ears generally do not make fine silk purses is true. Similarly, flawed, ill-written, ill-conceived dissertation chapters may not be salvageable. Let them go, and move on.

6. *Keep an eye on the clock.* A student who has been granted an extension does not have time to waste. When a dissertation advisor or coach negotiates a "due date" for revisions or for the concept paper, avoid making excuses for not delivering. These individuals are responsible for dovetailing your remaining tasks into the timeline delineated in your extension. When you disregard the clock, you are deliberately placing your extension in jeopardy. Extensions are not handed out *a priori*, just because you think you should have one or because you have suffered some real or imagined infraction. The forms required to secure an extension reflect detailed information, including a rationale for your failure to complete the degree within the specified time, a list of remaining tasks, timeline for degree completion, and other important information related to your potential to complete the degree. In addition, the extension form is vetted by a series of individuals whose approval is required at various levels. If your

university or college has granted an extension, consider it a gift and then employ it as a tool to get you where you need to go without wasting precious time.

Reference

Lovitts, B. (2005). Being a good course taker is not enough: A theoretical perspective on the transition into independent research. *Studies in Higher Education, 30*(2), 137–154.

Chapter 15

Dissertation Proposal and the Human Subjects Institutional Review Board (HSIRB) Protocol: Symmetry in Design

Individuals conducting research with human subjects are required to ensure protections for the target populations participating in research studies. Risks are to be kept to a safe minimum, and the overall benefit of the research should be clear, both serving as overarching principles of ethical research. Researchers must file for HSIRB approval of their proposed studies prior to data collection and ensure that the proposed research meets the federally mandated requirements for ethical research. We will return to this point later in the chapter.

In some circles, the dissertation proposal and the HSIRB protocol are thought to exist as part of a two-step, sequential process. However, perhaps it would be better to regard them as simultaneous elements designed with efficiency in mind. To a certain degree, the requirements of both documents are generally the same: statement of the problem, significance of the research, research concept/questions, literature review, and method for data collection and analysis. Protocols for HSIRB will include elements such as confidentiality/protection of data, as well as risks, benefits, and informed consent for participants, among others.

Symmetrical Design of Proposal and Protocol

As the dissertation proposal is being developed, the advisor and advisee may begin conversations with the research compliance office in an effort to create a tight Chapter III (methods for data collection and analysis). Let me clarify that it is not necessarily the responsibility of the research compliance office to plan and design the study; however, many research compliance coordinators are skilled at understanding what methods or procedures work most logically in real-world settings. Their expertise can be invaluable in conceptualizing a research study that intersects with human subjects. Sometimes, simply having access to someone who is willing to review the procedures, even orally, places researchers in an advantageous position. Concomitantly, advisees should be working with a statistician to determine the selection of statistical methods for analysis of the data. In this manner, the proposal reflects conversations focused on cultivating a document of integrity that aligns well with the requirements of the protocol.

The more closely the team (advisor, advisee, compliance officer, statistician) works together, the better. The advisor always maintains responsibility for the oversight and development of the protocol and is the principal investigator (PI) on the protocol. Advisees, however, should have the direct experience of writing and organizing the protocol, as well as managing the process and conferring with respective professionals in this circle. This management of the protocol requires but also teaches discipline, an integral aspect of the research process. One professor that I know insisted that his advisee submit an HSIRB protocol, even though the research compliance office made a determination that "no approval was needed" for a particular study. The professor concluded that his advisee needed to experience the HSIRB protocol process as a purely disciplinary exercise necessary to the advisee's doctoral experience.

The more closely aligned the experts are with the student and the student with the experts, the better the overall outcome: a well-shaped, professional proposal and protocol prepared for defense and HSIRB review, respectively.

As the advisor and advisee work together to conceptualize and develop the proposal, they can also begin to organize and write the

HSIRB protocol and to prepare it for eventual submission, especially as the corresponding sections integrate. This side-by-side approach permits for the HSIRB protocol to emerge out of the proposal, almost simultaneously, rather than as a second step in the process.

Proposal Defense

According to the two-step method, once students defend the dissertation proposal, generally the first three chapters, they proceed to write the HSIRB protocol. But above, I spoke of the complementary nature of the dissertation proposal and the HSIRB protocol as being closely aligned. As a point of clarification, it is important to state that the dissertation proposal varies from field to field, department to department, university to university. In some fields, at some universities, it may also be a one-page document, a prospectus, the first and third dissertation chapters, or a concept paper, for example. There is a significant degree of variance, even within the same institution.

Approval of the proposal may take place according to informal and formal procedures. Generally, in the case of the former, the advisor will authorize the student to provide a copy of the proposal to the dissertation committee. A meeting takes place to discuss continuation of the research, as described, and/or refinement of the concept. In the case of the latter, the student uses a more structured presentation approach that includes Microsoft PowerPoint and that guides the committee through the various phases of the dissertation, focusing on the same elements that inhere in the concept paper. The structure of the proposal defense in a more formal setting is similar to the dissertation defense, with the exception that it is a modified variation: there are no results or subsequent corresponding sections. Refer to Chapter 16 for information relevant to the proposal defense.

Revisions to the Proposal

With either of these two approaches, if revisions are necessary, the advisee should be given instructions to submit revisions in an amended proposal, which the committee may want to review one additional time to ensure the integrity of their recommendations, as those were implemented into the proposal. It is most important that changes to the proposal are placed into the formal context of a written document. If not, then instructions are left to memory only, which is not always reliable.

Proposal Approval

The committee should sign the *dissertation proposal approval form* if this procedure is used at your university. If your university does not use this form, then the committee should indicate approval in writing. The advisee is then cleared to work with the advisor on securing the HSIRB protocol, if indeed the research involves human subjects. A carefully delineated dissertation proposal results in a more expeditious filing of the HSIRB protocol because certain sections of the proposal dovetail into the requirements for the protocol: the methods section, for example, as described above.

A poorly assembled proposal will necessarily impact the process of writing the protocol, and so each step must be planned carefully and with attention to detail. The proposal and the protocol should align at the critical points of intersection. Think of it this way: you can't get to the HSIRB protocol without the proposal. You can't get to the proposal unless the research methods/data collection/stats analysis pieces are in place. Overlapping is built into a successful system, and so the more overlap, the better, in terms of ensuring efficiency. Regard the process as a recursive one: it draws back upon itself in an effort to move forward. You're hitting two birds with one stone and working smartly. Amendments to procedures can and must be made when or if problems or complications arise, of course. But it is best to spend time constructing viable, working concepts that result in excellent proposals and protocols, as these are the foundations for the proposed research.

The Difference Between Filing the HSIRB Protocol and Securing Protocol Approval

It is imperative that students understand an approved proposal does not mean they are cleared to conduct research at this point; the approval of the HSIRB protocol is necessary before any data collection that involves human subjects takes place, as stated previously. By the same token, the simple filing of the HSIRB protocol does not mean the student has been cleared to collect data. These distinctions are important and must not be confused. The advisor and the advisee will receive formal notification of the protocol's approval, if or when approval may be granted. There should be no research activity unless or until such formal notification is received. Bear in mind that each university or organization has its own processing time for HSIRB protocol review, and so it is important to inquire about this turn-around time frame. At my university, protocol review is generally completed in approximately 10 days, or less in some instances.

Other Clearances

Other types of clearances are more obvious in terms of the necessity to file a protocol: research with animals, hazardous materials, and recombinant DNA, for example, all require IRB clearances, which are typically filed by the faculty member (dissertation chair/principal investigator), who lists the student as the co-principal investigator/student investigator on the project. These are more *obvious* categories; students working within these categories *know* they are working with these elements and, further, they do not initiate the protocol in quite the same manner as one appropriate to human subjects.

The area of human subjects is less clear and may be complicated by a series of factors that require clarification and further interaction with the research compliance office. This is why it is important that graduate students and their advisors consider the benefit of establishing solid working relationships with the research compliance office early in the process. It is also critical that they avoid guessing about whether a project requires HSIRB approval. *Never guess*. Always speak with the research compliance coordinator or submit the protocol directly and wait for the determination.

Research Compliance Office as Resource

The research compliance coordinator is an integral factor in the research procedure. For many years, I observed that faculty and students alike seemed wary of research compliance coordinators and their perceived control or power over a complicated process. They were viewed in certain circles as individuals who could stall out your research and block your progress. This perspective may well have been unfounded; the reality is that research compliance is a specialized area of the research process that requires intervention and oversight, in a one-on-one, customized approach that takes into account the individual variations of a research agenda. Coordinators are highly trained, capable individuals whose skills enable them to serve as mentors to faculty and students. Rather than regard them as *gatekeepers* to success, perhaps it is best to regard them as *conduits* to success. Advisors should consider the value of maintaining open lines of communication with the research compliance staff and encourage their advisees to do the same.

When writing the HSIRB protocol, consider the following:

1. *Value of the Team.* Advisors and advisees should consider the collaborative value of writing the proposal and protocol together, as a team. Advisors should have oversight of both processes and aid the student in creating the narrative texts for both documents. I would encourage advisees to take the lead in such projects, as they will benefit from the discipline of writing and organizing. However, the oversight of the advisor is necessary. Should the HSIRB recommend revisions or clarifications, it is the responsibility of the dissertation chair/committee to review the amended/revised protocol to ensure the accuracy and comprehensive implementation of all adjustments. Refer to item 8 in the list below.
2. *Ethical Role of HSIRB.* The primary role of the HSIRB is to ensure ethical best practices and protections for human subjects participating in human research. Due to the ethics of conducting research with human subjects, advisees must complete an online training course designed and sponsored by the Collaborative Institutional Training Initiative (CITI Program) that intersects into the Responsible Conduct of Research (RCR) course or by a self-made product at certain other universities. The certification granted as a result of taking the CITI Program training is in effect for 3 years, and for 4 years typically for RCR, whereupon additional refresher modules must be taken. Advisors, as principal investigators of the project, must also have successfully completed this training as well as updated training.
3. *Anticipating Review Questions.* When reviewing an HSIRB protocol, the board will hold the authors of the protocol accountable for responding to a series of questions built into its review process. Questions such as why, when, where, how, with whom, under what conditions, for what purpose, and for how long, among others, frequently come to mind in the board's review process. It is up to the authors to provide detailed information that anticipates these questions and that

very clearly responds. The HSIRB protocol anticipates that authors will employ a *process analysis* discourse mode; that is, writers will use a step-by-step process that delineates each and every step in the research agenda, from the rationale for the study to the maintenance of confidential data and their eventual destruction. The second discourse mode that will serve authors is *exposition*: to explain very clearly to an audience of non-specialists in your particular field.

4. *Considerations of Informed Consent.* The HSIRB protocol includes informed consent and the manner in which that information is communicated to potential and willing participants. (This list is not exhaustive.)
   A. What is the purpose of conducting this study?
   B. Does this study involve protected populations: children, prisoners, for example?
   C. How will you invite participants into this study?
   D. What does your Informed Consent document/entire process look like?
   E. Have you explained how individuals can stop participating in the study if they no longer wish to continue?
   F. How will confidentiality of data be maintained? Where will data be stored and what is the time period before destruction of these data files takes place?
   G. Do you understand the use of incentives in your research and are you cognizant that some incentives can appear to be coercive?
   H. What is the period of time required of individuals who wish to participate in the study?
   I. What are the benefits to participants, and have these been intentionally or inadvertently overstated or overpromised in any manner so as to give the appearance that certain outcomes can be realizable?
   J. What are the risks to participants?
   K. What are the costs to participants?
5. *Disciplinary Lexicons and Standard Language.* Use a combination of the disciplinary lexicon in your field as well as standard, clear writing. Remember to use the terminology in your field, but stop for a moment to define your terms so that they are understandable from the perspective of non-ex-

perts. Remember that the HSIRB is comprised of individuals from different disciplines, mostly all with Ph.D.s, but it may even include student representatives who do not have a vote, but who do attend meetings and contribute to the discussion. These will be the individuals asking those questions addressed in item 3 above. The board's objective is to understand your protocol and to ensure that it aligns with federal standards. It is up to you, as author, to clearly and cogently state that information. This requires the use of language as a vehicle to communicate, and as we all know, language is a slippery creature that can easily squirm away from us. Moreover, the board is charged with averting potential difficulties, harm to human subjects, federal violations, and similar issues. Think of the board as an advisor of sorts who oversees, cautions, guides, and mentors researchers through the research process. In this manner, you will tend to see it less as a gatekeeper and more as a resource.

6. *Proofreading of Protocol.* In addition to the development of solid concepts framed in good writing techniques, use appropriate grammar and mechanics. If you cannot manage your writing, your grammar, and your mechanics, then you come across as an individual who may not be able to manage the research process either. Fair or not, that's what happens when poorly written protocols come across the HSIRB desk for review. The same happens in articles for publication, research grants, and other competitive endeavors reliant upon narrative acumen.

7. *Returned Protocols.* Protocols can be returned for continued revision for a variety of reasons: unclear writing (which translates to the idea of muddled thoughts), lack of understanding your own research process and what you intend to do and how you will do it, failure to protect the data, failure to protect the human subjects in your proposed study, and failure to ensure confidentiality, among others. Generally, if the full board is being convened, the student and the advisor will be brought into the meeting together. One or two individuals will be assigned as *primary reviewers* on the protocol, but the entire board will also review the protocol as *secondary reviewers*, prepared to discuss their findings, rec-

ommendations, and suggestions during the scheduled meeting. The board secretaries (generally two) will each take down notes, carefully recording statements from the primary reviewers first, and then recording additional notes from the secondary reviewers. These notes are provided to the advisor and advisee pair several days after the meeting adjourns, and in this manner the pair receives written documentation of the changes/revisions recommended by the reviewers.

8. *Implementing Revisions.* Take care to heed the directions of the board for implementing revisions to the protocol narrative. These may vary from institution to institution, but you should find out before you begin. Visit the IRB's website or speak directly with the research compliance officer. At my university, revisions are to be highlighted so they are clearly identifiable to both the authors and the chair of the board, who is responsible for ensuring that the recommended changes do indeed appear in the revised protocol. This step illustrates the importance of having a written copy of the revisions: the advisor–advisee pair can use the copy as a checklist of sorts when implementing the revisions. In addition, the HSIRB chair will also use the checklist when ensuring that those changes are reflected in the revised protocol, a double benefit. The value of using the checklist cannot be overstated. If you are careless and leave out any of the recommended changes, your protocol will be returned to you again. So, if time is an important element in your research plan, you will do well to exercise care. Remember the value in collaboration: both the advisor and the advisee should use the checklist together to ensure they have covered all the bases. Refer to item 1 in the list above.

9. *Be Specific.* The board appreciates detailed information. If you are uncertain about a precise statistical method that you will use in your protocol, for example, then get that information before you begin to write the protocol. HSIRB is certainly going to want that information, and so leaving it out will not serve you. Your protocol will be returned. More time wasted. Go back to the previous section in this chapter in which I talk about the complementary nature of both the dissertation proposal and the HSIRB protocol: these two docu-

ments share a logical, congruent connection. In that section, I advocate that the advisor–advisee pair collaborate with the research compliance officer and a statistician or a committee member serving as the statistician. If it is the research procedure itself that is causing difficulty, then go back to the question of *how* and ensure that each step in the process is clearly delineated. This means that the authors are *anticipating* the HSIRB's questions and concerns and that they are clearly stating precisely how the research will be conducted and managed, as well as the manner in which human subjects will be protected. The more specific you are and the more detail you provide, the better.

10. *Filing a Protocol Does Not Equate to Approval.* I am returning to this point because it is a critical one. Do not *ever* embark on data collection unless or until you receive formal notification from HSIRB that your protocol has been approved. Such notification will come to you in the form of a written approval letter that bears the signature of the HSIRB chair and is printed on university letterhead, in most instances. At my university, an email notification with the very same language is sent first, but it will always be followed by the formal letter, on university letterhead, delivered in hard copy. The language will always be the same, regardless of format. Some IRBs may have implemented an electronic letterhead and, therefore, the letter of approval can be typed on electronic letterhead and emailed directly. Check with your institution's IRB to determine its procedures. The main point to remember is to receive official approval first and then collect data. At my institution, the email notification signals authorization to begin the research.

Gail's Story

Gail was a Ph.D. student who had defended her dissertation in November several years ago. She planned to graduate in December and was thrilled to be at the end of the dissertation pathway. A review of her dissertation by the thesis and dissertation coordinators revealed an absence of the HSIRB protocol, and clearly human subjects research had commenced, and on a restricted/protected population. Gail had been asked to submit the protocol as an appendix to the dissertation. But there was no evidence that a protocol had ever been filed with HSIRB. Neither Gail nor her advisor could produce an approval letter or even a copy of the protocol. The exhilaration of coming to the finish line slowly morphed into a terrible dread. A committee was convened to determine next steps, the first of which was to cancel her graduation. Gail was devastated at the outcome and beside herself at the loss of years of work. The research could not be used for the purposes of a dissertation, a conference, or an article for publication; in essence, it was off limits to any academic purpose. And further, whatever could be salvaged from a study that was not approved for human subjects research but had *already* been conducted was negligible.

Episodes like this do not often end well and generally spell devastation for the student and the advisor, who together are held responsible for such breaches. In this instance, sanctions were imposed on the advisor. Gail eventually produced another dissertation and went on to graduate. However, let me be clear that this outcome is exceptionally rare. Most people do not have the time, energy, temerity, or financial solvency to undergo a second dissertation. In most cases, a situation such as this one is its own endgame.

~ The Take Away ~

1. Recognize the value of designing the dissertation proposal and the HSIRB protocol in a simultaneous manner, so that the documents are synchronized.
2. Proceed with proposal defense, revisions, and final approval.
3. Know the differences between *filing* the HSIRB protocol and *approval* to begin data collection.
4. Consider the research compliance office as a resource for advisors and advisees.
5. When writing the HSIRB protocol, consider the following: the value of the team, the ethical role of HSIRB, the anticipation of review board questions, the necessity for informed consent and its implications, the use of disciplinary lexicons and standard language, the value of proofreading, returned protocols and the revising process, specificity/detailed information, and filing a protocol versus approval.

6. Remember that human subjects research carried out without HSIRB approval *cannot,* in almost all instances, be presented in articles, at conferences, or in any formal academic writing endeavor, including the dissertation and the thesis.

Chapter 16

Preparing for the Oral Defense of the Dissertation: 17 Easy Steps

For many doctoral students, the dissertation defense, the apex of doctoral study, resides in the distant future. But without warning, students find themselves bracing for the final hurdle. They wonder how or if they will manage to pull off this "last hurrah" as graduate students and enter into the scholarly realm as *bona fide* academics.

Students are never quite as prepared for this event as they would like to be. This rite of passage looms before them as a mysterious and unknown event, a gothic terror in its own right. It certainly should not be this way, and some forethought and preparation will go far in fostering confidence.

The following suggestions will help students take control of this nerve-wracking experience and transform it into the exciting, memorable, and joyful event that it should be.

1. *Attend dissertation defenses.* The best way for graduate students to prepare for the dissertation defense is to regularly attend the defenses of their colleagues, those internal and external to their respective fields of expertise. They should be doing so throughout their programs, not just several weeks prior to their own defense.
2. *Know the rituals.* What happens at a dissertation defense lends to an important learning experience. Students should discuss the intricacies of the defense with their advisors, as there are many variations. Generally, the dissertation chair reserves a conference room or meeting room for the defense. At some universities, dissertation defenses are held in the

graduate college or graduate school. Attendees may or may not be invited to sit at the same table as committee members. After the presentation, the student and the attendees are usually dismissed from the room while the committee members deliberate. Then, the candidate and the attendees are brought back into the room and the candidate is congratulated and referred to by his or her new title for the first time. At this point, the committee meets privately with the advisee to discuss revisions or other relevant matters.

3. *Know the time allocated.* Students should ascertain how much time their particular departments allocate to the complete oral defense, presentation and questioning, and should confer with their advisors. Most defenses last approximately two hours, including deliberation time for committee members.

4. *Use PowerPoint.* Using a PowerPoint presentation is a professional approach that does justice to the vast research that comprises the dissertation. PowerPoint slides should encapsulate the study and focus on its most salient findings. In preparing, students should ask these questions: "What do I want people to know about my dissertation? What is the most important information that I can present and talk about?" Presenters should consider the rules of chartsmanship, creating a goal-oriented presentation that navigates attendees through a logical, point-by-point sequence of information that builds to the conclusion in a clear and focused direction.

5. *Prepare slides.* Prepare PowerPoint slides by using information in the dissertation's first chapter (which actually is the overview of the dissertation) as a framework or outline that reflects the logical sequencing of information. However, substantive information in the entire dissertation should correspond with the slides and also with the notes (see suggestion 7 below). In essence, presenters reduce their dissertation to a PowerPoint format. The information presented should correspond to the time allocated for the defense presentation. Ensure the internal and external quality of the slides, and make certain there is integrity of information, as well as integrity in appearance of the slides. Slides should be readable and professional-looking. PowerPoint provides a

framework for the presentation, but it should not become the epicenter of the dissertation defense. Slides should reflect the following:

- *Title*: Title of the dissertation, including the presenter's name, department and/or program of study, and date.
- *Committee acknowledgment*: Include the names of the dissertation advisor and committee members. Presenters should speak briefly about the contributions of each to the success of the work. It is appropriate to acknowledge the spouse, significant other, family members, friends, and others who have lent support. Presenters may describe to the attendees why they chose their research and what informed that decision; attendees are naturally curious about how researchers arrived at their topics.
- *Statement of the problem*: Include a brief statement that draws researchers' attention to a particular critical situation revealed in the scholarship. Presenters are encouraged to incorporate several slides that reflect statistics, data, and information about the problem. Elements of the literature review should be included to provide a viable framework that stands as evidence of the agreement among critical experts in a given field that there is merit in conducting the research, which fills a particular need for increased scholarship (see "Literature review" below).
- *Significance of the research*: Presenters should address the importance of the research to a wide pantheon of shareholders, from those most invested as beneficiaries to those least. This segment of the presentation focuses on the wider applications of the research to the community at large.
- *Research question(s)*: List all of the research questions exactly as they appear in the text of the dissertation.
- *Literature review*: Presenters should provide an overview of salient critical studies. Such slides serve two functions: (1) they delineate the current critical perspective, and (2) they justify that the research advances the scholarship through its research objective.

- *Method*: Such slides provide an overview of the application of particular methods through which research questions are answered. Presenters should include references to critical information that addresses the rationale for the selection of a particular method and addresses issues of validity and reliability.
- *Results and analysis*: Slides should reflect graphs, tables, or charts that demonstrate critical elements of the research findings or outcomes. Presenters sometimes include their hypotheses and the corresponding results or analysis.
- *Discussion*: Presenters should list and discuss salient findings and their applicability to their field of expertise.
- *Limitations of the study*: Generally, limitations emerge out of the research process or after the research has concluded and prompt these questions: "If I had to do this study again, in what way would it differ? Would another approach affect outcomes, and, if so, how?"
- *Recommendations for future study*: Where do students see the logical continuation of their work? This opens the pathway for future scholars and extends the opportunity to enter into the academic conversation.

The conclusion of the discussion, limitations, and recommendations segments intersects naturally with the questioning phase of the dissertation defense. Presenters should anticipate the round of questions from committee members at this point.

6. *Provide PowerPoint handouts.* Prepare hard copies of the presentation for each committee member and attendees and distribute them before the defense; it may be useful to delegate this responsibility to a colleague (see suggestion 11). Send electronic copies to committee members who will attend the defense remotely.
7. *Prepare PowerPoint notes.* A notes section appears at the bottom of each slide and should reflect discussion points, culled from the text of the dissertation. Notes enable presenters to remain focused and on track in an organized manner that sets up a series of bullet points to jog the memory and

help the presenters to discuss additional details or elements of interest. The opportunity to elaborate may calm nerves and help presenters rise above the formality of the defense by dovetailing into interesting conversational elements that heighten audience interaction.

8. *Be the authority figure.* When presenting, students should think of themselves as authorities who best understand the information being presented and who stand in an ideal position to instruct attendees. The presentation should be instructional or expository, so they should consider themselves as teachers, experts in their own right, informing the audience about the research findings. This perspective reverses the power differential and re-centers the student in a position of authority, one who has wisdom and knowledge and who teaches the committee the knowledge acquired.

9. *Anticipate questions.* Successful graduate students are generally adept at anticipating test questions, as their years of experience bear out. Applying these skills to the dissertation defense provides students with a clear advantage. Students should consider the academic expertise of their respective committee members. In what areas would they most likely be focused? Advisees should be familiar with advisors' theoretical or methodological penchants, the manner in which they think and reason, and the emphasis placed on certain elements of the dissertation as they confer throughout the dissertation process. Exposure to committee members as they serve at other defenses provides excellent insight into how they work together as a group and as individuals. Anticipation informed by knowledge is an important tool in students' dissertation defense tool kit.

10. *Conduct a dress rehearsal.* At some universities, it is common practice to schedule a pre-defense or a mock defense of the dissertation, an opportunity to field possible questions from committee members and other faculty. Students are not provided with the committee's actual defense questions, but gain experience in responding to questions that relate to their research. This preparatory experience initiates students into the defense experience and inspires confidence. Several days prior to the actual defense, students should schedule a dress

rehearsal in the same room reserved for the defense. Exposure to the surroundings, ahead of time, engenders comfort and reduces stress. Tech-smart rooms equipped with state-of-the-art technology make the setup for students somewhat easier. If tech-smart rooms are not a possibility, students should set up their own computer, projector, and other equipment, such as phones, speakers, or video conferencing for an offsite committee member.

11. *Delegate.* Students should delegate to a trusted individual some of the smaller but important responsibilities of the defense well ahead of schedule. This chosen person could set up the equipment for the presentation, prepare the room on the day of defense, and make copies of the PowerPoint presentation and distribute these and other handouts.

12. *Consider the X factor.* Although there are no guarantees of technological integrity or flawless appearances, having Plan B as a backup is a good thing. Handouts can save the day if technology fails, and an additional fresh shirt for a spilled coffee can be a salvation for the X factor.

13. *Dress for success.* The defense is a formal event in which the entire university community is invited. The event signals a critical rite of passage for most doctoral students and for the faculty who have supported them throughout a long and challenging process. Though there are no general rules governing appropriate attire at most universities, the event should be regarded with dignity and respect. Presenters should dress as if they were delivering a paper at a conference or going to a job interview.

14. *Prepare the night before.* Keep everything as normal as possible, including sleeping and eating patterns. Save the heavy celebratory meals and desserts for a post-defense treat.

15. *Remember to laugh.* Despite our best efforts and planning, we do not have complete control. Laugh at what does not go according to plan and move on.

16. *Think about post defense.* After the defense, committee members may decide the dissertation requires revision and will refrain from signing off until adjustments have been implemented. Such revisions may include minor changes to the text that can be dealt with immediately. Other adjust-

ments may require elaborate restructuring, and there may be additional work to do. Students should immediately address the committee's concerns and implement all changes. Students need to remain focused on graduation and complete the work that will take them there.

17. *Consider professional editing and formatting services.* The dissertation is not complete until the monograph is in final form according to departmental or graduate college/school specifications. But at the end of this process, students are exhausted intellectually, psychologically, spiritually, and perhaps financially. Thus, it may be wise to make life easy for yourself, and if your budget permits, it is advisable to secure the professional services of a formatter or editor who can put the document into final form; in other words, purchase the services you need in order to lighten the burden. Check with your graduate school or college to determine if a list of approved editors/formatters is available to you. Generally, these individuals are skilled in various formatting styles that are required by your discipline and university. Moreover, to save a few dollars, you can separate editing tasks from formatting tasks, although the two are best combined to ensure a professional final product.

The journey to the doctoral degree is long and often arduous, but knowing how to navigate the course sustains those who venture on the pathway to the Ph.D. The end of the process does not differ from the beginning in terms of the need for students to understand the procedures and rituals that comprise the dissertation defense. The preparation of faculty and their advisees is key to the safe harbor of degree completion and graduation.

~ The Take Away ~

1. Planning for the dissertation defense by conducting a mock defense or dress rehearsal and by making prior arrangements inspires confidence and sets the stage for a smooth experience.

Chapter 17

Bill of Rights for the Advisee and the Advisor

When we think of the Constitutional Bill of Rights, we reflect upon the first 10 amendments to the U.S. Constitution, which came into effect in 1791 to protect the rights of the citizenry. The Bill of Rights makes clear various freedoms or expectations that were not necessarily articulated by the Constitution. In later centuries, various forms of Bills of Rights evolved to protect patients in hospital settings or passengers in airplanes, for example. University and college program handbooks also articulate students' Bill of Rights, but those rights may be limited to the actual program requirements or relevant ethics issues that concern students' trajectory to degree completion, but seldom include those rights associated with the dissertation.

Because the advisor–advisee relationship can sometimes be difficult or challenging, with the rights of both sides not clearly expressed, I propose two versions of a Bill of Rights for advisees and advisors at the dissertation stage.

Advisee's Bill of Rights

1. You have the right to be treated with respect, fairness, and dignity.
2. You are entitled to the timely return of your dissertation chapters.
3. You are entitled to the timely return of your phone calls, voice messages, texts, and email.
4. You are entitled to sound, ethical advice and guidance from your department, graduate program advisor, dissertation advisor, and committee members on matters that relate to your curriculum and to your dissertation.
5. You have the right to expect a dissertation advisor to treat your dissertation concerns with patience and understanding.

6. You are entitled to the confidentiality, privacy, and protection of your intellectual property.
7. You are entitled to regularly scheduled appointments for which your advisor and committee members are prepared with materials, information, feedback, and resources.
8. You are entitled to receive an accurate accounting of your progress to degree completion.
9. You are entitled to play a role in the academic recommendations and decisions of the dissertation committee to the extent that you can prove your point and defend it for the committee's consideration.
10. You maintain the right to change advisors if the advising relationship should prove to become unworkable and after careful and consistent attempts to rectify it fail. With this as a given, you have the right to assemble a new committee, the formal appointment of which is not subject to an unrealistic timeline connected to an unrealistic policy. You have the right to re-convene the new committee without prejudice or bias toward yourself or your new committee members and your decision.
11. You are entitled to work with a group of professionals who respect your desire to complete the Ph.D. and who are dedicated to the successful completion of your dissertation and your timely graduation.
12. You are entitled to be informed of the range of policies that can help to promote and protect your scholastic health throughout the degree-earning process: leave of absence, continuous enrollment, annual review, and research policies, among others.

Dissertation Advisor's Bill of Rights

1. You have the right to be treated with respect, fairness, and dignity.
2. You are entitled to your advisee's timely return of edited chapters, based upon your recommendations.
3. You are entitled to timely responses to your phone calls, voice messages, texts, and email.
4. You are entitled to the right to withdraw your professional

association from a student who will not heed your guidance, who refuses to or cannot meet your expectations or adhere to your instructions, or who becomes belligerent, uncooperative, and disagreeable.
5. You are entitled to the right not to have your time wasted.
6. You reserve the right to inform your advisee that your advising relationship is moving off track and is no longer serving the purposes of completing the dissertation, thereby resulting in the decision to resign.
7. You, in consultation with and approval by your department, reserve the right to "counsel out" a student who continuously is not performing according to program expectations.
8. You are entitled to the professional training, mentorship, guidance, and resources of your department and university so that you can deliver the highest quality of professional advice/support to your advisee.
9. You are entitled to work in a collaborative environment in which duties and responsibilities of the dissertation are shared by the dissertation committee and not carried by you in isolation.
10. You are entitled to your own time to research, write, publish, teach, conference, and continue to develop your professional aspirations.
11. You have the right to direct the student's dissertation in a manner that comports with the rigor of your discipline, according to your professional experience.
12. You are entitled to be informed of the range of policies that can help promote and protect your department's scholastic integrity throughout the degree-earning process: leave of absence, continuous enrollment, annual review, and research policies, among others.

~ The Take Away ~

For Advisors and Advisees

1. *Know your rights.* Be familiar in your own mind with your rights and what you require to be successful in this process to get the job done. Don't be shy about identifying those ele-

ments that are integrally connected to success. You have to work together, and so talk to each other about the best ways to reach those ends.
2. *Insist on your rights.* Articulate your rights. Talk about them. State them outright. Expectations that are not met are almost always disappointments, and disappointments can ferment into resentments. Resentments can morph into retaliations, and thus it goes. You get the picture.
3. *Respect the rights of others.* There is a "Golden Rule" for advisors and advisees. You don't get *more* respect because you're an advisor or *less* respect because you're "just" a student. You also do not get to reign supreme and call all the shots because you are a student or because you are the advisor. This is an equal opportunity arrangement; do what is best for the *other* individual, with the idea that if you do this, positive outcomes for *both* of you are possible.
4. *Focus on the dissertation.* Make the *dissertation,* not your compromised relationship, the focus of your energy and passion. Defining your rights keeps the focus where it needs to be.
5. *Think like a team member.* Winning teams work together in unison. Think and act like a winning team, and you will succeed.
6. *Know when it's over.* Despite all efforts, there are times when transgressions occur on both sides of the aisle and when the Bill of Rights, whether formally created or simply a tacit arrangement, no longer functions in its protective capacity. When there is growing opposition between advisor and advisee that cannot be assuaged, rectified, or resolved, it is time to part ways. People who have lost confidence in each other will not survive the dissertation ordeal. Try to graciously and gracefully manage this parting of the ways, and move on. Refer to Chapters 13 and 14.

Chapter 18

Combating the Dissertation Blues: Comprehensive Examinations — The Prelude

Once program courses are completed, doctoral students enter into the beginning of what for many of them is a long, solitary journey to degree completion.

Comprehensive examinations signal the first step along this pathway to candidacy. The definition of candidacy frequently varies from institution to institution and can even vary from department to department in the same university, but essentially, students enter into doctoral candidacy after they complete certain requirements beyond the comprehensive examinations. At my university, for example, candidates are in good academic standing, have completed all program requirements with the exception of the dissertation defense, and have in place a formal committee and an approved dissertation proposal.

Students frequently experience the beginning of the separation from their peers and from their respective institutions at this particular point. Suddenly, the familiar context of their educational world is disrupted; there are no longer formal classes to attend, along with examinations, assignments, or other course requirements to fulfill. Literally, students find themselves outside of a group environment that has served, in a certain sense, to unify the members in a common cause. Some, moving forward into comprehensive examinations, may be lock-stepped in a cohort or other singular group framework, and hence, they find themselves accompanied by others on this next leg of the journey. However, countless others find themselves on isolating pathways, with no associates to accompany them. An educational process which at first appeared to be integrative and collaborative, supportive and clear, suddenly tilts on its axis and seems not in league with the fellowship that once characterized the initial forays into the program. It is not surprising that many students find themselves isolated and somewhat distanced from once-familiar colleagues; the road has forked and students are on their own pathways.

Balancing Isolationism and Collaborative Interaction

This time alone actually represents a two-edged sword. While I am not an advocate of isolationism, the time alone benefits the student in preparing for comprehensive examinations in a deeply penetrative manner. Without distractions, students should become autodidacts and learn to teach themselves and acquire the information necessary to the successful completion of the examinations, perhaps their first inundation into scholarly demands on such a heightened and indeed isolated level. This activity may work well for certain fields, where examinations are customized to individual students and to their specialized content area. However, by the same token, the actions of studying or preparing in a group may also lessen the isolation and actually serve academically those individuals who are indeed in a cohort. Lock-stepped together in a common comprehensive examination, they may be given segments as part of a take-home examination, for example. Strategizing together is a team-building enterprise that can solidify individual efforts because, at the end of the day, comprehensive examinations are about the individual, not the group. However, the *group study* approach may solidify the journey, lessen the separation, and keep peers motivated and on task. Moreover, the group dynamic plays into synthesis and analysis of ideas and helps to sharpen the thought processes.

But first, let me clarify the need to observe ethics; students should not collaborate on answers so that they are actually writing responses to a common examination together, but more so that they engage in discussion of test-taking techniques or the logistics of test taking or the understanding of particular questions geared toward a winning approach, in terms of "technique" or thought process—not in terms of producing exact answers. They should consider whether there are common courses in their doctoral programs that lead up to the examinations or that can contribute to the test-taking experience. Advisors and faculty play an important role in articulating such viewpoints and can advise students accordingly. If the curricula are designed in a way that leads to successful completion of the comprehensive examinations, then students need to hear this. They should also understand if the examinations are completed via independent study; in other words, coursework plays only a minor role in the test-taking preparation. At the University of South Florida, my degree-granting university, coursework played a minor role, and a period of at least 6 months of independent study was imposed as comprehensive examination preparation time.

Other examination models include take-home examinations that must be submitted by a certain date. Yet others are set up as individual examination appointments: students show up and take the exam over a period of days, according to scheduled hours allocated to them. Some fields require both an oral and a written examination.

Most of these sorts of comprehensive examinations, however, require a great deal of expansive writing, with the cultivation of logical ideas, using literature and other sources to support main ideas. These are not *point and click* or *multiple-choice* questions, and so conferring together on test techniques does not disrupt the ethical balance inherent in any test environment, in my opinion. In fact, consider the success of problem-solving techniques that lawyers and medical students use when exploring a medical or legal case that may open to multiple possibilities for resolution or when preparing for the bar examination or medical boards. The value of collaborative preparation for comprehensive exams is clear. These are scenarios in which students teach each other through their unique perspectives that include the reading and understanding of the phraseology of those questions and the information sought, as well as the spectrum of responses that demonstrate students' proficiency and expansive knowledge.

In many respects, this is a team-teaching or team-learning technique that points test takers into probable questions or areas that comprise the test-taking experience. I am certain that as students we all mused about potential questions that professors might or could ask on tests. If we projected correctly and structured solid responses, we were delighted to see them included in the examination, but if we missed the mark and failed to see them as possibilities and thus were not prepared, we may have been horrified. One of my professors once catapulted his students out of their predictive security by testing them on material in the footnotes of texts. The point is this: if you participate in a more collaborative type of comprehensive examination preparation, you lessen or at least forestall some of the isolation that is experienced by those who "go it alone." Furthermore, you gain via a collaborative interchange that capitalizes upon the team strategy.

It is not uncommon at all for students to experience the *blues* during this time period. Students at this stage are in transition, between course taking and the dissertation, and, as we all know, periods of transition are generally uncomfortable, characterized by uncertainty and a kind of hesitancy. To compound the matter, many students do not have exposure to examples of superlative comprehensive examinations that could serve as emulative models. Neither do they necessarily have access to failed examinations. Students can always access completed dissertations that their advisors may recommend for review as they (students) prepare for their dissertation journeys, but seldom do departments offer examples of sterling or not-so-sterling comprehensive examinations, and these could be invaluable heuristics through which students learn the art of mastering this kind of test. The object of the exams is *to show what you know* or, as one of my committee members proclaimed, *to strut your stuff*—not to fail. Yet, think of how many students fail the comps because they have no idea of what is expected, nor are they necessarily aware of the test-taking strategies that yield successful exam completion. Failed comps equate to lost time and certainly more blues.

This transitional stage will not be their last, however, for the blues experienced during the comprehensive examination process return, in many instances, during the time that students are writing the dissertation and even after, when all is said and done. But we will return to this point later.

~ The Take Away ~

1. *Strategize as a study team.* Use the medical school/law school model and consider the value of problem solving as a group, rather than as a lone individual. Yes, you'll have to write the examinations as an individual, but if you align yourself with the right people, you'll have the team approach behind you and the ability to avail yourself of varied problem-solving perspectives: deciphering questions to ensure that you are responding in a manner that comports with the question's objective, and providing theoretical background information balanced by relevant literature.
2. *Recognize that some isolation is normal.* Isolation to the point of total seclusion is most likely not conducive to success during the comprehensive examinations. However, there is a degree of necessity in being somewhat secluded during this time, and so advocate for the appropriate balance. Working with a group offers great advantages: solace, comfort, support, and academic/disciplinary reassurance. But time alone in contemplation reinforces the ideas discerned during contact with the group.

Chapter 19

The Dissertation Writing Blues

Walter Isaacson writes that as Michelangelo was confronted by the enormous challenges of painting the Sistine Chapel, he wrote in a poem, "I am not in the right place, and I am not a painter." According to Isaacson (2018), Michelangelo was a sculptor at heart who "preferred the chisel to the brush" (p. 375), a statement indicating that he may have been out of his element and clearly uncomfortable with the task at hand. A moment must have arisen when Michelangelo felt constrained, clearly melancholy and "petulant" as was his nature (Isaacson, 2018, p. 367), and perhaps even *blue,* with the enormity of the Pope's request upon him; he may have desired to escape the drafty chapel ceilings and an irate Pope and flee to the solace of his chisels and white marble, the price of this creativity proving to be too exorbitant.

What we know is that creative, innovative impulses all exact a steep price of those who execute them. Dissertations count among those creative works. During these activities, people tend to feel the weight of their engagement, and that frequently makes them sad and forlorn, and perhaps, like Michelangelo, temperamental and agitated. Why? Perhaps because they think the project is beyond their capabilities; because they think the project costs more than what they want to invest in it; because it hurts to be locked up interminably in an office or a library somewhere pounding on a word processor or, like Michelangelo, lying under a wet ceiling with a barking Pope at your heels; because it feels terrible to tell your kids you don't have time to read *Strega Nona* or toss a ball in the back yard; because you don't have a real job and your significant other keeps asking when you will. For centuries, creative artists, whether rich or poor, have had to safeguard their time, and that careful apportioning of time comes with a price. Dissertating students really are no different, it seems, only they do not generally refer to themselves as artists. Either way, when you're alone, you may tend to feel a separation from others or a separation from what you really would like to do, as we can see from the example of Michelangelo who perceived himself *"not in the right place."*

Dissertation blues depart somewhat from the blues experienced during the comprehensive examinations. True enough with the comps, there will still be periods of isolation; even if you work within groups, you still have to produce committee-approved examinations yourself.

Once comps are completed, there is generally a feeling of euphoria, a celebratory moment in which students relax and rejoice, and rightfully so. However, the dreaded dissertation is just around the corner, and students are catapulted out of the joyful moment to face the realities of moving through the dissertation. As I've said before, if you are in a STEM field (science, technology, engineering, mathematics), your topic may well be a resurrection and a continuation of your advisor's topic. If you are in education, the health sciences, social sciences, or the humanities, for example, your topic may be something that you must discover. That process may take some time and may contribute to feelings of uncertainty and gloom.

Getting started, however, is its own anodyne to inactivity and stasis, and by using the tools that I talked about before, the concept paper and conceptual conversations with the advisor, you should be able to overcome inertia and move into purposeful action. However, these tools, in and of themselves, are not always all that is required. Taking the tools and actually implementing them into dissertation chapters is the next logical step, and failure to do so may account for some of the less-than-optimistic perspectives that students frequently experience. It is sometimes very difficult to operationalize a plan of action because the project seems overpowering, even dreadful.

If I told you to sit in a room and write a book by a certain deadline, you would probably panic at the idea. However, if I tell you that we can break down your book-length project into 5 or so doable pieces, each with a clear direction and focus, you would feel more relaxed, more able to meet the objectives.

Think about it this way: by the time you've written the proposal (3 chapters), you are about ¾ of the way through the dissertation; you will need to collect and analyze data, and then write up the results and analysis and fine tune the editing for the entire 5 chapters, that is, if you are writing a traditional dissertation. By using the concept paper as a frame for the entire dissertation, you keep the project moving and deliver each section, piece by piece, ensuring that each meets its objectives.

Consider the value and symmetry of the Kaizen system, with its emphasis on continuous process improvement and quality attained through incremental small steps. The word *Kaizen* translates to "continuous improvement": *kai* means "change" or "to correct" and *zen* means "good" (Lean Six Sigma Definition, n.d.). Kaizen is a system of improvement in Japan that extends to both the domestic and the professional circles and, thus, it is holistic, encompassing all aspects of individuals' lives, not just the corporate level. It is this system of improvement that also guides the entire dissertation process, but this process is often painstaking and isolating, whereas the Kaizen system is collaborative and collective and understands that improvement is an incremental process, executed in stages. The results are evolutionary rather than immediate. You are drafting, writing, researching, thinking, creating recursively, or so it would appear.

The blues enter into the picture because you are indeed alone, without the benefit of your peers during this stage. Yes, you may have friends, associates, and family members who are willing to commiserate with you about your dissertation woes or even read your chapters, but that is not quite the same as being enrolled in courses with easy access to a university support system populated by your peers who are also going through the same experience.

What you must bear in mind is the essential necessity to plan your dissertation as if it were a project that requires the best management skills available. The dissertation is a book-length study that departs in depth, breadth, and scope from the master's thesis; however, if you wrote a master's thesis, then you already have a realistic sense of the requirements. Remember that knowledge is power, and that awareness alone puts you in the driver's seat.

When you are planning, consider the following:

1. *Decide on a realistic completion date.* Use the *backward calendar* that I discussed before as a guideline to getting there. You wouldn't invite people to a dinner at your house without making a great number of arrangements beforehand; from the dinner menu to the seating arrangements, you would work out a systematic plan that takes you from invitation to the sit-down affair. That's how a suc-

cessful dinner unfolds. Similarly, successful dissertations do not just happen, *a priori*. They are born out of deliberate actions that have been well thought out and planned according to the individual components that equate to the whole. In my own dissertation experience, I realized that, in the end, I had produced one finished page of narrative for approximately 8 hours of reading, analyzing, and advancing the study, a great deal of alone time. In no way does that equate to a great productive leap, but that was the nature of that particular work. Again, be realistic about what it is possible to do, or not to do.

2. *Beware of procrastination.* We all procrastinate from time to time, and there may even be a salvo in doing so; perhaps we don't have the energy today to contend with a task, let's say, cleaning out a closet. But after a little break, we find renewed strength to handle the task the next day. Then, it doesn't seem so bad, after all. Our minds, at the time we contemplate taking that closet apart, might have encouraged us to think of the project as insurmountable, and so we postponed doing anything at all. Procrastination is a natural tendency in all of us, but it becomes problematic when it is chronic in nature and when it leads to an ongoing and unbroken chain of "tomorrows," each not typified by evidence of progress. You may think of the dissertation as a Herculean task that is beyond what you can deliver. If you just break it down into smaller pieces, you will see that it becomes doable. Use the modular method that I described earlier, as this is an economic, efficient way of breaking down the dissertation into manageable parts that do not intimidate. You have to take the first step. Think of the words of the Chinese philosopher Lao-Tzu: *A journey of a thousand miles begins with a single step.*

3. *Set aside the optimum time in which to write.* What is the best time of the day for you, as an individual? Throughout history, women writers, particularly those with young children or large families, took advantage of the early morning in which to write. If this seems a likely time, then setting the clock for an early alarm may be just the right approach; asking significant others to take over domestic responsibilities on the weekends or late in the evening may also be another option. In other words, select times and days that best coincide with your schedule and use that time wisely to write the dissertation. Engaging in this practice will be a boon when you are writing articles for publication to secure tenure.

This approach will also boost your self-esteem and self-confidence and persuade you that you are making progress. There is nothing worse than feeling as if you are on a treadmill, working hard and not getting anywhere.

4. *Remember that being alone is part of the world of writing the dissertation.* In the end, you are the one who must deliver it. Yes, you have a dissertation chair and a committee, but in the final analysis you will need focused time in which to produce it, and there is no escaping this fact. So, I suggest that you embrace this concept and work with it, as it is the reality of the scholarly work you are producing. You do not need distractions. Yes, a brief escape here or there is understandable, and we can all benefit from a Starbuck's coffee or a movie, but remember that continued interruptions lead to perpetual laxity and, for many students, signal the end of the momentum necessary to a completed dissertation. Sacrifice is built into the equation, but remember that the sacrifices are not forever. Eventually, if you stay the course, you get the Ph.D. Life goes on.

John's Story: John, now a tenured professor, recalls the time when he was approaching his dissertation defense. He desperately needed a break and wanted to drive to Chicago with his partner for a weekend's reprieve from his dissertation. He told his advisor that he was ready for a break; the advisor asked him to quickly calculate the number of hours he would take from his dissertation defense preparation, and John arrived at 16. The advisor said, "If you go to Chicago, figure it this way: you'll be 16 hours short of what you need in order to get ready. If you go, I can promise you that you won't graduate when you want to. If that's worth 16 hours of fun in Chicago, then go."

Not surprisingly, the trip to Chicago was postponed.

5. *Self-management is key.* No one is going to chase you around to find out if you have completed your research, run the stats on your data, transcribed your interviews, implemented the latest set of edits into your chapters, or set up your graduation audit. That is just not going to happen, and most advisors would agree that you need to manage yourself and your work. You are your own CEO, in charge of your own company. How you run it is your business. Remember that your advisor and committee have their own lives. In addition, if you disappear and move off the radar, other students will arrive to take your place and your faculty members' time and attention. It's not pretty, but this is what can happen when you fail to stay on task,

and, in essence, disappear, even if your reason for doing so seems logical. You become a statistic in the world of ABDs (all but dissertation), and believe me when I tell you that those are not the three initials you want to appear after your name.

Arial's Story: Arial was a dedicated Ph.D. student who was interested in pursuing a tenure-track position upon completion of her degree. Realizing that she did not have a sufficient number of publications on her CV (curriculum vitae), she decided to take a break from writing the dissertation and publish articles. For a period of over a year, she barely touched the dissertation. By the time she had accrued what she deemed an appropriate number of publications, according to her own imposed estimate, she announced her return to the committee, fully anticipating they would all pick up where they had left off and move her immediately to defense and graduation. That was not the case. The committee members had already assumed other obligations with other students; in addition, they had become distanced from the nuanced elements of her dissertation chapters. Lastly, they were somewhat put off that Arial had postponed her graduation by failing to complete her dissertation, which had advanced to the point that it could have been defended in the months prior to her hiatus. Somewhat perplexed, Arial did not understand why she was not immediately welcomed back to the fold with open and ready arms. But it was true. While the committee did not necessarily forget about Ariel, they also did not run after her to plead with her to finish; in short, her withdrawal, although temporary, was not something they would oppose. And so, with benevolent apathy, they permitted her to go her own way. She would have to wait her turn to regain their attention, which she eventually did.

6. *Establish parameters for the dissertation.* Don't let the dissertation grow beyond the objectives set in the concept paper: students who are intently researching naturally are drawn to ancillary areas of research interest and frequently want to move in those directions. Avoid the temptation of watching your dissertation exponentially grow away from your target goals or grow away from the parameters you have set for it. However, it is critical to consider the objective of your dissertation and the manner in which that objective connects to your future career. You do not want the dissertation to be the somewhat limited last exercise "that a scholar completes as a student" (Olson & Drew, 1998). The dissertation should bear the

imprimatur of the emerging scholar, "the first major project that a scholar completes as a 'professional.'" This is a different mindset (Olson & Drew, 1998; see Chapter 2). It is not, nor should it be, the culmination of all of your scholarly endeavors. It is a first, but an important step, and if you view it in this way, you will maintain a realistic hold over it and not let it take hold of you. If you allow yourself to be perpetually dissatisfied with your study, seeking always toward ancillary goals or objectives, most likely you will always be working toward some future, evanescent goal that is always out of reach, unattainable. Concerns about the veracity or value of any study should be discussed with the dissertation chair and the committee members well before too much work is expended in a certain research direction in which you may lack confidence.

7. *Reevaluate your quest for the Ph.D.* The entire dissertation process is often rife with complications, both professional and personal, and you may find yourself contemplating program withdrawal. This is a critical decision that should be discussed with your dissertation advisor and committee members to help you determine if it is indeed your intention not to complete. It is important for students to bear this recommendation in mind and not to depart their programs in silence: attrition for many students remains an invisible act, and students simply leave without the benefit of discussion and potential intervention. Some students do make the decision not to continue with their dissertations, and they mean it. They no longer want the dissertation or the Ph.D., nor do they see the degree to be of value to them in their future lives. Still others arrive at this decision because the idea seems good at the time, an escape from a process that may have been less than ideal, and they just don't see a way to get past the barriers. For additional information on this topic, read Sydni Dunn's (2014) article in the Chronicle of Higher Education: "In Hindsight: Former Ph.D. Students Reflect on Why They Jumped Ship."

Remember that there are alternatives to stopping out; students need to be aware of policies such as leave of absence or program extensions that will get them past the time limit on their degrees and into a safe haven, a respite. They need to assess whether a problem has surfaced that requires some intervention, or whether they really do not want to continue with the degree and are confusing the latter with the former. Escape seems like a good idea, but escaping from a life goal because of an underlying issue is not wise. The questions are these: What are the problems? Can they be resolved? How?

Remember that all kinds of unforeseen occurrences can and do happen during the dissertation process. The idea is to strategize for a solution and to safeguard the process so that it moves forward and is not derailed. If you don't communicate your concerns, those issues will remain unresolved, or they will be resolved in a way that you may regret later.

~ The Take Away ~

1. The "dissertation blues" manifest for many diverse reasons and fall into an ironic category that I would describe as *normally abnormal*. You may be struggling with beginning the dissertation or struggling through it, feeling as if the entire project is a waste of time. You want to marry it and divorce it in the same moment. You might feel regret over what you have sacrificed to get where you are currently, perhaps sacrificing getting married, having children, buying a home, taking a vacation, and myriad other quality-of-life events. You may find yourself resenting your dissertation because it extracts a high price and absorbs your life. All of this may be true for you, but realize that everything worth doing is worth doing well. There is always a price to pay. The pathway to the Ph.D. is not smooth and even, and if you thought so, you were mistaken.

References

Dunn, S. (2014, April 15). In hindsight: Former Ph.D. students reflect on why they jumped ship. *Chronicle of Higher Education*. Retrieved from https://community.chronicle.com/news/445-in-hindsight-former-ph-d-students-reflect-on-why-they-jumped-ship

Isaacson, W. (2018). *Leonardo da Vinci*. New York, NY: Simon & Schuster.

Lean Six Sigma Definition. (n.d.). Kaizen. Retrieved March 23, 2021, from https://www.leansixsigmadefinition.com/glossary/kaizen/

Olson, G. A., & Drew, J. (1998). (Re) Reenvisioning the dissertation in English studies. *College English, 61*(1), 56–66.

Chapter 20

The Dissertation Aftermath Blues

Is that all there is? Is that all there is? If that's all there is, my friends, then let's keep dancing.
Jerry Leiber and Mike Stoller

As a professional in my field, I first came upon what I call the "dissertation aftermath blues" years ago when Peter, a recent Ph.D. graduate, called to thank me for working with him. But that wasn't the real reason he had called; he was feeling "a little down," and he couldn't quite put his finger on the reason why he felt this way. In fact, he admitted that he felt guilty for this admission. He had worked very hard, delivered the dissertation, graduated, and now was startled, a few weeks later, to find himself not as deliriously happy as he anticipated he would be.

He felt lost and adrift, without direction, especially now that the dissertation was complete and he had graduated. He wondered what was next on his life's journey; he thought of publishing his dissertation, but then reeled back from that idea as he was not up to that kind of task; he thought of going on vacation, but then he recanted that idea because his doctoral education had been costly, and he had debt to repay; he wasn't certain of new career possibilities that might be available to him, especially those that required an out-of-state move. All in all, he settled for a weekend trip to Saugatuck and a spin on Lake Michigan in his boat. I didn't hear from Peter again after that, but I assume that he went on with his life in a productive manner, having quelled his discomfort. Clearly, he had been suffering from the blues.

Dissertation blues are a real fact, and they can catch recent graduates short, because generally there is limited foresight regarding this phenomenon. As students, they maintained a tight routine with a strict schedule and, in those initial moments of freedom, are caught almost entirely unaware that they may be spiraling downward. Ironically enough, this realization comes on the heels of the most joyous and exhilarating moments of their lives, and they learn the hard way that the culmination of the Ph.D. does not always bring the lofty rewards one might imagine.

The battle for the Ph.D. is formidable, and those last months prior to the dissertation defense are often fraught with administrative tasks beyond the imagination: dissertation revisions, formatting, completion of numerous forms, among others. Instead of the pace slackening at the end, the pace actually quickens, and students are almost breathless as they strive to pull together the last requirements. Lurking behind the blur of colorful regalia and the pageantry of the graduation ceremony lie real concerns about next steps: future employment, repayment of debt, and publishing, for example. Several years ago another graduate, Ryan, confided in me that his feelings of uncertainty and foreboding surfaced during his commencement ceremony. As he walked across the stage to receive his degree, he realized that he didn't have the number of publications he thought necessary to be competitive on the job market; there were few if any job prospects in sight; he questioned the wisdom of postponing a family in order to earn the Ph.D. In short, he felt that his degree resulted out of some sort of cosmic mistake. As we spoke, we agreed that having a job would at least have lessened the impact of the dissertation blues and eased the sense of lost-ness or drifting without purpose that seemed to dominate our respective situations following the award of the Ph.D.

If a straight line existed from graduation to a position, perhaps the momentum would smoothen the effects of the blues somewhat. At least, this is what some students admit to me. I know this was true in my own experience: When I graduated, I did not have one position. Instead, I had cobbled together a kind of job out of several adjunct positions, but without benefits or the promise of long-term employment. I was not qualified to teach on the high school level (no education courses in my curriculum and no certification); not qualified to teach on the community college level (I had experience predominantly at 4-year institutions); and not qualified for a tenure-track position (no book, no articles). At a prestigious event, I refused to allow myself to be introduced with my title (I didn't have a job, an idea somehow incongruent with having a Ph.D.). All in all, it was a dismal reality that left me feeling not at all well prepared for an academic life, and I came to the conclusion that my Ph.D. was nothing more than an entry-level qualification for a very chimerical position. I felt that I had been shackled to unrealistic expectations about what the degree could do for me, unaware that others may have felt this way too. Usher in the blues—bad enough. And then, usher in its companion, the Imposter Syndrome, and the idea that I had somehow serendipitously discovered a framed Ph.D. diploma—with my name on it, no less.

From time to time, I still come across graduated students plagued by the blues. I don't think our stories differ vastly, despite the time frames in which they unfolded. The bolder graduates are discomforted enough to voice their opinions and signal their discontent. Others, no doubt, remain silent, unwilling to voice their experiences, which really should be told. Still others, like Ryan or me in our early post-graduation days, considered themselves imposters who arrived at the Ph.D. by some quirk of fate or wild lottery game.

Those who already were working professionals in their respective fields and acquired the degree make for an interesting group to study. Unquestionably, some went on to achieve promotions and to advance. If these individuals were on the tenure track, then the Ph.D. may have sealed the bid; some were not on the tenure track and simply wanted to earn a Ph.D., but this fact may not have necessarily altered their lives to the degree they had hoped. It didn't get them a better job. It didn't help them to advance or to move in another career direction. Much depends upon where they were in their careers at the time of their Ph.D., the discipline itself, as well as the vibrancy of the economic markets.

Dr. Ilse Schweitzer VanDonkelaar has generously granted me permission to include her blog posting in which she describes her experiences with the blues.

Ilse's Story

Post-Dissertation Blargh

POSTED ON MARCH 10, 2014 UPDATED ON MARCH 10, 2014

by Ilse Schweitzer VanDonkelaar, Ph.D. (finally), English

It's been about four months since I defended my dissertation and three months since I graduated with a Ph.D. from WMU. I fully expected to be living in a state of elation after the defense and walking across the stage, and thought that euphoria would last at least until summer. After all, I had been working toward graduation for 8 years, and had the Ph.D. in my sights since sometime during undergrad. I had reached the final fruition of my academic goals, and had been unburdened of writing, revising, editing, and researching the diss... I should be walking on air!

But now I find myself experiencing a funk for which I was completely unprepared. Instead of feeling finally relaxed, I'm increasingly anxious about jobs (exacerbated by a horrible job market for both academic and non-ac positions), money (hello, student loan payments), publications, and how to improve my chances on the market for next year. After years of managing my time and living with the pressure to read, write, and get the darn dissertation finished, my mind is going in a hundred directions, unsure of what to do now. Without classes or writing groups to attend, I feel disconnected from my fellow scholars. After only a few weeks, the excitement of being unburdened has worn off and now I'm faced with a bit of an identity crisis: I'm no longer a student, yet not a member of a new faculty. I'm stuck in "Ph.D. limbo-land," a place between identities.

Fortunately, just a few minutes on the Google-machine assures me that I'm not the only one who feels like this (see blog entries on Portrait of a Supposed Scholar, Academic Cog, and Mathemagenic, and this PSA on YouTube). I'm afraid that we don't really prepare ourselves (or our students) for the shift back into real life after years of working toward a degree. The common assumption for departments like mine is that we prepare for teaching or research jobs in academia, and begin in those positions several months after graduation OR we continue working as adjuncts at WMU or at other institutions. In each of these situations, there's some continuity in our identities as scholars and as teachers. But what about our graduates who don't secure these kinds of positions? What about the students who want to pursue alt-ac tracks, or who are unsuccessful in the academic job hunt? What becomes of us?

This is all related to larger issues of employment within and without the university, but my immediate concern is the experience of uncertainty, transition, and anxiety that comes with ending one's tenure as a student. The experience of completing the largest research project you've ever undertaken, and moving slowly and unsurely (if you have no immediate career on the other side) into your new identity after graduation. For my entire life to this point, I've been a student... every degree and certification has led into and been preparation for the next, so I've never had any fear or uncertainty about the next phase of my life. It's always been "back to the classroom," or "back to the library." And now, I might not see the classroom again...

so what do I do? Where do I go? And who am I now that I'm not a student?

Alongside this quandary comes the (strong) possibility that I should have stopped thinking of myself as a student LONG ago. The moment I entered grad school, I should have started thinking of myself as a professional, and maybe this distinction has hindered my ability to be able to launch myself into a post-doctoral career. Well, live and learn…

I have no immediate answer or solution to these issues, no bullet-points of advice at the end of this blog post. What I want is for people to know that this feeling, this experience EXISTS. I'm lucky that I've been able to find part-time work this semester, and that I have a wonderful spouse who DID manage to put his Ph.D. to good use and landed a teaching job. (So there's hope out there!) Still, I wonder how many students have dealt with this kind of post-dissertation funk / limbo / let-down, but lacking a continued connection to their university, they don't know to whom to speak. It seems that students like me need to be better informed of [sic] prepared for the challenges and anxieties of this post-academic transition, and we need to know that counseling, support, and sympathetic mentors are there to help us through.

Ilse's blog resonates with the reality of the dissertation blues, a blindside hit that can dismantle and undermine confidence and self-esteem, ironically at the very moment when students have achieved one of the highest accomplishments. For so many students, the challenges in securing it have assumed the relevance of a career. It is difficult to think beyond the degree when, in and of itself, it seems such a prize. The *getting there* and the subsequent *arrival* represent the entire journey when in fact that viewpoint, though myopic, represents the reality of the way in which many doctoral students perceive the degree.

However, the value of the Ph.D. depends for the most part on what you can do with it, beyond displaying it on a wall. This degree does not live apart from your real-world goals and objectives. Obviously, a person doesn't sign up for a Ph.D. for the fun of it all. And so, if the return on investment is not quite there or if it seems slow in happening, then one naturally questions one's choices or motivations in the first place. Most significantly, one begins to question one's worthiness or entitlement to the degree. Those who are not able to fit the degree into meaningful and purposeful employment commensurate with the doctoral degree may find themselves sorely disappointed in the outcome. Moreover, a person trained in a certain career field who has the qualifications for that position but cannot secure it can easily perceive himself or herself as a failure. This is the most hideous outcome of reaching "the other side" of the Ph.D.

The *Blue* Job Market

Departments that proffer the *tenure track only* philosophy, and corresponding curricula, also set their students up for grave disappointments, and concomitantly for the blues, as currently there are limitations on the availability of many of these positions, given the national employment climate in higher education. Teaching recent graduates or Ph.D.s-in-progress how to market themselves in diverse career fields is smart. *Although the purpose of the Ph.D. primarily is to prepare students for the professoriate, the fact remains that there is a dearth of opportunity among the professor ranks. Moreover, changes in curricula to accommodate alternate Ph.D. careers will be long in coming, and so we cannot look there for an expedient amelioration.*

It is indeed interesting that translational, intersectional career preparation is not part of many traditional degrees, such as the Ph.D. in English. Consider, for example, the value of incorporating medical writing into the English curriculum with the inclusion of science-based writing preparation. The medical writing field is lucrative and abounds with innumerable possibilities for qualified candidates; yet, the English degree alone is not sufficient for this purpose because it lacks the medical/science-based components. Similarly, the straight science Ph.D. in physics or chemistry or biology does not include medical writing-centric preparation. Thus, the requirements for a position as a medical writer are almost exclusively eclipsed by the straight Ph.D. in English and the straight science Ph.D., because at least one half of the qualifications are missing from the respective curricula, and unless some generous soul designs to give an individual a chance, there is scant opportunity to break into this field. Given the current critical challenges to university and college enrollment, it is disconcerting that such program restructuring is not a consideration. As a result, few individuals outside of the medical writing discipline can break into it and utilize their advanced degrees in a viable manner. Students who sign up for degrees in English and other humanities degrees, for example, must be prepared for the disconnect between their degree preparation and the reality of the job market. Many of us have been beguiled by the pursuit of the Ph.D. alone, without cognizance of the next step: employment. As the sister of one of my adjunct professors once proclaimed to him when she became aware of his dismal career opportunities, "You can't eat liberal arts."

Earlier in this book, I mentioned The Versatile Ph.D. as a resource that can be used to bridge students in their trajectories from Ph.D. to career. Yet, it is important to note that the emergence of this resource occurs because of institutional recognition that jobs in the career fields for which students have earned their degrees are not there. If you do not diversify your career expectations and re-envision/re-package yourself in a viable manner, you may find yourself struggling to secure a position that equates with the level of your educational preparation and that provides you with the financial means not only to repay your college debt but to live your life.

Given this, the most important element to remember is that you are more than your Ph.D. Secondly, you have talents that surpass your discipline, and so if you are experiencing difficulty in securing a career in your field, explore the potential opportunities in the out-of-the-box perspectives that inhere in The Versatile Ph.D. Lastly, do not think of yourself as dead-ended; you have the highest degree offered by any nation, and it has transferrable value. Your job is to find a career *home* for you and your Ph.D.

~ The Take Away ~

Advisors and Advisees Together

1. *Dissertation Blues Aftercare*: Advisors should acquaint their advisees with the fact that it is normal for students to experience a letdown after a major accomplishment such as completing the Ph.D. Students often are not aware that they can feel blue and may be alarmed or disconcerted by the flood of divergent emotions they are experiencing. Speaking about this phenomenon together to signal this possibility might prevent students from feeling as if their reactions are untoward or abnormal. Students are often surprised by these re-

actions, feeling guilt and recriminating themselves for their failure to be happy. Advisors should refer their advisees for professional counseling if students perceive a deepening or a persistence of these reactions. Students should be told that it's okay for them to seek professional assistance.

2. *Be Realistic in Determining Career Goals*: If your goal is the tenure track, then aim for that *during your program of study*, not when you are already out the door with degree in hand. (CVs of students who are potential faculty should reflect the tenure triumvirate during their degree trajectories: teaching, research, and publication experience.) Advisors should consciously cultivate their advisees throughout their programs of study and not tack on those initiatives late stage as an afterthought. Set realistic expectations; advisors and advisees should study the current disciplinary markets out there and strategize for careers apart from the tenure track, as well. Utilize The Versatile Ph.D. and any other resource that will help you gain a clear perspective of alternate career possibilities, just in case. This is a "belt and suspenders" approach. You aim for your main goal, but if securing it should not succeed, at least you have a solid Plan B in the works.

3. *Tenure Track or Bust*: This is a dangerous attitude that can undermine recent graduates who are struggling with challenged job markets. The Ph.D. is multifaceted, and it equips individuals with myriad skills that are indeed translational and that can serve in diverse markets. Some of these markets may be connected to the primary discipline only in ancillary ways, or perhaps not at all. Avoid shackling students to a one-dimensional philosophy regarding their future success. If curricula prepare students *only* for tenure-track positions, when the reality is that tenure-track positions are far and few between, then departments should (a) expand upon curricula to incorporate alternate fields into which their primary disciplines may fit, and (b) implement career counseling for Ph.D.s not going onto the tenure track. This type of preparation makes sense and safeguards against an *all-or-nothing* perspective that results in feelings of shame, failure, the blues, and perceiving oneself as an imposter. Before enrolling in an advanced degree program, students should

have clear indicators regarding the career opportunities their degrees will accord them and avoid enrolling in dead-ended programs that take them into unemployment/underemployment and debt.
4. *Think Beyond the Ph.D.*: People are more than their degrees, and degrees themselves do not always signal success. Consider your intellectual interests, talents, skills, passions, dreams, and goals, and realize your life's works by keeping an open mind to the possibilities that lie before you.

Chapter 21

Debriefing: An Essential Final Step in Doctoral Education

The value of debriefing has never been lost on the business or the military community, both elements quite expert in engaging in the art of inquiry regarding all details relevant to a completed mission. Whether it is a business venture or a military strategic initiative, nothing better serves those vested in the process than a focused, in-depth conversation about goals and objectives, timetables, decision-making practices, communication efforts, and the protocols that figure necessarily into engagement.

Strategists learn invaluable lessons through the sheer acts of reflection and conversation, and their insights better inform the process for the next go-round, utilize resources and avoid waste, and ensure a more productive, efficient process upon which they can continue to improve.

Unfortunately, graduate education does not formally engage in such a review of its dissertation or thesis processes; hence, the opportunity for an exchange of insights and ideas is frequently lost as busy dissertation advisors and committee members move on to meet the demands of new advisees. Similarly, recent graduates, harried as they are, escape to the tasks of finding jobs, carving journal articles out of their dissertations, and rediscovering their spouses and significant others. Understandably enervated by their respective ordeals, faculty members and graduates alike often do not discuss what happened or what did not happen during their time together and therefore miss out on a rare opportunity to engage in productive intercourse.

Years ago, Sherry, a doctoral graduate, came into my office terribly upset by a series of unpleasant experiences that had been brewing and had finally erupted in an icy standoff with her committee members, just weeks prior to her dissertation defense. It seemed that she and her committee were at odds regarding a content issue, and the bridge back to sustaining a good working relationship appeared to have been burned on both sides. Clearly, an impasse seemed imminent, but when the realization dawned on her that there was more to lose than gain by holding to her objections, she reconsidered and graduated. Nevertheless, what brought her to my office was a lingering sense that the communication process had utterly failed— and long before the differing opinions on content had arisen. Disconcerted by what had transpired, she had arrived at my doorstep after the fact to sort out the events that led up to the schism.

In a previous section of this book, I mentioned Peter, the student who had experienced the blues after he had completed the dissertation and graduated. He was struggling with converting the dissertation into publishable articles but discovered that he did not have the desire or the inclination to embark upon this endeavor and was concerned about finding a position and paying off debt, considerable challenges that descended upon him like an emotional tsunami. However, he had enjoyed a positive dissertation experience, engaged productively with his committee, and generally experienced a rewarding journey to the Ph.D.

In both instances, it might appear that these students would have benefited by speaking with a psychologist or a counselor. In all reality, however, a debriefing with their committee members would also have served them well. The ability to objectively communicate observations and perceptions is an invaluable tool through which faculty and students enlighten each other by focusing on the strengths and weaknesses of their interactions and the processes that bound them together throughout the advising experience.

Dissertation advisors and committee members need to hear about the value of their sustained commitment to students and the attainment of their degrees. Wouldn't Peter's committee be gratified to know their diligent oversight of the complicated dissertation process made a positive difference in the life of their advisee? As well, had they been aware of the student's emotional letdown after the completion of his doctoral degree, a common enough phenomenon frequently noted by psychologists, perhaps they could have forestalled some of those negative effects by normalizing the possibility that students sometimes do indeed experience a temporary sense of "lost-ness" after a great accomplishment.

Conversely, overfilled faculty email accounts and voice mailboxes, broken or missed appointments, and protracted turnaround times for chapters spelled apathy to Sherry. She felt absolutely dependent on maintaining her committee's good will for the successful completion of the degree but did not express her mounting discontent regarding their disagreement over a content issue or the management of the dissertation process in a forthright manner. Faculty members also need to hear this.

Faculty also can play a critical role in helping students to recognize their (the students') resistance at each step of the editing process, as well as the penchant for refusing to take constructive criticism with grace. Such circumstances frustrated the good will of Sherry's committee, and she should have been made aware of her role in cultivating that frustration, if not during those interactions, then surely after.

As I have stated previously, expectations about what will occur in the dissertation process, or any process for that matter, often lead to an imbalance because unvoiced expectations are frequently dashed. It is far better to articulate those expectations up front and to delineate the Rules of Engagement. Then everyone understands what will happen and what will not.

After the dissertation process is completed, it is always advisable to engage in a debriefing during which committee members and their advisee reflect on the process and collaboratively engage in a critical review by which advisors and advisees benefit through continuous process improvement. Ultimately, the application of metrics to ascertain process improvement could prove to be a viable tool; if we do not measure appropriately, we will fail to know if what we are doing is effective or not.

The following steps are for students and dissertation committee members, as well as professional facilitators in the academic setting:

- *Schedule a debriefing.* Prior to the student's graduation, but after the defense when all formal paperwork has been signed, ask for a meeting during which the student and the dissertation advisor and committee members come together to critically review the entire dissertation process and their joint and individual roles in that process. Reserve a quiet room for this meeting and provide some light refreshments. If circumstances warrant, a virtual meeting can be arranged instead. Make certain that the meeting will not be interrupted by other duties or obligations. Such approaches ensure more of a celebratory tone and indeed bring closure to a long and demanding process. As well, the meeting itself reinforces best practices and affirms the value of the collaborative process. Any member of the committee or even the student may conduct the meeting; however, a professional facilitator or an administrator may offer a skilled, objective approach.

- *Prepare for the meeting.* To prepare for the meeting, consider all factors that worked to make the dissertation engagement rewarding, successful, and productive, and then write them down. By the same token, consider those elements that may have protracted or confused the process and note them. These could include the following:
  - Quality and level of communication among and between committee members and the student.
  - Expectations of the committee regarding editorial/conceptual revision of chapters.
  - Turnaround time to receive and send chapters.
  - Frequency, productivity, and outcome of meetings.
  - Availability/accessibility of the committee to the student.
  - Level and quality of mentoring support.
  - Level and quality of interaction guiding research methodology and statistical computation.
  - The committee's level of interest and commitment to the completion of the project.
  - The student's level of interest and commitment to the completion of the project.
  - The degree to which the student was prepared for the dissertation defense.
  - The degree to which the student complied with the committee's expectations and directives.
  - The level of support and interaction of the Institutional Review Board (IRB) if research involved human subjects or other compliance concerns.
  - The degree to which the graduate college or school facilitated the student's trajectory through the degree process.

Questions that encompass these elements, for example, establish a more complete appreciation for the intricacies of a highly complicated process that can easily fall prey to misunderstanding on the parts of both advisors and advisees.

- *Communicate positive and negative variables as well as outcomes.* Everyone at the meeting should take careful notes, discussing the strengths and the shortcomings of the process. Begin with the positive elements and make clear responsive statements that indicate an appreciation for what worked well and then explain why. Include a results section that shows the outcome of these positive features upon the dissertation. Committee members should acknowledge each other's contributions in this process; after all, it is likely that they will encounter each other on yet another dissertation committee in the future and should therefore help to establish or reaffirm solid working relationships to benefit future students. Students should acknowledge the contributions of individual committee members, who also should acknowledge the student's positive involvement. In addition, factors that did not lend positively to the process should also be discussed, along with the outcomes generated by these negative elements. Again, include a corresponding results section that indicates the negative impact upon the dissertation process. Strategies to ameliorate the negative variables provide new plans of action for the future. For example, a student who experienced delays because she ignored the committee's directions for submitting a Human Subjects Institutional Review Board (HSIRB) protocol, obligatory for any researcher conducting research with human subjects, needs to understand that she is accountable. In addition, a student who is clearly advised about the manner of submitting revised chapters to the committee and who then does not comply with those directives is responsible for the resulting outcome.
- *Remain calm and quiet.* It is far more difficult to listen to a list of shortcomings, rather than a litany of hosannas. Remain calm and objective, and try to avoid personalizing negative statements you may hear. Rising above the situation to examine process and actions, rather than the individuals who are the doers of those processes and actions, actually serves

to depersonalize the debriefing and keeps everyone focused on process improvement, rather than improvement of particular individuals, always a negative in itself. That part will unfold as individuals self-reflect.
- *Mirror back responses.* It is important to affirm that participants in the debriefing actually listen to each other and respond to each other. One way to do this is by mirroring back responses. An advisor could say, for example, "Do I understand correctly that when I missed our scheduled meeting you felt that I didn't care about you or your dissertation?" or a student could say to a committee member, "When you asked me to revise a section of my dissertation and found that I hadn't, you felt that I had just wasted your valuable time and didn't care about improving the quality of my work." Such initiatives affirm that good communication is taking place and that people are really interested in seeking resolution to issues that complicate the process. The opportunity to clarify these issues, offer an explanation, or simply acknowledge the fact and then move forward positively reinforces the process. Also, expressing gratitude to each other for seemingly insignificant kindnesses reinforces the spiritual nature of individuals bound to each other through commitment. A committee member could admit, "I didn't realize that my weekly phone calls and emails meant so much to you. I will keep that in mind as I work with other students."

~ The Take Away ~

1. Advisors and advisees alike may be surprised by what they can learn and by what they can teach through the process of debriefing. Benefits extend beyond the individuals and coalesce as one of many evolving best practices in graduate education.

Chapter 22

New Forms and New Paradigms

The form of the traditional dissertation has been changing, the old form not necessarily dying out altogether, but rather joined by newer, more progressive forms that allow for more creative, accessible research. In addition, technological advances permit for innovative forms of the dissertation to emerge, and many of these forms are interdisciplinary and collaborative. Diverse groups of individuals with diverse, specialized skills are often brought together to lend their talents to an evolutionary dissertation model that expands the capacity for intellectual engagement, as well as scholarly contribution. This is not to say that the traditional dissertation fails in this regard, because it does not. Simply put, the opportunity to incorporate new dimensions into the dissertation is an exciting endeavor that opens to limitless possibilities.

Think of digital humanities dissertations in the same context that you would think of three-article dissertations when that approach to the dissertation was launched decades ago. Many advisors availed themselves of this model because they had been exposed to it at one point in time, had constructed their own dissertations in this manner, or were persuaded to see that the new model was actually effective and efficient in helping students to produce publishable articles as a starting point for the dissertation, rather than creating the dissertation first and crafting articles *after the fact*, a time-consuming, labor-intensive, cumbersome activity. The last thing that doctoral students want to think about after crafting their dissertations is to consider how to take them apart and make them congeal logically into journal articles. Framing articles from the onset makes good common sense and is catching on as an alternative to the traditional monograph.

The value in doing so is clear, particularly when educators consider the complexity in converting dissertations into publishable *ar-*

ticles versus the value of submitting *extant* articles to journals, where timely dissemination of information remains the priority. Peter Klein (2013) comments on the "pragmatic" value of the traditional dissertation or treatise, versus the value of published journal articles, especially in fields such as "economics, management, finance, accounting," for example, where the emphasis is on the exchange of scholarly information in a format most accessible to information users. Klein cites Wendy Stock and John Siegfried (2013) in their publication, "One Essay on Dissertation Formats in Economics," in which the authors address the changes in economics dissertations over the last 40 years that move from the treatise format to the journal article or essay format. Stock and Siegfried conclude that Ph.D. graduates in economics who assume faculty positions were more likely to have used the essay format for their dissertations, whereas those graduates who took governmental positions were more likely to have chosen the traditional dissertation format. Moreover, they found that in the field of economics, students at top-ranked Ph.D. programs, international students, and those with specializations in microeconomics were more likely to have used the essay format for their dissertations than the traditional monograph. The Interdisciplinary Health Sciences Ph.D. program at my university uses the three-article format almost exclusively for its dissertations, thereby giving its students a critical tool to boost publication opportunities. Similarly, other programs such as the Interdisciplinary Ph.D. in Evaluation and certain engineering programs have slowly adopted the three-article framework for the dissertation, and so interest in this model has increased.

Klein (2013), zeroing in on the efficiency of the dissertation, questions the relevance of the standard literature review, which is a feature of the traditional model and, in his view, "redundant," as opposed to the value of the student's engagement in the actual analysis of research outcomes, a more focused outcome of individualized articles or essays. Klein advises his students not to "waste time putting anything in the dissertation that is not intended for publication!" For additional information on three-article dissertations, refer to the University of Texas at Austin model (*Three Article Dissertation,* 2011).

Adaptability of the Three-Article Dissertation Format to Other Disciplines

The applicability and value of this format in the field of economics seems clear. However, there may be some disciplines for which the three-article dissertation may not always be a viable option. Some humanities disciplines, for example, almost always require publication of a book to position candidates for the tenure track. It is therefore up to those departments, up to those advisors, to cultivate dissertations that will position students for the tenure track by virtue of sustaining the rigor, intellectual elegance, and scholarship in the dissertation that are necessary to this end, as that "end" plays out in specific disciplines. These dissertations, then, necessarily contribute to candidates' attractiveness to potential hiring universities. From there, candidates need to consider next steps in cultivating articles for publication and potential books. The information produced as a dissertation is a preliminary grounding for potential positions and is not always and in all cases the ready-made *book*. There are exceptions: consider books of poetry, for example, which may also stand as dissertations in fields such as creative writing. But there are few dissertations in any field that are written to be both *dissertation* and *book* simultaneously. One caveat for programs interested in utilizing the three-article dissertation is to avoid requiring students to actually secure publication in a journal; the publication process can be long and involved, requiring a protracted time frame for editing and finalization that might compromise the graduation timeline. The critical element to bear in mind is that the articles should be "publication ready" and reflect the high standards of respected journals. In addition, the author guidelines for respective journals and the formatting requirements of specific universities will differ, and so the first step in this process is to format the three-article dissertation according to a university's guidelines, not according to a specific journal's guidelines. That part will come later, when the student is actually ready to submit the article.

Holding Up the Mirror to New Forms

New modalities for dissertations will require new ways of conceptualizing them, as well as new ways of justifying such out-of-the-box projects, especially when considering how those projects will be evaluated by hiring institutions. A graduate student attending a talk on digital publishing told the presenter, Kathleen Fitzpatrick, professor of media studies at Pomona College, that "while I want to do a digital project [for my dissertation] that would make my argument in an innovative form, I know the safe thing to do is to be conservative, to write something traditional and leave experimentation for later. What do you advise?" (Fitzpatrick, 2011). Fitzpatrick responded that she should "Do the risky thing." However, her recommendation was not that the student engage in reckless professional decisions, but that she should ensure she had the support, mentoring, and backing of her advisor, who could defend the decision to employ the innovative format, indicate its merit, and demonstrate how it contributed to the scholarship—in short, deflect any negative commentary away from the advisee and justify the decision to take the less-traveled pathway. Such a stance would necessarily have to be reflected in letters of commendation/recommendation for tenure-track opportunities, particularly at more traditional universities, where the standard dissertation is still the hallmark for the Ph.D.

The introduction of new forms always signals a certain skepticism and perhaps, at times, an outright rejection. But how will that rejection play out? Certainly there are considerations regarding the manner in which a digital dissertation will be received within various institutions of higher education, such as whether these forms will harm candidates for tenure-track positions or whether they will advance their candidacy; whether these forms truly further the scholarship; whether collaborative digital dissertations actually reflect the presence of multiple authors, not just one single author, and therefore stand as a dissertation for multiple individuals; or whether the substitutions for the narrative frame are acceptable given the guidelines for what currently stands as a *dissertation*, among other considerations.

These facets play out importantly, especially given the fact that digital dissertations can reflect many electronic, highly technical formats that depart significantly from the traditional standard dissertation and that draw into question the manner in which advisors will interact with their advisees on both the technical and the advisory levels, amidst the new technological demands that digital dissertations bring. Celeste Tuong Vy Sharpe (2019) writes that "incorporating digital methods, presentation, and tools in an individual sustained research project is largely uncharted territory" (para. 1). And yet, the technological momentum pushes past disciplinary boundaries to find new expression, and in varying dissertation forms. Peter Monaghan (2006) acknowledges that while dissertations today may reflect some media elements, few of them begin with a multimedia frame as a beginning point. For example, the digital dissertation of Virginia A. Kuhn, a doctoral student at the University of Wisconsin, "is not a printed document" and was "born digital in a multimedia format." Monaghan (2006) describes Kuhn's thesis as a dissertation

> ... based on that of a regular book, but with many nonstandard features. Its online pages are heavy with text, like a printed book, but when a user moves the cursor over the pages, hyperlinks pop up, leading to embedded information. And images, when clicked on, open windows containing more-detailed captions, or a film clip, or citations. An electronic "sticky note" feature lets users record comments and reactions for their own later reference. (para. 13)

If all of this sounds exciting, it is. However, the questions concern the manner in which these dissertations fit within the established parameters for a dissertation, as recommended by respective universities and colleges. In addition, Monaghan (2006) points to the complicated issues of copyright when attempting to cite a multimedia source, such as a video or photo. And Sharpe (2019) considers the manner in which digital dissertations intersect, if they do at all, with "career trajectories" (para. 10). The concern of the graduate student who attended Professor Fitzpatrick's talk on digital publishing is not misplaced; Kuhn faced her own standoff when officials at her university debated for a period of 4 months whether to accept her dissertation, which they eventually did. Of course, its nontraditional format resulted in an extreme departure regarding how a dissertation should be defined.

The Council of Graduate Schools (1991) defines the dissertation as "a unified work with a single theme, including an introduction and literature review, a description of methods and procedures used, a presentation of results, and a concluding discussion of the meaning of the results" (p. 12). It may be possible for these elements to be recast into different presentation modalities within the digital context and, thus, they will be extant, just in different forms. Nevertheless, concerns are well placed; Fitzpatrick (2011) raises the real possibility that "untenured digital scholars [may] run the risk of burnout from having to produce twice as much, traditional scholarship and digital projects, as their counterparts do." We do not have all the answers or, in fact, all of the questions, and yet technology itself becomes the beckoning force that urges emerging scholars to experiment along these pathways.

Fitzpatrick's (2011) point regarding the portended duality of scholarly efforts may well be a familiar argument, one that academia continues to witness in the Scholarship of Teaching and Learning (SOTL) momentum versus straight disciplinary approach to the publication realms. SOTL scholars know that it is imperative for them to establish themselves in their own disciplines first, before venturing into the publication world of SOTL, as that may not necessarily be a viable destination for those making the tenure bid. If SOTL publications will not count toward tenure, and yet if they are a viable outcome of teaching within a certain disciplinary perspective, then Fitzpatrick's point regarding the necessity to do double duty, so to speak, is a point to consider.

Modern Language Association's Four Main Issues

Four main issues arose from the third Modern Language Association preconference workshop (2012) on the assessment and evaluation of digital projects for faculty tenure and promotion; these are applicable to doctoral students interested in producing digital dissertations, as well as to potential faculty.

The first point concerns the fact of educating the audience; dissertating students will have to educate their committees regarding the viability of their research as well as "justify the field of the digital humanities itself" (Koh, 2012). Further, they will have to acknowledge the diversity of such projects, as well as communicate the collaborative nature of these projects and the necessity to document individual roles and contributions to these projects. Lastly, they will have to explicate the new forms for peer review: "'post publication' rather than 'pre-publication' review" (Koh, 2012). These ideas, then, undergo peer review and may lead to revision and subsequent publication in "traditional scholarly venues."

Dissertation advisors and committee members interested in additional information on assessing digital projects should visit http://www.mla.org/guidelines_evaluation_digital where they can access MLA's Guidelines for Evaluating Work in Digital Humanities and Digital Media. To visit information on humanities digital scholarship, as well as information relevant to other fields, such as science, please visit the following URL, which will take you to *Creating the Texas Digital Humanities Consortium* (TXDHC, 2014): http://digitalscholarship.wordpress.com/2014/04/23/creating-the-texas-digital-humanities-consortium/

~ The Take Away ~

1. Technological innovations and new ways of perceiving the world of the dissertation lend to higher-ordered evolutions of the monograph. Because we see the world around us differently, we also know that our observations must necessarily filter into new forms that also permit for renewed intellectual investigation and expression. The "either/or" argument does not fit within these parameters because both the traditional and the non-traditional forms stand on equal footing. Displacement of forms is not the issue. The issue is that as technology advances, so too will the dissertation format advance and evolve. Doctoral students and their committees must be prepared to accept the notion of an evolutionary dissertation world and step boldly forward to enter into new dimensions of scholarly investigation.
2. Despite the form used, at the end of the day, it is the value, integrity, merit, and contribution to the field that must win out over the vehicles through which these end products are produced.

References

Council of Graduate Schools. (1991). *The role and nature of the doctoral dissertation.* Washington, DC: Author.

Creating the Texas Digital Humanities Consortium. (2014, April 23). Retrieved from http://digitalscholarship.wordpress.com/2014/04/23/creating-the-texas-digital-humanities-consortium/

Fitzpatrick, K. (2011, September 25). Do "the risky thing" in digital humanities.

Chronicle of Higher Education. Retrieved March 22, 2021, from https://www.chronicle.com/article/do-the-risky-thing-in-digital-humanities/

Klein, P. (2013, May 11). *Rise of the three-essays dissertation.* Retrieved April 30, 2014, from http://organizationsandmarkets.com/2013/05/21/rise-of-the-three-essays-dissertation/

Koh, A. (2012, January 25). The challenges of digital scholarship. Prof. Hacker. *Chronicle of Higher Education.* Retrieved March 22, 2021, from https://www.chronicle.com/blogs/profhacker/the-challenges-of-digital-scholarship

Modern Language Association (MLA). (2012). *Guidelines for evaluating work in digital humanities and digital media.* Retrieved March 22, 2021, from the MLA website: https://www.mla.org/About-Us/Governance/Committees/Committee-Listings/Professional-Issues/Committee-on-Information-Technology/Guidelines-for-Evaluating-Work-in-Digital-Humanities-and-Digital-Media

Monaghan, P. (2006, April 28). Digital dissertation dust-up. *Chronicle of Higher Education.* Retrieved March 22, 2021, from https://www.chronicle.com/article/digital-dissertation-dust-up/

Sharpe, C. T. V. (2019, April 19). Digital dissertations and the changing nature of doctoral work. *Perspectives on History* https://www.historians.org/publications-and-directories/perspectives-on-history/april-2019/digital-dissertations-and-the-changing-nature-of-doctoral-work

Stock, W. A., & Siegfried, J. J. (2013). One essay on dissertation formats in economics. *American Economic Review, 103*(3), 648–653. Retrieved March 22, 2021, from the American Economic Association website: https://www.aeaweb.org/articles?id=10.1257/aer.103.3.648

Three article dissertation. (2011, March). University of Texas at Austin. Retrieved March 20, 2021, from https://socialwork.utexas.edu/wp-content/uploads/2020/09/Three-article-dissertation.pdf

Chapter 23

Personalizing Academic Misconduct: An Approach for the Graduate Classroom

This should be the shortest chapter in the book and reduced to just one sentence: *Don't even think about doing it.* However, such a statement does not suffice in a world of academic responsibility to self and others.

Plagiarism is an equal opportunity transgression. Repercussions impact students and extend to faculty and their respective colleagues. Plagiarism sullies communities of scholars and thinkers, violates standards of excellence and integrity, and sets poor examples for future scholars. Its frequency lends to a certain evident but dangerous normalization. This chapter explores the overt nature of the impact and discusses strategies that professors and dissertation advisors can impart to graduate students to inform them about ethical obligations to the research process.

Plagiarism is not an act necessarily restricted to inexperienced, unsophisticated individuals. Vladimir Putin's dissertation came under scrutiny because large sections are alleged to have been plagiarized from the work of two University of Pennsylvania professors. Doris Kearns Goodwin, the famous historian, allegedly plagiarized large sections of her novel *The Kennedys and the Fitzgeralds* and paid an undisclosed financial settlement to another author who claimed that her work had not been formally acknowledged in Goodwin's novel. Bob Dylan allegedly plagiarized his Nobel Prize lecture from the SparkNotes summary of Moby-Dick (Pitzer, 2017). In 2006, a number of engineering students at Ohio University were alleged to have plagiarized their theses and dissertations, an action that cast shadows on the integrity of their degrees, as well as the advising capability of their faculty committees. Many stories abound regarding the conscious and sometimes unconscious manifestation of plagiarism. Yet it is clear that the deliberate, intentional kidnapping of another's words, ideas, or intellectual property falls into the former category, and it is that category that I am focused upon in this chapter. However, it is important to touch briefly upon the unconscious variety.

Examples of unconscious plagiarism mystify and call into question the mechanisms by which the ideas and words of others may infuse an author's works. Their phraseology, presentation, linguistic singularity, and even their memory may seep inadvertently into a writer's work. Helen Keller writes of her dismay at having unconsciously recast Margaret T. Canby's story "The Frost Fairies," published in a book titled *Birdie and His Fairy Friends* before Keller was born, into a story she (Keller) wrote at the age of 11 titled "The Frost King." In her autobiography, *The Story of My Life,* Keller writes of the autumn of the year after she had learned to speak. Her teacher, Anne Sullivan, described the foliage at Fern Quarry to Helen, and it reminded her of a story that someone must have read to her at one time and that she "must have unconsciously retained." Keller concluded that she was "making up a story" and she captured it in writing—in her words, "before the ideas should slip from me," filled with "joy in the composition." Blind and deaf, Keller states in her autobiography, "At the time I eagerly absorbed everything I read [in Braille] without a thought of authorship, and even now I cannot be quite sure of the boundary line between my ideas and those I find in books." Keller describes her astonishment and grief at discovering that Canby's story must have been read to her and that her (Keller's) story was "a plagiarism," admitting that "no child ever drank deeper of the cup of bitterness than I did. I had disgraced myself; I had brought suspicion upon those I loved best. And yet, how could it possibly have happened?" (Temple, 2018).

It is important to note that deliberate, conscious, line-by-line plagiarism differs markedly from this example, especially given the idea of intentionality, purpose, and intent, absent from the Keller chronicle.

Miguel Roig (2015), psychologist and specialist in academic dishonesty with a focus on plagiarism, has dedicated his career to teaching students and faculty about the complexities of learning to write ethically in an effort to avoid "plagiarism and other inappropriate writing practices," circumstances that can easily destroy careers and blight university reputations. Interventions in the form of instructional guides, such as the one that Roig has produced, may quell what appears to be an expanding trend as students are confronted by pressure to succeed in highly competitive environments. Donald McCabe's study of 63,700 undergraduates and 9,250 graduate students from 2002–2005 revealed statistics that confirm the possibility of a rising trend. In these two groups, 36% of the undergraduate students and 24% of the graduate students admitted to "paraphrasing/copying few sentences" from the internet, without the use of footnotes; in addition, 38% of the undergraduates and 25% of the graduate students admitted to "paraphrasing/copying few sentences from a written source," absent footnotes. A total of 14% of undergraduates admitted to falsifying a bibliography, as did 7% of graduate students ("Plagiarism: Facts & Stats," 2017).

What is apparent is that incidents of academic dishonesty in the form of plagiarism may simply have become normalized in a competitive world in which *topping out* is key. The fact remains that ideas are the stock and trade of successful people, whether those ideas appear in print, are offered up as part of collaborative interactive conversations during meetings, appear on the internet, or are gleaned through any accessible informational venue. The entire concept of intellectual property, who actually *owns* ideas and who has the right to *access* those ideas through appropriate attribution, is at stake in a world in which there are dubious boundaries between originators (owners) and users. Consider the almost unconscious behavior of appropriating ideas exchanged in a business meeting, for example, and it is all too apparent that even *conversational attribution* has become a lost art.

As educators, we are courting deep ethical insolvency if it is indeed true that students are no longer conscious of, or tend to disregard, these untoward tendencies, the initial steps toward normalization. Moreover, we are courting a great misconception if we cling to the notion that "students should know better." In a highly competitive world in which information is readily accessible and in which authorship is not always apparent, we are obligated to admonish and educate.

Plagiarism as Deception

Plagiarism is a fraudulent activity that distorts and misrepresents, even when the intent to do so may not be deliberate. (I am compelled to exclude Helen Keller's story from this description and, in so doing, join the ranks of Mark Twain, who supported Keller and who considered those on Keller's "Plagiarism Court" as "a collection of decayed human turnips" (Twain, 1903, as cited in Temple, 2018).

International students, for whom the tendency to incorporate unattributed information in scholarly venues is a manifestation of cultural norms in their own countries, may find themselves at particular risk in American educational settings where documentation and citation are requisite and where faculty may not always be aware of cultural proclivities to take ideas or language verbatim, without attribution. Moreover, the degree to which faculty and international students are counseled, trained, and educated about plagiarism on both sides of the international borders is debatable. Ignorance, however, does not relieve accountability.

The nature of such infractions as fabrication, falsification, and plagiarism is "deceptive," and this factor is what qualifies them as "wrong" and causes "readers or viewers to have false beliefs about the work" presented (CITI Program Training, n.d.). Readers expect to believe that what they read is true, and it is this very expectation that is dashed.

Paradoxically, these beliefs *appear* to reflect the "scholarly or scientific inquiry" of the researcher, that is, veracity in research and reporting (CITI Program Training, n.d.) and suggest that information presented is the logical outcome of a truth-seeking enterprise. Plagiarized texts do the opposite; they violate trust. Miguel Roig (2015) refers to the relationship between the writer and the reader as an "implicit contract," through which readers make the assumption that the writer is the "sole originator" of the text and that references to the scholarly work of others are clearly delineated within the framework of that text. According to Roig, this "contract" extends not only to ideas appropriately *attributed* to originators, but also to accurate *representation* of those ideas. Roig's concept of an "implicit contract" between writer and reader, through which a lineage of ideas can be traced, parallels Abigail Lipson and Sheila Reindl's

(2003) perspective of responsible scholarship as a "family tree of intellectual kinship," sustained through "proper documentation," into which writers marry their ideas (p. 9).

Writers have a duty and obligation to uphold standards of ethical conduct, actions that Michael Grossberg (2004) refers to as a "collective ethical responsibility" that has been heightened by our awareness of the "vulnerability of our scholarship to misappropriation." While there is no justification for infractions of ethical conduct, adherence to standards of integrity may be a recurring challenge in today's fast-paced, high-tech world. Access to the internet and to new technologies promotes opportunities for plagiarism to proliferate: information appears to be free for the taking.

Students feel pressured to meet timelines for research papers, and faculty researchers must compete for scarce funding as well as enhance opportunities for tenure and promotion amid the requirements of a *publish or perish* imperative. The stress to produce, and *quickly,* cultivates a philosophy of risky entitlement to the ideas, concepts, narratives, and published works of others, without attribution. Research paper mills lend an air of legitimacy to the acquisition of another's work, and even theses and dissertations can be purchased for a fee, often unstated on web advertisements. An advertisement for one such company ensures the timely production of dissertations so that students can be free to concentrate on career preparations and other interests (Quick Writer, 2020). The dissertation comes with a "plagiarism-free" guarantee and, despite the ironic fact that it is being written *for* a customer, the promise is that the product will pass plagiarism detection software checks. The lure is clear: someone can be paid to do the hard work, and the student can occupy his or her time in working on resumes and networking. The company also offers master's theses or papers on the high school and undergraduate levels.

If students fall prey to these captivating ads but lack necessary budgets, they may find a bottomless resource in the internet. A survey of 23 college campuses revealed that 38% of undergraduate students surveyed admitted to "cut-and-paste plagiarism" at least once or more during the previous year and almost half did not consider this form of plagiarism an act of "cheating" (Rimer, 2003). (A smaller survey conducted 3 years previously indicated that only 10% of students surveyed admitted to cheating.) According to the study, students cited the increasing pressure of gaining entry to graduate schools and landing "top jobs" as reasons for cheating (Rimer, 2003). Burke (2005) observes that students' "thirst for knowledge has been replaced by a quest for good grades" that will give students entrée to the best schools. Ironically, students are unaware that the very same challenges will confront them in the graduate schools they cheated to get into in the first place. One student respondent wrote the following comment on the survey: "This isn't a college problem. This is a problem of the entire country!" (Rimer, 2003), a statement that alludes to the globalization of cheating observed by the respondent.

The repetition of this thought process and ensuing behavior *appears* to lessen the negative impact. But those closest to the issue know differently.

Plagiarism as Failure

Educators and administrators question the genesis of such misconduct breaches. Isabella, an ABD (all but dissertation) doctoral student, came to my office in distress. In grading research papers for her class, she discovered one of her students had plagiarized the majority of a paper. She personalized the act of the student's plagiarism not only as an effrontery, but as her own failure. She spent inordinate time familiarizing students with the project requirements: formatting style, literature review, methodology, required citations, citation sources. She offered to review an outline if students chose to submit one. However, she had not discussed plagiarism, primarily because, as she herself admitted, "I never thought students would do that—I'm always so good to them." Her supervising faculty advisor suggested a formal misconduct hearing available via university channels, but Isabella was reluctant and sought my advice about options.

Initially, she was uncertain about *how much* information had been plagiarized. Her review revealed two violations. We reviewed the entirety of the paper, and I verified clear examples of plagiarism throughout by conducting a comparative study of the original document and the student's paper. The student culled information directly from the literature review section of an article located on the internet, without attribution. The most original section of the paper included the student's own commentary, which was completely uninformed by the working principles of the literature that she had seized from the internet. Reflecting a complete lack of understanding or a working knowledge of the ideas at play, her own words unmasked the fact that she did not understand the fundamental concepts of her topic. Further, the differences in writing style, tone, and phraseology between the student's own writing and that of the author whose work had been plagiarized established a sharp contrast, the tip-off that the work was not her own.

Intervention, Next Steps

How to contend with the student was the next question, and, after we discussed options, Isabella decided against levying a formal complaint, opting to work directly with the student in an instructional mode of interaction, as I recommended.

One effective approach is to have professors discuss the many facets/dimensions of plagiarism with students as part of ongoing classroom activities, define these elements, and educate students about appropriate citation according to scholarly conventions. Another approach is to incorporate the method we used in our review of the student's paper: the professor looks up the original citations and compares them with the student's version to demonstrate mechanisms resulting in plagiarism. The quiet, dignified, and personalized interaction between professor and student results in a civil, humane way to approach and overcome the problem, as it did with Isabella and her student. The use of Endnote, RefWorks, and Mendeley Reference Manager citation management software can be incorporated into the writing phase of research papers, theses, dissertations, grant proposals, articles, and other writing projects to track citations and organize bibliographies. Lost or missing citations often account for many instances of plagiarism, and so the use of software systems to manage them is a bonus for seasoned as well as novice writers.

The issue of plagiarism, both intentional and unintentional, raises concerns. Isabella's student claimed she was unaware of elements that constitute research misconduct and, in fact, appropriated material without forethought. Some students are not aware that they must cite information taken from the internet or even from class lecture notes and may make an "honest error," which does not necessarily constitute research misconduct. In these instances, students are not thinking about intellectual property issues or considering the individuals who actually *own* the material, especially in the depersonalized, anonymous virtual worlds accessed for information. Moreover, they are ignorant of such exotic transgressions as "self plagiarism" or "salami slicing." (See Miguel Roig's [2015] online guide for a host of different kinds of plagiarism.)

But lack of awareness as a justification takes students only so far, and in the case of two Harvard University law professors, not far enough in extricating distinguished reputations by claiming they had "unintentionally misused sources" and that "their errors were accidental" (Rimer, 2004). More college and university courses should include components that identify plagiarism and other forms of academic misconduct and establish clear guidelines to prevent it. Professors and instructors can sponsor awareness projects showcasing questionable research behaviors and preventing proliferation of *free for all* environments, the antithesis of the standards of scholarly conduct institutions of higher education must foster. Universities should implement rigorous honor codes and policies and hold students accountable. One variant of the honor code concept appears on a proposal approval form currently in use at Western Michigan University. It includes a statement that authenticates the originality of the dissertation, thesis, or specialist project and represents the student's pledge to provide appropriate scholarly attribution ("Proposal Approval," n.d.).

Efforts by the National Science Foundation (NSF) to promote and foster a culture of ethical integrity through the development and implementation of a research ethics training program at universities receiving federal funding are particularly encouraging (Federal Register Online, 2009). These efforts resulted in sustained training for undergraduate students, graduate students, as well as postdoctoral researchers who participate in NSF-funded research. Roig's (2015) guide mentioned previously represents an extension of this initiative and is grounded in ethical writing practices aligned with scientific inquiry. This initiative has also drawn the support of the Council of Graduate Schools, and while these efforts exist at the macro level, educators should reinforce the principles in their interactions with students at the micro level—in courses, seminars, workshops, the research bench, and other educational venues—so that ethical awareness and training are woven within the context of the university and made relevant to all students.

Conversations on campuses must address the need for academic honesty and research integrity in holistic, integrated ways. The infrastructure of the campus community should reinforce these conversations by offering assistance to students in welcoming, learning environments. Faculty can direct energies toward preventive measures, reinforced as a natural concomitant of daily interactions with students. Too often, vast efforts are expended *after the fact* of violations, when damage has been done and when students may proceed to penalty stages of formal misconduct hearings, for it is within the realm of academia that plagiarism plays out as an *academic* violation, not a *legal* violation that plays out within the court system: plagiarism versus copyright infringement (Cronin, 2003). (For differences in these concepts, see Charles Cronin's paper at http://abacus.bates.edu/cbb/docs/Cronin.pdf)

The academic community permits and encourages access to a wealth of scholarly materials upon which progress and advancement in respective fields are founded. The purpose of academic writing is to advance the scholarship and to contribute to the academic conversations, and this is accomplished by acknowledging the work that serves as predecessor through the act of appropriate citation. Academic papers, conference presentations, class notes, books, etc., are all viable sources of information that can be incorporated into the scholarly work of others. Academics relish being formally cited, and their professional advancement often figures centrally not only in numbers of publications but in numbers of citations. However, they would eschew the appropriation of their intellectual property without attribution. This is the point that students need to know. Moreover, this awareness necessarily implies that students must be taught the technical elements of writing or expressing information that will be cited: how to summarize, paraphrase, annotate, synthesize, analyze, and quote, and how to establish the differences between and among these elements (Roig, 2010); how to keep track of citations; and how to proofread final copy and conduct a crosswalk between cited information in the narrative of the text and actual references. To assume that students, both domestic and international, come to the university with these skills intact is to court folly.

Personal Costs

As faculty admonish students about the technical circumstances that result in plagiarism, they should also focus upon the human toll wrought. Consider the case of Judy Tzu-Chun Wu. In 2002, Wu discovered her dissertation on Margaret Chung, the first American-born Chinese female physician, condensed into one anthology chapter written by Benson Tong. Wu set about to distinguish her own research within the 15-page essay that Tong authored and discovered only one paragraph that Tong could claim as his own. Worse yet, Tong even appropriated Wu's footnotes (Bartlett & Smallwood, 2004). She filed a complaint with the American Historical Association, as well as with Tong's publisher, but colleagues advised her to let the issue go, warning her that the process would be "long [and] exhausting" (Bartlett & Smallwood, 2004). She ignored the advice.

Wu describes the nature of her attempt to wrest back rightful ownership of her intellectual property as indeed "exhausting" but admitted that having the "validation" of the American Historical Association was "important" ("A Plagiarized Writer Speaks Out About Her Case," 2005), even though Tong's anthology was not retracted. A writer's enervation, however, may be the least costly outcome of suffering from a plagiarist's transgressions. Some victims do not have the stamina or resources to fight. Maurice Maeterlinck, Nobel Prize Laureate, appropriated at least half of the research of South African scientist, lawyer, and poet Eugene Marais on Marais' masterpiece, *The Soul of the White Ant*. Maeterlinck's published version, *The Life of the White Ant*, is thought to have contributed to Marais' eventual suicide in 1936 (Maartens, 2006).

My own experience with plagiarism mirrors the sadness and disappointment that accompany the discovery that one's work has been stolen. Several years ago, as I prepared for a presentation, I came across an article that I thought would be appropriate, but as I reviewed it I experienced a sense of déjà vu, as if I had come across this information before. My initial thoughts were that this author writes *like I do*, but those thoughts were rapidly displaced by the realization that *those were my words*, taken, and without attribution to me. A faculty advisor and his doctoral advisee had taken the majority of my article, kept the title intact, removed my name, and placed themselves as first and second authors. Conducting a crosswalk between my original article and the "kidnapped" version was painful and demoralizing. I notified the Vice President for Research at my university and my dean of these circumstances. I then provided the faculty member's institution with the results of my analysis, which proved conclusively that my article had been plagiarized. At the faculty member's institution, the kidnapped version was then subjected to Turnitin, a plagiarism detection software program—a step that cemented the case for the benefit of the investigatory committee, which then went on to conduct a year-long investigation, after which I received a not-so-apologetic letter of apology from the faculty member. I did not hear from the student. However, this is not the end of the story: several months later, I came across an article that referenced the plagiarizer and the advisee as authors of *my* work. I contacted the writer who had attributed the material to the two thieves. She was upset and asked me what she could do besides contact her publisher. It was then that I realized the horrific impact of being erased and not being able to do anything about it. Like a cancer that metastasizes without warning, so too does plagiarism cannibalize our scholarly efforts and poison those who lead lives of integrity. I understood that there would be no way to pull back the pathological tide of circumstances and to right the wrong.

This saga, like those sagas of the Wus and the Maraises of the world, remind us of the personal cost to researchers and scientists alike, who spend countless hours in pursuit of *truth*, only to have it eclipsed by others who lay claim to the prize, without toiling to reach the lofty heights that distinguish the *true scholar* from the *poseur*. Like Isabella, faculty suffer when students plagiarize. Many perceive their integrity violated and may internalize students' transgressions as failure. Failure, though, belongs to the plagiarists, who cheated themselves out of the opportunity for intellectual growth and development that comes with scholarly pursuit. Remarking about her own plagiarist, Wu stated that "he put a lot of effort into plagiarizing. He could have spent that time researching something else" ("A Plagiarized Writer Speaks Out," 2005).

Paraphrasing the American Historical Association's statement on plagiarism, Michael Grossberg (2004) writes that "historians … have a fundamental responsibility 'to oppose deception'" and that such "responsibilities cannot be delegated to others." "Each of us must be prepared to act," says Grossberg. So too must all educators embrace what he refers to as a "renewed commitment to collective vigilance and collective action." If the problem of cheating is a "problem of the entire country," as one student's survey response indicates (Rimer, 2003), then the answer must certainly lie in the collective action that Grossberg advocates.

~ The Take Away ~

Recommendations for Advisors

The following are some approaches that all educators can employ to kindle that renewal process. Plagiarism creates a no-win situation. Dissertating students who have plagiarized face serious consequences and, in many instances, are removed from their programs of study and from their universities. Those who find a way to survive the charge, by virtue of someone's good will or by happenstance, often find themselves *persona non grata* in their departments or programs, without the faculty support necessary to complete their dissertations. International students face far greater consequences and may be forced to return to their countries without their degrees, a reality often complicated by strict funding repayment policies. Even graduated students whose dissertations and theses are found to be compromised are not isolated from the consequences, as evidenced in the case of the engineering students at Ohio University in 2006. The emphasis should be on prevention. Here are some ideas:

1. *Initiate research ethics training.* Implement strategies/systems that interface with the demands of graduate education; students are expected to conduct independent research, run statistical analyses, write results, portray data in tables, and publish. These tasks often challenge responsible conduct for researchers, and time spent in preventing infractions through intensive online training is beneficial (refer to CITIProgram.org). Such training can be supplemented by presentations, workshops, and seminars conducted by recognized experts in ethics.
2. *Be proactive.* Provide students with examples of plagiarized writing and other forms of academic misconduct, and compare against the original copy as part of ongoing class sessions *prior* to a misconduct incident. Faculty who mentor on

a daily basis address unique questions and forestall misconduct situations.
3. *Educate and ameliorate.* If plagiarism occurs, consider the opportunity to educate and teach the student, in a calm and respectful manner that preserves dignity.
4. *Use citation management software.* Incorporate Endnote, RefWorks, or Mendeley Reference Manager programs within a class schedule to assist students in professional citation management. Library staff can also teach these sessions outside of the classroom setting. Professional writers as well as novices often discover that the effective management of citations is a painstaking task, not always mistake proof. Technology may offer a boon and facilitate the management process.
5. *Implement honor codes and corresponding policies, and instruct.* Such codes/policies hold students accountable and focused on ethical responsibilities. However, as Roig (2010) indicates, it is not sufficient to simply articulate a code or policy or to include it in course syllabi in the absence of more rigorous instruction about plagiarism and how it occurs.
6. *Design discipline-specific ethics courses.* Ethics courses should be part of all university curricula and should intersect with unique/specific disciplinary concerns in an ongoing manner.
7. *Implement ethics certificate programs.* Design/develop a certificate in ethics/interdisciplinary ethics to distinguish graduates via this special credentialing that values ethics and integrity. Permit for ethics courses to stand as recognized electives in programs of study and encourage interdisciplinary accessibility.
8. *Personalize misconduct.* Teach students the human toll of plagiarism and other forms of misconduct, for those who plagiarize as well as for those whose intellectual property has been stolen, misused, or misrepresented.
9. *Avoid overuse of plagiarism detection software.* Employ such initiatives sparingly, and only after initial instructive methods have been employed. Writing is distinctive and singular; deviations in style, tone, language use, and even punc-

tuation signal an untoward departure that should be apparent to instructors. Instructors should work closely with students, honing drafts of papers and using peer-evaluation groups or class editing to demonstrate the evolutionary nature of good academic writing. Use of plagiarism detection software begins with the unfortunate notion that the student is dishonest, *a priori*. The pedagogical use of these tools is somewhat dubious, especially if penalties are enacted as first-step. Direct access to the software, prior to submission of a writing project, would provide students with a learning opportunity to examine their own work and to ameliorate possible violations. The no-risk environment is more conducive to learning.

10. *Be aware of daily ethical infractions.* The opportunity to violate ethical standards exists on a daily basis, as part of our lived world experiences. Educators need to look past habits or other recurring behavioral patterns and examine practices and procedures from objective viewpoints. For example, do doctoral programs violate ethical standards when students are permitted access to resources for assistance with comprehensive examinations? Do graduate students violate ethical standards when they plagiarize a dissertation and then maintain university scholarships and other funding advantages? Do dissertation advisors violate ethical standards when they intercede so extensively in the dissertation writing/editing process that there is little to distinguish the advisee's contributions from theirs? Is it an ethical violation to rewrite an international student's grant proposal so that the language sounds better, more erudite, and therefore results in a more competitive document?

Good intentions do not always equate with sterling standards of ethical behavior, and institutions of higher learning must look beyond individual circumstances to see the implications of such behavior within the larger societal framework. Are ethical standards *true* standards evenly applied to everyone, or are ethical standards merely flexible suggestions that bend according to will?

Concluding Thoughts

Advisors must teach their advisees about plagiarism and warn them of the losses—not only potential failure of a paper or a course, not only a squandered learning opportunity. They must tell sobering tales that illustrate the full impact of stealing someone's ideas and words, from the human, *the personalized*, perspective.

References

Bartlett, T., & Smallwood, S. (2004, December 17). Special report: Plagiarism. Four academic plagiarists you've never heard of: How many more are out there? *Chronicle of Higher Education, 51*(17), A8.

Burke, M. (2005). Deterring plagiarism: A new role for librarians. *Library Philosophy and Practice, 6*(2). Retrieved from https://core.ac.uk/download/pdf/188041019.pdf

CITI Program training: Publication and responsible authorship in humanities. (n.d.). Retrieved from https://about.citiprogram.org/en/homepage/

Cronin, C. (2003, October 15). *Plagiarism, copyright, academia and commerce.* Paper presented at the Conference on Information Ethics and Academic Honesty, Colby College, Waterville, ME. Retrieved from: http://abacus.bates.edu/cbb/docs/Cronin.pdf

Federal Register Online. (2009). *Federal Register, 74*(160), 42126-42128. Retrieved from https://www.govinfo.gov/content/pkg/FR-2009-08-20/pdf/E9-19930.pdf

Grossberg, M. (2004). Plagiarism and professional ethics—A journal editor's view. *The Journal of American History, 90*(4), 1333–1340. https://doi.org/10.2307/3660352

Lipson, A., & Reindl, S. (2003, July–August). The responsible plagiarist—Understanding students who misuse sources. *About Campus, 8*(3), 7–14.

Maartens, W. (2006). *Eugene Marais: Baboons, termites, and the evolution of the human psyche.* Retrieved from http://www.authorsden.com/visit/viewshortstory.asp?AuthorID=40804

Pitzer, A. (2017). *The freewheelin' Bob Dylan.* Retrieved January 5, 2021, from https://slate.com/culture/2017/06/did-bob-dylan-take-from-sparknotes-for-his-nobel-lecture.html

Plagiarism: Facts & stats: Academic integrity in college and graduate school. (2017). Retrieved March 17, 2021, from Plagiarism.org website: https://www.plagiarism.org/article/plagiarism-facts-and-stats

A plagiarized writer speaks out about her case. Special report: Plagiarism. (2005).

Chronicle of Higher Education, 51(30), A27. Retrieved from http://chronicle.com

Proposal approval. (n.d.). Retrieved March 20, 2021, from the Western Michigan University Graduate College website: https://wmich.edu/grad/proposal-approval

Quick Writer. (2020). *Buy original dissertation, thesis papers online*. Retrieved December 18, 2020, from https://quickwriter.com/dissertations/buy-dissertation-online.html

Rimer, S. (2003, September 3). A campus fad that's being copied: Internet plagiarism seems on the rise. *New York Times*. Retrieved from http://www.nytimes.com/2003/09/03/education/03CHEA.html?pagewanted=1

Rimer, S. (2004, November 24). When plagiarism's shadow falls on admired scholars. *New York Times*. Retrieved from https://www.nytimes.com/2004/11/24/nyregion/when-plagiarisms-shadow-falls-on-admired-scholars.html

Roig, M. (2010). Plagiarism: An ounce of prevention. *American Society for Quality (ASQ) Higher Education Brief, 3*(4). Retrieved from https://asq.org/edu/2010/06/continuous-improvement/plagiarism-an-ounce-of-prevention-.pdf

Roig, M. (2015). *Avoiding plagiarism, self-plagiarism, and other questionable writing practices: A guide to ethical writing* (2nd rev.). Retrieved March 20, 2021, from Avoiding plagiarism, self-plagiarism, and other questionable writing practices: A guide to ethical writing (hhs.gov)

Temple, E. (2018, March 29). *12 literary plagiarism scandals, ranked from Helen Keller to Jonah Leher, some more legitimate than others*. Retrieved January 5, 2021, from https://lithub.com/12-literary-plagiarism-scandals-ranked/

Chapter 24

A Visionary Perspective for an Academic Resource Matrix

The wave of the future in doctoral retention lies in focused specialization and not in the random placement of initiatives sometimes dropped into place. The challenges to doctoral education require varied retention resources that align with student needs and degree completion. These must be comprised of an expansive framework of specialized interventions that reflect specific areas of expertise. Fields such as medicine, law, and engineering are framed within specialized components or disciplines that account for the exceptional levels of expertise required to meet a diverse, sophisticated range of clients. But this approach is not always extant within the realm of graduate education. It remains, for the most part, typified by arbitrary approaches.

Resources that are essentially invisible and/or tucked into place within existing institutional structures, not originally designed for those purposes, do not address the complex needs of graduate students. For example, undergraduate writing centers that endeavor to expand into scholarly/academic writing but that lack the staff, expertise, and financial institutional support cannot address the rigor of the dissertation on a consistent, sustained basis. Based upon their design, they address the needs of an undergraduate constituency, but not necessarily on the level required of the dissertating student. A specialization in one area does not necessarily equate to expertise in another area: the radiologist is not the neurosurgeon, and the structural engineer is not one suited to aeronautical engineering. All specializations reflect limitations.

I do not in any manner disparage the function, purpose, and philosophy of writing centers, for they play a significant role in higher education and optimize undergraduate student learning outcomes in the discipline of writing. So too do academic centers for success that provide tutoring in specific fields, such as mathematics, biology, and chemistry, among others. However, the specialized nature of dissertation writing and research too frequently resides within the isolating confines of dissertation committees, which are left to puzzle through the isolation, the lack of collaborative interventions, and the specific expertise that both students and faculty require. In light of the almost consistent 50% doctoral attrition rate, we should not have to ask how this has been working for us.

Hidden Resources

Several concepts developed in this book lend to the observation that the dissertation process is essentially an isolated and isolating experience for dissertating students and their committees. Individuals work in compartmentalized, siloed units frequently challenged by flawed communication and abstruse definitions of roles, functions, and responsibilities, let alone the lack of formal training. In Chapter 1 of this book, I cited the Council of Graduate Schools listserv of November and December 2020 that reflected questions regarding *how* and *if* other universities defined qualifications for the position of *graduate program director,* which is intriguing given the fact that many such positions have been filled over the years in the absence of these very questions now raised as considerations of the selection process. Such a position represents a pivotally important connection to department faculty.

Often, those individuals with graduate faculty status are not aware of the various administrative forms required and their coinciding timelines, let alone the policies, procedures, or resources available. An example of a student who was about to depart his program because he was caught between trying to salvage his marriage and trying to meet the demands of his Ph.D. program, both in conflict, serves well. Neither he nor his dissertation chair were aware of the leave-of-absence policy that provided him with a respite from program demands so that he could work on his marriage: the policy literally "stopped the clock" on the seven-year program limitation and permitted him the time he needed to resolve marital issues without sacrificing his program. Yet another example serves: Committee members in my most recent work this year indicated that neither the student nor they were aware of the free statistical consultation offered by my university, an arrangement that I initiated with the Department of Statistics in 2006. Given the expanse of time from initiation of this arrangement to the present, it is indeed remarkable that awareness of the availability of this resource never came to light. The student had been paying a statistical consultant at another university out of his own very limited funds. An individual in the role of graduate program director, trained for this position, could have connected these students to available resources.

Such examples point to the lack of institutional leadership in supporting these initiatives and then marketing them to students and to graduate advising faculty across the university. The leave-of-absence policy was created to protect students experiencing a legitimate interruption in their degree process: military service, illness, childbirth, death of a family member, among others. The statistical consultation service was designed as part of a toolbox of comprehensive, integrated instruments to be employed and utilized to advance student success. But it wasn't, and begs the question, *Why*? in both circumstances.

The communication gap aside, not all units within a university actually support such resources, ironically enough. When I first announced the need for statistical support for dissertating students' research at a Graduate Studies Council meeting in 2005, the initial response was "shock" (*the actual word used*) that the Graduate Center was engaging in the "hand holding" (*the actual word used*) of such advanced students who should already possess statistical acumen. The reality, however, is that students often do not possess the statistical skill levels sufficient to meet the demands of the dissertation, despite the required research methods or statistics courses in their curricula; many of these courses are taken at the beginning of the program of study and therefore lack relevance at the time of application to the dissertation, many years later. Neither are students necessarily quantitative or qualitative experts or content gurus, a point that supports my previous recommendation that dissertation committees must be configured with such specialists in mind or at least have access to such expertise. Committee misconfigurations can spell potential disaster, especially if they are discovered late in the dissertation game, when the student approaches the defense, for example. The end-stage discovery that committee members lack the expertise to evaluate and assess the advisee's research and do not know where to locate a quantitative or a qualitative expert within the university community will jeopardize the student's opportunities for degree completion. Further disaster also looms when it becomes apparent that the student lacks the competence and training to operationalize the method, or when it becomes apparent that a content expert has not been invited to join the committee.

Now, there is absolutely no harm in a student's or the committee members' *not knowing* and in requiring assistance; but there is great harm in remaining silent, ignoring the fact that *one does not know* and proceeding anyway throughout the entire dissertation process. Further, there is great harm in a committee's refusal to ask probing questions about their own and an advisee's qualifications because that individual *appears* to be qualified.

Committee members, as well as their advisees, must avoid making assumptions about each other's qualifications, similar to the Council of Graduate Schools listserv faculty mentioned above who are now asking the hard questions and not assuming that any and all faculty members are qualified to serve as graduate program director just because they hold faculty rank. Committee members must close the communication gap or they will surely suffer the consequences of not knowing what is needed—or where to look for it. This is a top-down initiative, and unless senior leadership steps up to the plate and takes ownership, the situations described will remain unabated. But are they doing so, or are they just cherry picking politically correct solutions and not enacting bold, encompassing, quality-driven mechanisms that really go to the heart of the dilemma and that serve the needs of both doctoral students and graduate advising faculty? In the absence of interventions, faculty will operate in a lacuna regarding policies and resources centered in best practices; committees without the appropriate expertise will continue to operate; students will enter into the dissertation process, unqualified and unprepared for the research at hand; and the production of "good enough" dissertations will become the norm for our institutional output.

The dissertation itself, *as process*, must be integrated consistently within the curricula, from the beginning, and not serve as an exercise simply tacked onto the end of the doctoral program, pro forma. If it is true that "You are your dissertation," and if it is also true that career potential aligns with the excellence of the dissertation, its research and writing acumen, then the entire concept of the "good enough" dissertation flies in the face of the rigor that should typify this last step in doctoral education.

How can we address these impediments to the success of graduate students and graduate advising faculty in their mission to cultivate emerging scholars of merit?

Operationalizing Resources: Graduate Centers for Scholarship and Professional Development

I envision that universities and colleges will build Graduate Centers for Scholarship and Professional Development that are staffed by dissertation experts, mentors, statisticians, qualitative and quantitative methods experts, professional writing experts, conceptual editors, formatters, proposal developers, research program officers, digital technologies gurus, career advisors, and transcribers. Conduits to psychological counseling will also be aligned with such Graduate Centers, and not simply appear on a list of website resources. Students will also have access to an individual charged with administrating various awards and prizes for thesis/dissertation completion, research, and travel to conferences. In other words, the entire complex of student needs will be housed, *umbrella style*, in a one-stop-shop (an outreach) environment that serves as a centralized conduit to the array of available resources: the center could be housed in a Graduate College/School/Office of Graduate Studies or in the Office of the Vice President for Research, for example. It should connect logically to offices of institutional effectiveness that can manage data and produce statistical reports on retention and attrition, thereby permitting the center to function in a data-driven capacity.

Administration on this centralized level will be key to advancing student and faculty access. Students on all spectrums of their doctoral educational programs, as well as those working on master's level theses, will be welcome to partake of a center's resources, whenever needed, and free of charge. This means that students and faculty can engage with the center's staff and receive support and training or just touch base to ensure they are on the right pathway via *Dissertation Wellness Checks,* which represented an invaluable resource that I implemented into the center that I directed. Students responded very well to the opportunity to discuss their dissertations and to cultivate career plans on a monthly basis. One student confided that she appreciated the opportunity to confer with me simply because I was *not* on her committee and *not* in her department, a freedom that eliminated stress and permitted her to speak freely and without restraint about her concerns. In addition, these Dissertation Wellness Checks ensured that she remained on track in meeting her dissertation and career goals, especially given the fact that she was a self-described procrastinator. Once we set the calendar for our monthly meetings, she understood my expectation that she meet a defined goal we had previously established, whether that be researching the author guidelines for a particular journal, applying for a dissertation completion award, or simply conferring with her advisor. So, Dissertation Wellness Checks accounted for any dimension of an academic process in which a student might be engaged and require additional mentoring and oversight. Such checks can be arranged within a virtual context via Zoom or Webex and also can take place via phone calls. The point is simply to establish contact on a basis that is as frequent as the student desires, and it is the student who can set those parameters. This resource remains in place with the students whom I currently advise as a dissertation committee member and it serves as a catalyst to the myriad facets of degree completion, including the resources, since I know the key players and where to find them. In addition, the phone calls, virtual chats, texts, and email solidify personal and professional connection to the student, signal that "we care," and counter the sense of isolation and disconnectedness inherent in the dissertation process. Similarly, dissertation committee members and chairs can also avail themselves of such wellness checks to discuss students' progress and to apprise themselves of next steps, collaborate, voice concerns, and communicate.

The Role of Chair/Advisor

So, how does the dissertation chair/advisor fit into all of this? In such a Graduate Center for Scholarship and Professional Development, the chair/advisor (hereafter referred to as the *advisor*) remains at the epicenter of the dissertation process, but surrounding him or her is the pantheon of resources/experts described above with whom he or she would communicate and establish a viable professional relationship. Thus, an advisor's time is focused in the content research, its accuracy, and the manner in which it fits within the context of the discipline. The day-to-day management of the dissertation process will be left to a major coordinator/facilitator who will consult with the advisor regarding the ongoing facets of the dissertation process and then reach out to the various resource "arms" for individualized support that each student requires. The advisor's oversight will be further engaged when chapters are in *clean copy* format, ready for the advisor's intervention, when minimal adjustments to the narrative, minimal tweaks to a literature review, for example, minor organizational restructuring, may be all that are required. In other words, advisors receive what is essentially a penultimate draft for their review or could request a series of drafts that are in almost final form. The individuals involved would establish the working relationship that best suits their needs. Given the wide circle of experts at the helm, advisors' time would be conserved for the most salient requirements of the dissertation. The collaborative model described above still permits advisors to maintain control over the process, but the array of experts lends to best practices in terms of project management and quality outcomes. Consider the advantages for all faculty when they serve simultaneously on multiple committees.

 A student in a STEM field (science, technology, engineering, mathematics) will obviously discuss the idea for the dissertation with the faculty member who sponsors the research. As indicated previously, faculty in STEM fields work closely with their advisees, almost from the inception of students' programs. However, students in other fields have a different model, as discussed previously. When they have an idea for the dissertation, they will come to the Graduate Center and meet with proposal developers who will listen to the student's ideas and help craft a viable concept paper, with the goal of securing approval from the dissertation advisor. At least this approach puts ideas on paper and provides the advisor with a potential topic from which a dissertation can potentially emerge. In this manner, the student is engaged in the process of research discovery and comes to the advisor armed with a potential topic that has been thought out and that represents the initial place where collaboration or the conceptual conversation can begin.

The advisor will be accountable for the assessment and evaluation of the concept paper, the final document, and intervening documents (theses or dissertations or articles) at various stages, if so desired, but the majority of the work will be handled in the expert collaborative environment of the Graduate Center, which will have more of a "hands-on" approach. In other words, the arduous work of editing and revising will be dealt with by the center's staff, with penultimate documents provided to the advisor. The advisor will receive a stream of evaluative reports to share with the dissertation committee but will not necessarily be involved in the daily ongoing activity of the dissertation writing/editing process with its stops and starts, *unless he or she so insists*.

Oversight of lab research/content research will remain with the dissertation advisor, but the other dimensions of the dissertation will remain with the Graduate Center's expert staff. The student's advisor will become an ad hoc member of the center but will dovetail his or her content expertise into the entirety of the center's work. Since the center's staff will all be experts in what they produce, the quality of the dissertation will be enhanced; in other words, the actual research elements will remain with the advisor, but the structural, organizational, and technical parts of the dissertation will reside with the center's experts. In this manner, the advisor's expertise and time are preserved for those areas most necessary to the integrity of the project: the research.

Again, the idea is to create an umbrella of specialized services and resources to graduate students and to graduate faculty in an effort to streamline the process, as well as provide a pantheon of elements requisite for graduate student success via best practices. The economic/financial matters regarding how such a center will be staffed and funded certainly are considerations, but perhaps one solution inheres in the idea of utilizing the vast faculty resources already extant within the university environment. Arrangements via release time to serve in the center may be one approach: these individuals will not require designated office space but will operate out of their own departmental office space and confer with students and other associated faculty in a one-on-one and/or virtual space that permits for ongoing collaboration. The role of the center's coordinator/facilitator (director) would be filled best by an individual with a Ph.D. but not necessarily an individual who is a faculty member at that university, and there is a rationale for this decision: Individuals who are faculty members could conceivably carry with them a certain preference for or bias toward their own department's style of dissertation management, and, because of departmental affiliations and commitments to colleagues in that department, potentially dismantle the capability of working across diverse disciplines in a more egalitarian manner that respects disciplinary singularity.

An Emerging Specialty

Dissertation advising will eventually assume the importance of a disciplinary specialty, with trained individuals who ensure that advisees have access to appropriate and timely support mechanisms. Think of this idea as part of a natural progression in higher education or a more contemporary approach to contend with the complex issues surrounding doctoral retention. At the moment, this may seem a foreign concept: programs often operate in their own siloes and not necessarily according to more standardized, cohesive, or collaborative procedures that lend to best practices. Such isolation permits for the idea that "We are different," and this is true to an extent, but it does not account for the fact that difference itself does not always constitute quality outcomes.

However, let's reflect on the practice in years past when emergency rooms were staffed by doctors who essentially had to *pull a shift in the ER*. Their field of medical specialty or expertise was not necessarily a consideration: a psychiatrist, although trained as a medical doctor, could end up delivering a baby or treating a patient for meningitis; a general practitioner could end up performing a cardiac procedure. As outcomes were evaluated, hospitals must have realized that this approach was not efficient, or safe. Over time, the specialty of emergency medicine emerged as a bona fide medical specialty.

In my opinion, dissertation advising eventually will become its own specialized area of doctoral education, administrated and staffed by trained experts who understand, appreciate, and are responsive to the singular needs of doctoral students and graduate advising faculty. However, the academy will have to undergo radical changes, and students will have to press for more diverse forms of support than ever before as we move further into the 21st century.

~ The Take Away ~

1. Standardized approaches to the dissertation eliminate the potential for variations that may pose threats to the integrity of the dissertation project. Specialization of the dissertation process ensures that experts work together collaboratively and with cognizance of quality outcomes.
2. Dissertation advising will emerge in time as its own specialty in graduate education.

Chapter 25

Blurred Lines: Ethical Considerations for Committee Members

One of the most complex processes that doctoral students experience concerns the critical transition from the coursework phase of their programs to the research and writing process of the dissertation. It is important for graduate advising faculty and their advisees to be aware of this transition period and for doctoral curricula to include strategies that assist both groups in this process. However, the process is defined by blurred lines that are difficult to negotiate. Let's explore.

"Deliberate Practice" as a Component of Critical Transition

Doctoral students' academic and intellectual *preparedness* to meet the demands of the dissertation raises concerns. Consider the intensive work of graduate advising faculty and subsequently students' reliance upon it to *make the dissertation right* without their (the students') acquisition of requisite skills. Consider also that students have not practiced the art of the dissertation during the course of time that intersects with its delivery: their programs of study do not include the "deliberate practice" that constitutes a foundation for the excellence and mastery of skills (Ericsson & Pool, 2017, p. 97). Ericsson and Pool (2017) write that if we want to improve anything about ourselves, a game of tennis or writing or chess, for example, we need to comply with the principles of "deliberate practice" to become "the best in the world," and not just "good enough" (p. xxiii). Are we lowering expectations for our doctoral students and denying them the opportunity for professional growth and development when we reduce our standards to the "good enough" dissertation?

The implementation of solid training for our students may be one conduit to rising above this point and cultivating *capability*. Ericsson and Pool's work is replete with examples that demonstrate individuals' capacity to expand upon and to increase their skills levels in ways that actually create physiological and neurological responses to those task demands.

Ericsson and Pool (2017) cite the study of neuroscientist Eleanor Maguire, who used magnetic resonance imaging (MRI) testing to study the brains of British taxi drivers who had undergone intensive navigational skills training to qualify for positions as licensed taxi drivers in London, a city that departs from the grid-like designs of other cities and is difficult to navigate, even with GPS systems. She compared the MRI results with those of prospective taxi drivers who had either stopped the navigational skills training or did not pass the test for licensure. Maguire's results indicated that the posterior hippocampi of the brains of those individuals who persisted in their training and became licensed had increased in volume when compared to the group of individuals who did not. According to Ericsson and Pool, Maguire's study provides "dramatic evidence" of the brain's ability to grow, change, and adapt to intense training. They liken this change to what happens to the muscles of an individual who undergoes intensive training to become a gymnast and experiences a "bulking up" of the muscles. The same occurs with the brain: it bulks up to meet the demands imposed upon it (Ericsson & Pool, 2017, pp. 31–33) and reflects an element of "plasticity" or "adaptability" (p. 34). This phenomenon also manifests in Braille readers, sports enthusiasts, and musicians (see Ericsson & Pool, 2017, pp. 35, 40, and 43). Interestingly, acquired skills can dissipate over time if not practiced consistently, as evidenced by Maguire's follow-up studies of the licensed cab drivers who had retired and no longer relied upon their navigational skills (Ericsson & Pool, 2017, p. 47). This outcome may also be applicable to those of us who studied international languages years ago and are no longer as proficient as we once were.

Principles of Deliberate Practice

Deliberate practice consists of a joint relationship between the learner and an instructor who assesses the student's current abilities and then will "push him or her to move just beyond the current skill level" (Ericsson & Pool, 2017, pp. 97–98) via the assignment of specific practice sessions designed in a way that increases performance levels, regardless of a specific discipline. Ericsson and Pool cite two important requirements of deliberate practice (1) a field that is "reasonably well developed" and in which those performing have distinguished themselves from novices just entering the field, and (2) a teacher who provides specific practice activities aligned with the goal of enhanced performance (p. 98). This last point will be clarified later in this book.

Deliberate practice shares these characteristics: it "develops skills that other people have figured out how to do and for which effective training techniques have been established"; it takes place "outside of one's comfort zone" and requires that a learner "try things that are just beyond" the level of "his or her current abilities"; it involves "well-defined, specific goals" and "improving some aspect of the target performance, . . . not aimed at some vague overall improvement"; it is purposeful, requiring "a person's full attention and conscious actions"; it involves "feedback and modification of efforts in response to that feedback"; it "produces and depends on effective mental representations," the ability to become "more detailed and effective" and therefore to improve further; it involves "building and modifying previously acquired skills" and focusing on particular aspects of them to improve performance (Ericsson & Pool, 2017, pp. 99–100).

The concept of deliberate practice is grounded in the logic of process improvement over time, not relegated to a specific course and certainly not within the context of dissertation committee work, where actual student learning and the acquisition of skills are not necessarily apparent on the levels that open to sustained practice, learning and refinement. Students' writing may be just "good enough" to take them to the finish line of the dissertation, but the degree to which students have actually acquired and improved upon their writing and research skills is debatable. It is further questionable whether the use of quality indicators for the dissertation are established, taught, and applied—or not. If the purpose of serving on a committee is simply to produce the dissertation with passable or marginal quality, then that is the debatable endgame, for the solid preparatory framework is not in place: students have not been provided with the opportunity to enhance their skills in preparation to meet the demands of the dissertation. They may well be out of their comfort zones, but that is because dissertations are uncomfortable environments; the fact is that there is relatively little investment in practiced learning and development and application of skills. There is no internalization of the writing process on a conscious level that permits for the acquisition of knowledge and proficiency. Instead, the work with a committee may be rote: the committee issues an order or a directive, and the student responds, almost unconsciously.

The Deliberate Practice Gap

For the most part, the "bulking up" of skills required of dissertation writing and research are relegated to dissertation seminars, bookended in some programs or sometimes just included as one of the last steps in a doctoral program. Generally, there is no "deliberate practice" for the dissertation exercised throughout the curricula. Intensive writing and researching throughout the entire course of doctoral study is not the norm. But it should be. Students must engage consistently in the skills training that facilitates excellence and that strengthens opportunities for successful transition. Researchers have long pointed to the value of introducing students to research experiences that also include interdisciplinary intersections (Golde & Gallagher, 1999, pp. 281–285), but the implementation of formal approaches that reach across all disciplines unilaterally are not in place consistently. And despite the fact that students may be exposed to research via participation in grants, conferences, or faculty research projects, these events may not be structured in meaningful ways that meet the demands of the dissertation and that bridge the gap.

Students often struggle at the dissertation phase and perhaps may not recognize the fact that the writing/researching of the dissertation is not a skill acquired preliminarily or at the end of doctoral study via dissertation seminar, but rather a skill that should be cultivated carefully throughout the entire course of doctoral training. If they did, the outcome would be more positive. Ericsson and Pool's (2017) research indicates that individuals who excel at something—sports, music, dance, for example, are not innately blessed with a "gift" or a genetic composition that makes them good at what they do: they practice, *deliberately*. But doctoral students are not necessarily practicing these skills in most instances. Students in STEM fields routinely practice research, but not necessarily formal technical writing, which they generally encounter at the end of their programs as it intersects with their research. In many other disciplines, students encounter both research and writing at the very end of their programs, where complications and the risks to degree completion are significant. Bowen and Rudenstine's (1992) research indicates that 15–25% of doctoral students do not complete the dissertation after advancing to candidacy.

In short, students are generally not prepared technically or psychologically as they undergo the *critical transition*, and their programs are not necessarily designed to account for it. As a result, they may not be able to establish the rigor that the late stages of a Ph.D. program demand, even though, according to Nancy Schlossberg, this type of transition is typically classified as an "anticipated" transition, an event that is expected (Meyer, n.d.).

This factor of students' unpreparedness may exert significant pressure on advising faculty. Are graduate advising faculty obligated to *push and pull* students through the dissertation process, and if they are, what are the limitations of this work before it breaches an ethical barrier or their patience, or both?

Several factors can be attributed, in part, to students' unpreparedness to navigate through this transitional phase.

Identity and the Student Scholar

Students may not even recognize or be cognizant of the *fact of transition* itself, the migration from "one form or type to another" as they move from the state of acquiring knowledge to the state of producing research (Cambridge Dictionary, n.d.) According to Goodman, Schlossberg, and Anderson (2006, as cited in Meyer, n.d.), transitions result in "changed relationships, routines, assumptions, and roles" (p. 2), and the migration from the certainty of the coursework stage to the ambiguous research stage exemplifies these changes. Anderson, Goodman, and Schlossberg (2012) state that moving through transition periods in life requires a "letting go of aspects of the self" as well as "former roles and learning new ones"; in addition, they urge for the necessity of individuals to evaluate the changes in their lives, changes that include "gains as well as losses" (p. 40). The "letting go" of the previous roles and the "learning [of] new ones" may be two contradictory impulses: students are enmeshed in a metamorphosis that involves both conditions almost simultaneously. They are aspiring scholars but they are also students, and so perhaps the term and the phase at which they find themselves can be described as *student scholar*.

In their student role, they enjoyed a certain identity: they may have held high GPAs and were provided with accolades such as awards, grants, and other significant accomplishments; they may have held positions in student government, served on search committees, or worked in deans' offices. It may be challenging for students to *let go* of those "aspects of the self" when confronted by the complexities of the dissertation that often frustrate degree completion, while simultaneously remaining open to the acquisition of new and complex roles such as those of researcher, writer, and scholar that represent formidable obstacles. Perhaps they need to reconsider: It is not that students must necessarily relinquish their accomplishments or the skills that transported them through challenges; it is that these same skills may no longer be sufficient in and of themselves to meet the demands of the next critical phase of their programs. Kralik, Visentin, and Van Loon (2006) write that transitions require the "reconstruction of a valued self-identity" that integrally reinforces the individual's ability to adapt to change. But safe and effective transitions may not always be possible as students grapple with past successes, which may have buoyed their confidence levels, amidst the new demands that may, ironically enough, dismantle them. The 4.0 GPA and the accolade do not necessarily symbolize safe transitions or knowable identities that lead to dissertation success, a sobering realization.

Underestimating the Critical Transition

Not only may students fail to recognize the *fact of transition* or anticipate the transition process, but they may also not visualize *themselves* as they enter into it; thus, they are further unprepared to navigate this uncharted territory, especially when they isolate the dissertation into a simple act that they have "only" to complete, as I have mentioned previously in the book. This phraseology alone dismantles students' awareness of the entire transition process from course taker to researcher, the "critical shift from the familiar realm" to that of the "independent scholar," and from a tightly controlled environment to one that is "uncertain" (Lovitts, 2005a). As a result of not completely understanding this shift in mindset, they may liken the dissertation to the *least* requirement, not the litmus test of doctoral study, its final arbiter, or as Lovitts (2005b) describes it, "the ultimate educational product" (pp. 18–23).

Dissertating students who cast the dissertation into the "only" category frequently cannot quite grasp the demanding context of dissertation production. Preliminary engagement in it conveys the appearance of something that is of slight consequence, not something upon which the degree itself is determined, and so their response is underwhelming: they have underestimated the technical complexity and the emotional demands. Perhaps if the emotional parameters of entering into the transitional phase of the dissertation could be a topic included in courses, dissertation seminars, or other preparatory courses, or even framed as a topic of discussion among dissertation committee members and their advisees, the journey would be less constrained by false notions, inherent disappointments, and poor performances.

Times of transition may be interpreted as life events that offer the possibility for individuals to metamorphose and transform; yet, the transformative power of the dissertation may also not be a conscious or even a desired outcome for dissertating students: many simply want to be *done* and move on to career opportunities, but *how to get there* remains the question that generates a kind of crisis. Approaching the dissertation may be likened to Corlett and Millner's (1993) interpretation of the Chinese "ideogram" for "crisis," which combines symbols for "danger and opportunity" (p. 34). Corlett and Millner write that the onset of a crisis is often typified by the perception of danger, later followed by the idea of opportunity and "new directions" or "new beginnings" that were not previously possible (p. 34.) They observe the presence of a kind of polarity that draws individuals in the midst of transition into two points of binary opposition—the knowable past and the unknown future, which creates "tension, doubt, and questioning" (p. 35), and that correlates to the relinquishing of a previous knowledge of the self and the acquisition of new roles as individuals undergo transition (Anderson et al., 2012).

Yet, the sense of a discontinuity between the knowable demands of the coursework phase of a doctoral program and the ambiguous demands of the dissertation/research process persists and casts students into an untenable position that may generate uncertainty and a lack of confidence.

It is not that students do not anticipate the dissertation. Certainly, they do. Rather, it is that they do not anticipate the *fact* of transition as a continuous process that takes them to the dissertation, and they are unprepared for the journey and initially unaware of just how transformative, challenging, and stressful this process can be. Anderson et al. (2012) write that transitions can only be deemed as "transitions" if the individuals undergoing them define them as such (p. 40). But what if the impact upon the individual resides more as an emotional reaction to a transition process, rather than a conscious intellectual awareness that transition is taking place and that certain adjustments will be required? Perhaps these individuals recognize only the discomfort engendered by the transition process but do not see the process itself. They may well find themselves broadsided, this realization manifesting not only for students, but for their committee members as well.

Collaboration vs. Plagiarism: The Critical Transition Dilemma for Advisors and Committee Members

The design and creation of a dissertation is generally collaborative, born out of the global sense of academic community that girds dissertation committee service. Members' experience and disciplinary acumen guide the conceptual framework and delivery of the monograph to ensure it reaches a level of excellence in research and scholarly writing that the committee and the institution view with respect. This outcome results from editorial intervention, from the positions of intellectual interrogation of the text and delivery of narrative responses that showcase the work.

But the role of this interventionist process is neither actually defined nor its extent articulated in the dissertation circle. As a result, the possibility of an ethical gap looms before every dissertation committee. If it is true, as Lovitts (2005a) suggests, that "researching and writing" a dissertation are "complex processes" that students must learn to "negotiate," then it is also true that students learn to write a dissertation through the act of writing the dissertation and through the committee's intervention; therefore, it must also be true then that the dissertation alone cannot be this proving ground, especially since it is an exercise not reinforced via Ericsson and Pool's (2017) concept of *deliberate practice.*

The degree to which committee members can ethically assume responsibility for the research and writing processes is debatable in light of the reality that students may not necessarily be good or even fair writers and that they have limited research experience. Further, students' coursework throughout the period of their doctoral studies may not have been writing-centric and therefore did not provide for the cultivation of a scholarly writing/research experience. It is not a wonder then that many students are hard pressed to negotiate the challenges of the critical transition process. The tools they require are just not in place, and even their perceptions of themselves as emerging scholars are not grounded in experiences that encourage confidence and self-esteem in this last stage of their doctoral studies. Moreover, where is the ethical line or the boundary for committee members whose *editing* of a dissertation blurs the distinction between collaboration and the possibility of their advisee's plagiarism?

Ghostwriting

My original career objective was not to be a ghostwriter, but during the course of my work as a conceptual editor, working with doctoral students on monographs or conferring with them on articles for publication, my evolution into *ghostwriting* has become apparent. I arrived at this designation unwittingly, for if someone had ever referred to me as a *ghostwriter*, I would have cringed at the notion. Now, I must accept the title and take responsibility for the ethical impasse at which I sometimes find myself. My ability to transmogrify students' leaden narrative texts into golden alchemical nobilities was purely unintentional, yet this is the outcome. How do I feel about that? Not so good.

I also am caught between the blurred lines generated by my role as editor, dissertation coach, committee member, mentor, and advocate, and the role of my students to produce the dissertation as evolving academic scholars. The expectation is that they will reach ideas through the power of their own critical thinking abilities, curiosity, intellectual passion, and willingness to do the hard work and enter into the academic conversations in their respective fields that will enrich, enlighten, and inform. But the equation is not balanced: I am doing a great deal of the hard work for those unable or unwilling to undergo the *critical transition* into the dissertation, and I have crossed that barely visible line. How have I missed it? In turn, students have ignored or chosen not to see the boundary lines, and in so doing, we each have entered into a kind of inadvertent deception that leads me to question the authorship of anyone's work for that matter, when editorial intercessions emblazon the entire monograph or journal article or grant. So, whose work is it, anyway? These are age-old debates to which many educators have been exposed, and while it is interesting to read about their linguistic, theoretical, and ethical frameworks (not the subject of this book), it is also disconcerting to be swept up in our personal experiences and to question whether we are truly collaborating or simply opening up a door to plagiarism.

Ericsson and Pool's (2017) research affirms that deliberate practice will help us to harness our talents and become better at cultivating our skills. As they tell us, we become better by becoming better. We do this by getting out of comfort zones that keep us anchored to the status quo and the ways in which we've always operated. The coursework that students undergo may not reflect the kind of practice that doctoral students require to be successful in the dissertation. They have little if any consistent training in writing and researching throughout their programs of study, and certainly not any *deliberate practice*. At the dissertation stage, most will require tremendous oversight and intervention on the part of their committee members. The extent of this involvement will impact committees in significant ways, and one of these concerns the ethics of that engagement.

Have we established a series of metrics that accompany quality indicators for dissertations so that students can align their objectives with these end goals and understand how committees will employ this information to evaluate and assess their work? Is the *good enough* dissertation the destination for the Ph.D. capstone experience, and does this differ from the *marginal* dissertation or the *barely passable* dissertation? Ericsson and Pool (2017) write that "good enough" in most instances in life really might be sufficient for us to "get by" in our endeavors, but they also suggest that "the option exists" for us to push those boundaries—if we are willing (p. 48). Superlative students who work autonomously in a self-directed, cognitively aware manner and blossom under the tutelage of the committee will not want to produce the "good enough" dissertation, the one that maintains them at an acceptable level of performance but bars them from excellence; instead, they will push those boundaries on their own by getting out of their own comfort zones, exploring, refining, and re-envisioning their work. In this regard, they also become their own teachers, a point that Ericsson and Pool affirm through the example of Benjamin Franklin, who taught himself to write (pp. 155–157). However, such students may not be the norm that educators encounter. The manner in which advising faculty contend with alternative scenarios bears exploration.

Madison's Story

Madison was a Ph.D. student nearing the end of her program. She had conferred for almost two years with Professor X, one of her committee members who had been tasked with helping Madison to conceptualize the dissertation and to produce three penultimate chapters to be presented to the entire committee for its perusal. Clearly disconcerted by his experiences in working with Madison, he sought my counsel regarding his problematic situation. He found that, absent of the self-directed critical thinking skills that lie central to analysis and synthesis, Madison had been only quasi-engaged in a dissertation process that appeared not to interest her. It seemed to him that she had not researched the topic sufficiently and did not have a working knowledge of the concept. His work constituted the fulcrum upon which her monograph emanated, and he found that Madison had relegated him, or perhaps he had relegated himself—he didn't know which, to the task of assuming full responsibility for the entire dissertation, from the identification of its thesis to the method through which the study would be operationalized, and all tasks in between.

Professor X was growing uncomfortable with the level of his intervention in Madison's dissertation and perplexed by her lack of enthusiasm for the project. He found her becoming more dependent upon him and less inclined to assume responsibility for the work. The migration into her ownership of the study was not apparent, and he did not see her growth into a more independent frame of mind.

He was aware of the committee's penchant to adopt a position of habitual intervention when a problem arose, a willingness, conscious or unconscious, to enter into what he termed as "salvation modality," where Madison was concerned. In his view, this tendency was the antithesis of cultivating an independent scholar. To confound the situation further, Madison carried herself with an air of self-confidence that he considered misplaced, a façade that disguised the reality that she was not capable and also not aware of her lack of capability. She proceeded in her doctoral work without questioning herself or her actions or asking, "Am I on the right track? Am I doing this correctly? Let me ask my committee if this idea is sound, or not." These questions alone would have permitted her to establish a firm grounding for her work. But she never asked them, and neither did the other members on the committee ask them about her.

Discoveries

Professor X discovered that each successive draft of the dissertation proposal unmasked the unsettling observation that his editorial interventions had filled those linguistic spaces in the text, blending them into a *new voice,* an amalgamated version of the text now alloyed with his critical interpretations and expertise, but not Madison's own. In his view, it was a "phantasmagoria."

He had not anticipated that the presence of this new voice, this new author, had migrated into the HSIRB protocol. But it had. There, he noted that his editorial recommendations and suggestions in the first three chapters appeared verbatim, unaltered by paraphrasing. Madison had surrendered her voice to his and, in some manner, he had taken control and begun to speak *for* her. He was perplexed and did not know how he had reached this place. He questioned his own editorial style and wondered at what point the other dissertations he had worked on had been transformed through the act of an *Other*'s linguistic/rhetorical interventions to the extent that the writing was no longer reflective of one authorial voice, the student's, but rather a complex of authorial voices. *At what point in the dissertation process had Madison's dissertation become his dissertation?*

Most disconcerting was the fact that Madison's inability to write the dissertation and to conduct research had emerged latently, at the end of her doctoral program, when significant complications arose. Madison's bearing and demeanor may have beguiled certain committee members into thinking of her as entirely capable, when in reality her inability to contend with the dissertation and the required research had manifested at multiple points throughout Professor X's work with her. He described his work as bordering on "extreme intervention." He had not anticipated crossing over into this undefined space that was beginning to resemble a collision course, and he was losing confidence in Madison's ability. In short, he was saving Madison from herself. But was he supposed to be?

Did Madison even recognize her penchant for making mistakes and serious errors and cultivate a critical self-awareness about her work, consulting with committee members before venturing forward? No. She did not. The careful, methodical, studied approach to undertaking dissertation planning, research, and writing was missing. Professor X's repeated conversations with the committee to express these concerns exerted no response other than the members' acknowledgment of surprise that Madison seemed to be encountering a host of problems, so atypical for an accomplished student. Among themselves, the committee questioned Madison's interest in completing the degree and wondered if she had made the decision to abandon her studies. Nevertheless, they remained dedicated to the end goal of getting Madison to the other side of the Ph.D.

Professor X was in a quandary. He considered the outcome of that pushing and pulling and tugging to get someone over that line. He questioned what he and the committee actually produced when the majority of the work was their own. What did it mean when he and the committee had saved Madison from serious error after serious error because she failed to understand instructions or operationalize them? It was at this point that he considered resigning from the committee.

Analysis

Professor X's observations and experiences are worth noting, for it is striking that the seemingly innocuous act of editing, uncovering mistakes, and saving students from egregious errors holds the potential for transgressing ethical barriers. If we become self-reflective about our processes and actions as we engage in committee service, the issues unfold. The implications of committee service began to reflect the austere reality that ethical lines were being crossed in the effort to get Madison through. We do not always detect them at first, but they are revelatory over time. Professor X had arrived at an especially disconcerting place: his recognition of the intense degree of his involvement in cultivating the monograph. Madison had arrived at the end of her program: when her struggles to deliver the dissertation did not abate and when the threat of non-completion emerged.

Madison maintained an affable demeanor and did not oppose recommendations, though she often misunderstood them and did not apply them correctly. However, the difficulty for Professor X was that he never reached a point where her evolution as a scholar became apparent to him. She was making mistakes and he was fixing them. That motif did not change but only intensified, reaching its apex just weeks prior to the defense when major issues with the research procedures unfolded; these were issues that he had previously admonished the committee would occur unless it took decisive action to prevent them by putting certain resources into place prior to operationalizing the study. That warning went unheeded. Failure to do so exacerbated an already tense situation that jeopardized Madison's efforts and further convinced Professor X that he should resign. Without those resources in place, Madison proceeded to yet another impending disaster, and only at that time did her committee finally agree to act upon Professor X's last set of recommendations, further solidifying an already chilly atmosphere.

Perhaps the committee did not appreciate his advice and felt that he had overstepped his role as a committee member. Perhaps they did not appreciate the unmasking of Madison's limitations. Perhaps the committee held onto some hope that Madison could finally step up to the plate and deliver on her own. According to Professor X, that did not happen. She was still being *carried* (*abandoned* is a better word) by the thought that she was a good teacher and had good grades in her courses; certainly, she would pull through. The idea that Madison was struggling at this late stage seemed incongruous when perceived through the lens of her past accomplishments. This was an idea that the committee refused to believe or accept, despite Professor X's continued admonitions and interventions. Madison may have been abandoned, but Professor X had been as well.

Madison encountered the dissertation quite unprepared for the marathon. Whatever preparation she had received in her research courses, comprehensive examinations, dissertation seminar, or other program components was not reflected in her engagement with the dissertation. She did not recognize her own insufficiency and probably did not want to. But neither could she inherit all the blame, either.

At the end of the day, the committee may have created inadvertently a false narrative that they themselves bought into regarding Madison's capabilities to produce the dissertation. The fact remains that her previous accomplishments did not translate into the skills necessary to carry her through the critical transition and to produce the dissertation. Throughout, the committee members clung to the illusion that success on one level (her past identity during the coursework phase of her program) equated to success on other levels, without understanding that they do not always. If the committee considered this possibility, it did not articulate it among themselves or to Madison: they did not ask if it were possible for Madison to be an excellent student, but not capable of critical thinking and writing, or of discerning information, or of connecting the dots of an argument, or of operationalizing research without cognizance that she herself may not have accurately grasped the concepts at play. Professor X had apprised them of the status of the proposal at each revision and made them aware of the debilitating factors that were present. In the end, they simply did not want to see them and/or did not know how best to handle them.

Epilogue

Professor X consulted with several colleagues, I among them, who admitted that from their own professional and disciplinary perspectives it was too late in the process to do anything more than press on and see Madison off to graduation, which he did. Moreover, with all of the committee members' editorial changes and suggestions, the final product was no longer lacking, but now of acceptable quality. Madison had ventured this far, and there was no turning back. Either way, staying or leaving, brought the same consequences: gains and losses had been cannibalized. Professor X had become intellectually and psychologically separated from his committee colleagues, his clarion call unheeded throughout and recognized only when the unavoidable prospects of a compromised dissertation defense loomed ahead.

Reading Madison's dissertation does not unmask the reality that Madison was propped up throughout the entire enterprise, unable to take ownership of her project at any point because she did not possess the skills and the training necessary. The success of the dissertation hinged upon Professor X's ability to circumvent Madison's limitations, actions that the committee did not appreciate and yet, in some way, expected and indeed encouraged; it was clear that without such interventions, the dissertation would not have manifested. The committee too was caught up in the oxymoronic reality that a Ph.D. candidate had progressed to the end of her doctoral program and did not possess the critical thinking, research, and writing skills requisite to the dissertation. If you were to read Madison's dissertation, you would say that it was *good enough*. The final product did not reflect the student's problematic history because the committee put the matter right at all turns. It relied upon her past accomplishments as proof of her eligibility for conferment of the degree and refused to recognize or address her obvious deficiencies, even when warned and even with Professor X's constant interventions clearly in sight. The compensations, interventions, excuses, and adherence to Madison's image of previous success created a blindfold to the stark reality that she was not capable of producing a dissertation.

I do not like to consider that this dissertation was just a case of *smoke and mirrors*, but perhaps it was. Did Madison actually learn anything about herself or become more introspective about her own educational process? Did she ever recognize that Professor X's words, ideas, thoughts, and intercessions into the dissertation were not her own? Or, was it best for her to simply ignore that reality, as did her committee? I cannot say. She was moored at the critical transition phase of her program, one that neither she nor her committee anticipated. The episode leaves one feeling *not quite right* about what transpired on any level. An ethical line had been crossed, but it had been blurred. By the time it became apparent, it really was *too late*.

Perhaps this situation, and others like it, could have been different if procedures had been established to help students and faculty negotiate this transitional period. According to Schlossberg's Transition Theory, it is critical that individuals undergoing life transitions are supported with resources to help them cope with the changes, and in the case of doctoral students, I think, to alert them very early on to the psychological and technical challenges inherent in this process. Schlossberg's 4 S's represent resources that include the following: recognition of the *situation* from which the transition stems; the *social support* structures such as family, friends, colleagues and others; the *strategies* for coping with the transition; and the *self,* and having a sense of meaning and purpose that fosters a positive, more resilient perspective. These elements are grounded in practical approaches to the manner in which individuals negotiate through transitional periods of life (Schlossberg, 1984).

But the manner in which these elements find pragmatic application to the world of doctoral students undergoing transition is not always apparent in the current higher education environment. The creation of a comprehensive resource matrix for graduate students and graduate advising faculty that accounts for the critical transition can ease students through one of the most vulnerable periods of their doctoral training. Deliberate practice may be one variable that can open the pathways to a successful, critical transition.

Deliberate Practice: Easing Advisors and Advisees Through Critical Transition

1. Implement opportunities *earlier* in doctoral program courses for disciplinary and interdisciplinary research and writing experiences *throughout the curricula* to ensure that students meet the challenges of scholarly research and writing on a continuous, sustained basis. Every course should hold some level of these pedagogical approaches as a student learning outcome that expands opportunities for success throughout the program of study and that ushers students into the dissertation with requisite skills intact. Such an approach creates a viable bridge into deliberate practice and establishes predictors for success and/or shortcomings sooner rather than later in the dissertation process.
2. Establish *quality indicators* and *metrics* for the dissertation so that standards are defined on the departmental and committee level. In addition, students are better able to gauge their writing and research so that these skills intersect with

those standards and the ways in which their dissertations will be assessed and evaluated.
3. Cultivate critical thinking skills and expose students to the art of the literature review: how to read, interpret, and understand points and counterpoints across their respective disciplines. Critical thinking is a skill cultivated over time, not one acquired through the sole act of writing the dissertation.
4. Create *ongoing* graduate student orientations that are sequenced to meet each stage of doctoral study: admission/coursework to comprehensive examinations, comprehensive examinations to candidacy, candidacy to dissertation defense, and dissertation defense to graduation so that students are fully informed of the requirements for each stage and provided with resources.
5. Conduct needs assessments for both graduate students and graduate advising faculty and implement corresponding resources to support both groups through each stage. It is of no value to conduct a needs assessment without also implementing the resources necessary to meet those needs.
6. Provide training in critical transitioning to graduate students, advisors, and committee members and create conduits to psychosocial counseling to ease students through the transition process.
7. Align deliberate practice initiatives with efforts of institutionally sponsored Graduate Centers for Scholarship and Professional Development to cultivate and reinforce skills development in transitioning students and to assist graduate advising faculty in meeting this objective. (Refer to Chapter 24.)
8. Develop ethics training programs in graduate advising that create inroads into problem solving and boundary setting for graduate faculty and graduate students. Establish a working definition for *ethical editing* so that the parameters for engagement are more clearly defined.

~ The Take Away ~

1. Do not underestimate the difficulty of the critical transition period in doctoral programs and the ethical ramifications for both students and graduate advising faculty. Create viable informational/developmental programs and training throughout the curricula that address the inherent difficulty, both technical and psychological, that students and faculty encounter.
2. Create training programs that account for the *ethics of advising* for graduate advising faculty.
3. Reconfigure courses in the curricula to include more writing-centric/research-centric approaches and experiences that dovetail logically into the demands of the dissertation so that transition, as a process, occurs over time and coalesces with production of the dissertation.
4. Organize ongoing graduate student orientations that segue into each stage of doctoral study and that ensure student preparedness to meet the singular demands of each stage. Orientations should align with needs assessments on both the faculty and student levels and should reflect resource matrices to address respective needs at each stage.
5. Implement *deliberate practice* into doctoral curricula as a tool to cultivate expertise in research and writing so that students are better prepared to meet the rigor of the dissertation. Align deliberate practice initiatives within the framework of Graduate Centers for Scholarship and Professional Development to ensure collaborative approaches and unity of vision among graduate advising faculty and graduate students that account for the cultivation of future scholars.
6. Implement quality indicators and metrics for the dissertation so that students learn how to "write into" those standards and understand how their work will be evaluated and assessed.

References

Anderson, M. L., Goodman, J., & Schlossberg, N. K. (2012). *Counseling adults in transition: Linking Schlossberg's Theory with practice in a diverse world* (4th ed.). New York, NY: Springer.

Bowen, W. G., & Rudenstine. N. L. (1992). *In pursuit of the Ph.D*. Princeton, NJ: Princeton University Press.

Cambridge Dictionary. (n.d.). Transition. Retrieved January 6, 2021, from https://dictionary.cambridge.org/us/dictionary/english/transition.

Corlett, E. S., & Millner, N. B. (1993). Navigating midlife: Using typology as a guide. Palo Alto, CA: CPP Books.

Ericsson, A., & Pool, R. (2017). *Peak: Secrets from the new science of expertise*. New York, NY: First Mariner Books.

Golde, C. M., & Gallagher, H. A. (1999). The challenges of conducting interdisciplinary research in traditional doctoral programs. *Ecosystems, 2*, 281–285.

Kralik, D., Visentin, K. & Van Loon, A. (2006). Transition: A literature review. *Journal of Advanced Nursing, 55*(3), 320–329.

Lovitts, B. (2005a). Being a good course taker is not enough: A theoretical perspective on the transition into independent research. *Studies in Higher Education, 30*(2), 137–154.

Lovitts, B. E. (2005b). How to grade a dissertation. *Academe, 91*(6), 18–23.

Meyer, L. (n.d.). *Nancy Schlossberg's Transition Theory*. Retrieved January 23, 2021, from formal_theory_paper_6020.pdf

Schlossberg, N. K. (1984). *Transition Theory*. Retrieved January 27, 2021, from MARCR website: https://marcr.net/

Chapter 26

Quick Takes

Chapter 1: Dissertation Advising: The Need for Collaborative Training Models

- Be aware that dissertation training models have changed and are moving in the direction of collaborative, integrative, interdisciplinary styles. The old model of the student as *scholar in isolation* is passé.
- Generally, formal advising training for faculty to serve as dissertation directors is not a standard in place, and so, too often, faculty are relegated to self-reliance in terms of figuring out this process.
- Graduate Program Directors are conduits to best practices in graduate education for students/faculty but may be undervalued.
- Dissertating students will find ways to compensate for what they do not receive in the dissertation advising circle.

Chapter 2: The Rules of Engagement

- Dissertation advisors should establish and communicate a carefully arranged set of guidelines that serve as parameters for dissertation committee members and doctoral advisees. Doing so ensures heightened awareness of the dissertation process and its objectives.
- Use a Backward Calendar to keep track of student progress in meeting graduation timelines.

Chapter 3: Defining Editing Expectations: More Rules of Engagement

- Assumptions on the part of the advisor or the advisee regarding ways in which they communicate, interpret, and implement editorial commentary frequently pose threats to the integrity of the editing process. Assume nothing. Communicate questions, concerns, expectations clearly.

Dissertation chairs and committee members may find themselves enmeshed in unsatisfactory editing behavioral patterns that do not necessarily yield student productivity or advancement in completing the degree. Advisees' failure to progress is a sign that advisees are in trouble. Seek for alternatives to re-focus students and get them on the right track.

Chapter 4: The Toxic Committee

The essential anodyne to dissertation toxicity is communication.

Understand the impact of dissertation committee reconfiguration upon the advisee and committee members.

Advisors should not agree to serve on a dissertation committee unless they recognize their interest level, the degree to which they are dedicated to the process, and their available time.

Committees should meet on a regular basis.

Recognize that the dissertation chair's role is a leadership role and leaders are accountable for ethical management of the process.

Chapter 5: Considerations When Forming a Committee: For Advisees

When vetting potential committee members, recognize that you are the *rule*, not the exception.

Listen to your colleagues' views and experiences.

Learn the art of negotiation and compromise: determine if you can work with this individual(s) and, if so, then understand the most effective/least effective ways of doing so.

Determine the advantages/disadvantages of working with the potential advisor/committee members.

Learn the number of advisees the potential advisor has *graduated*.

Determine the resources you need in order to be successful in the dissertation process.

Consider whether you and the potential advisor/committee members are a good match for each other.

Remember that the advisor is your advisor, not your friend.

Chapter 6: Selection of the Advisee: For Faculty

Determine if the potential advisee is committed to the process of earning a Ph.D. and is capable.

Determine if the potential advisee can follow directions.

Determine if the potential advisee has the writing skills necessary to sustain the dissertation.

Determine if the potential advisee has research experience.

Determine if the potential advisee is capable of working autonomously.

Determine the potential advisee's motivations in seeking the Ph.D.

Ask yourself if you, as potential advisor, are capable of investing your time and energy in this process.

Review a writing sample from the potential advisee to ascertain writing capability.

Chapter 7: Other Considerations for the Advisor as Leader

Build a solid dissertation team: consult the graduate catalogue at your university to determine configuration requirements.

Configure the team: chair/advisor, faculty member, external committee member, content expert(s), methodologist, statistician, conceptual editor, and/or writing expert.

Determine the need for other support: professional editor/formatter.

Chapter 8: Vetting the Committee

Vet potential committee members for graduate faculty status at the beginning of the process, as soon as the decision is made to appoint them to a committee.

Be on the alert for university practices that synchronize the dissertation proposal approval process with the appointment to a committee process; these should be two distinct processes, with the faculty vetting process in place prior to the proposal approval process.

Chapter 9: Discovering the Dissertation Topic

Preliminary Literature Review: Unmasking the Gap

Ensure that advisees understand the concept of the preliminary literature review: discovery of the dissertation topic and the gap in the research that ***their*** research will fill.

Continue to discuss ideas relevant to the discovery of the topic and keep the lines of communication open as concepts are being framed.

Be accessible to your advisees and help them to manage the literature review, which often can overwhelm.

Ensure accessibility to research librarians.

Secondary Literature Review: Dual Roles

Ensure that advisees understand the appropriate frame for the secondary literature review and its purpose: to provide a critical backdrop that frames the research questions and that supports the study under construction.

Discuss the organization of the secondary literature review and its logic.

Mosaics and Modular Patterns

When writing the actual literature review chapter:

Use a set up or an overview.

Delineate component sections or the narrative plan for the literature review.

Sustain the logic and narrative flow between each of the modules so that they connect in terms of argument, point, and relevance.

Ensure that references are current.

Include an appropriate conclusion to the literature review chapter.

Ensure the appropriate use of the discourse modes of exposition and argument/persuasion.

Use headings and white space as signposts to direct readers through the entire literature review.

Chapter 10: The Concept Paper and the Quality Circle Review

Ensure that students begin the dissertation with two critical tools: the concept paper and the quality circle review. Sending students off to write the dissertation proposal without these elements in place is neither sound nor efficient.

Chapter 11: Implementation of Editorial Commentary and Technology

Knowing When It Isn't Working: For Advisors
The student lacks authorial control
Use of cutting and pasting
Textual excision vs. editorial change
Ignoring editorial commentary
Lack of conclusions
Lack of organization
Writing *around* the topic
Grammatical and mechanical errors
Repetition
Lack of awareness of *audience* and *purpose*
Parataxis
Lack of appropriate bibliography/lack of reference style
Lack of consistency/careless editing
Argumentative or confrontational behavior
Implementation of non-recommended changes

Knowing When It Isn't Working: For Advisees
Refer to all of the above (for advisors) in addition to the following:
Advisor's editorial commentary remains unclear
Contradictory editorial suggestions
Lack of understanding the goals or objectives of each chapter
Writing is not unified, coherent, or poorly organized
Writing meanders and lacks direction/focus
Missing or weak conceptual frame
Use of erudite, convoluted, or abstruse sentences

Chapter 12: Naming Conventions for Maintaining Draft Files

Use failsafe practices, technologies, and procedures to ensure safe trajectory of the dissertation from draft to completed document.

Committee members should use the same naming convention practices to ensure continuity and consistency of labeling.

Advisees can use separate memory drives for each committee member in order to maintain control over the editing process.

Emphasize *prevention*, rather than *recovery*.

Consider the value of using Microsoft SharePoint or similar software in the dissertation editing process.

Chapter 13: Working Against the Grain: For Advisors

Don't be an "asshole" advisor to your advisee.
Define your expectations.
Make yourself available.
Maintain civility.
Be accountable.
Ask for conflict resolution.
Write a formal letter of departure.

Chapter 14: Working Against the Grain: For Advisees

Avoid tantrums.
Cooperate and graduate.
Avoid escalating the issues.
Don't break olive branches.
Let go of your baggage.
Keep an eye on the clock.

Chapter 15: Dissertation Proposal and the Human Subjects Institutional Review Board (HSIRB) Protocol: Symmetry in Design

Recognize the value of designing the dissertation proposal and the HSIRB protocol in a simultaneous way, so that the documents are synchronized.

Proceed with proposal defense, revisions, and approval process.

Know the differences between filing the HSIRB protocol versus approval to begin data collection.

Consider the research compliance office as a resource.

When writing the HSIRB protocol, consider the following: Value of the team, ethical role of HSIRB, anticipating review questions, informed consent, use of disciplinary lexicons and standard language, proofreading, returned protocols, implementing revisions, specificity, filing a protocol versus approval.

Remember that human subjects research carried out without HSIRB approval *cannot,* in almost all instances, be presented in articles, at conferences, or in any formal academic writing endeavor, including the dissertation and the thesis.

Chapter 16: Preparing for the Oral Defense of the Dissertation: 17 Easy Steps

Planning for the defense by conducting a mock defense and by making prior arrangements inspires confidence and sets the stage for a smooth defense.

Chapter 17: Bill of Rights for Advisee/Advisor

Know your rights.
Insist on your rights.
Respect the rights of others.
Focus on the dissertation.
Think like a "team member."
Know when it's over.

Chapter 18: Combating the Dissertation Blues: Comprehensive Examinations — The Prelude

Strategize as a study team. Use the medical school/law school model and consider the value of problem solving as a group, rather than as a lone individual. You will have to write the examinations as an individual, but if you align yourself with the right people, you'll have the team approach behind you.

Recognize that some isolation is normal. Isolation to the point of total seclusion is most likely not conducive to success during the comprehensive examinations. However, there is a degree of necessity in being somewhat secluded during this time, and so advocate for the appropriate balance.

Chapter 19: The Dissertation Writing Blues

The Dissertation Writing Blues manifest for a variety of diverse reasons that fall into an ironic category that can be referred to as "normally abnormal." *Many dissertating students experience these feelings that frequently stem from isolation and from the uncertainty inherent in the dissertation process.*

Chapter 20: The Dissertation Aftermath Blues

Dissertation advisors should be aware of students' propensity for the post-dissertation blues and dispense Dissertation Blues Aftercare, which can include career guidance, as well as counseling with a professional therapist.

Advisors should mentor advisees to be realistic in determining career goals.

Tenure track or bust—consider all career options, not just the tenure track.

Think beyond the Ph.D.

Chapter 21: Debriefing: An Essential Final Step in Doctoral Education

Advisors and advisees alike may be surprised by what they can learn and by what they can teach by undergoing a debriefing. Benefits extend beyond the individuals and coalesce as one of many evolving best practices in graduate education.

Chapter 22: New Forms and New Paradigms

Technological innovations and new ways of perceiving the world of the dissertation lend to higher-ordered evolutions of the monograph. As technology advances, so too will the dissertation format advance and evolve. Doctoral students and their committees must be prepared to accept the notion of an evolutionary dissertation world and step boldly forward to enter into new dimensions of scholarly investigation; the three-article and digital dissertation are two such dimensions.

Despite the form used, at the end of the day, it is the value, integrity, merit, and contribution to the field that must win out over the vehicles through which these end products are produced.

Chapter 23: Personalizing Academic Misconduct: An Approach for the Graduate Classroom

Help to initiate research ethics training.
Be proactive.
Educate and ameliorate.
Advocate the use of citation management software with advisees as a "self-check" measure.
Help to implement graduate student honor codes at your institution.
Advocate for discipline-specific ethics courses at your institution.
Implement ethics certificate programs.
Teach students the value of personalizing academic misconduct.
Use plagiarism detection software only when necessary.
Be aware of daily ethical infractions that reside within our worlds.

Chapter 24: A Visionary Perspective for an Academic Resource Matrix

Educators must consider innovative ways of guiding students through doctoral study, particularly at the dissertation stage, where specialization is requisite. Lack of expertise and training in the discipline of dissertation advising has compromised the efforts of graduate faculty as well as their advisees. Implementation of effective training and development strategies is necessary to doctoral retention and student success. Dissertation advising will emerge as its own specialty in graduate education.

Chapter 25: Blurred Lines: Ethical Considerations for Committee Members

Do not underestimate the critical transition period.
Create training programs in the ethics of advising.
Reconfigure the curricula to include writing-centric/research-centric courses.
Organize ongoing graduate student orientations.
Implement deliberate practice into doctoral curricula.
Implement quality indicators/metrics.

About the Author

Marianne Di Pierro holds the Ph.D. in English from the University of South Florida and is the former director of the Graduate Center for Research and Retention at Western Michigan University (WMU). As a graduate education specialist, she has coached more than 100 Ph.D. students across a spectrum of disciplines to degree completion. She holds graduate faculty status at WMU and is experienced in curriculum design, assessment and evaluation, policy development, and conflict resolution. She has been engaged as an expert consultant in graduate education for a law firm and has worked as a training consultant to graduate advising faculty. Di Pierro has participated in national research projects on Ph.D. completion and is principal investigator on several of her own studies that examine variables impacting doctoral attrition and retention. She has published articles in peer-reviewed journals and presented her research at professional conferences. Di Pierro is the current editor of the *Journal for Quality Perspectives in Knowledge Acquisition* and serves on the leadership teams for the American Society for Quality (ASQ) Education Division and the Health Care Division. She may be reached at the following email address: marianne.dipierro@wmich.edu

Index

A

academic divorce 140, 144, 147
academic misconduct 29, 227, 234, 238, 281
advising models 14, 61
advisor as leader 79, 275
annual review 28-30, 48-51, 153, 155, 159, 186, 187
assumptions 36, 40, 246, 259
attrition vii, 1-2, 6, 12, 15, 50, 66, 74, 100, 102, 119, 201, 244, 247, 283

B

backward calendar 24-25, 30, 271
bill of rights 185-186, 188, 279
Bowen & Rudenstine 102, 257

C

collaboration 14, 79, 119, 135, 136, 173, 250, 260, 261
comprehensive examination 60, 102, 113, 138, 189-193, 196, 240, 267, 270, 279
committee reconfiguration 45, 51, 73, 274
communication 4, 17-18, 22, 30-31, 35-36, 43, 45, 47, 49-51, 60, 69, 83, 90, 113, 130, 139, 141, 149, 153, 170, 213-214, 216, 218, 244-246, 274, 276
concept paper 11, 18-19, 92, 99-105, 108-109, 111-113, 116, 119, 167, 196-197, 200, 249-250, 276
conflict 110, 144, 149, 244, 278, 283
Council of Graduate Schools 1, 4, 15, 58, 66, 101, 120, 223, 225, 234, 244, 246
critical transition 2, 102, 154, 253, 257, 258, 260-262, 267-269, 271, 281

D

death of a committee member 45
debriefing 120, 213-215, 218, 280
deliberate practice 253-256, 261-262, 269, 271, 282
digital dissertations 206, 208, 222-223, 226, 239, 280
dissertation advising 1-4, 6, 9, 14-15, 50, 59, 69, 119, 148, 251-252, 273, 281
dissertation aftermath blues 203, 280
dissertation committee 2, 8-9, 14, 17-18, 23, 26-27, 29-30, 40-41, 46, 49, 51, 53-54, 64, 73, 84, 87, 99, 101, 104, 112-115, 135, 147, 151, 158, 167, 186-187, 215, 217, 244-245, 248, 250, 255, 259-260, 273-274
dissertation defense 18, 24-25, 35, 56, 80-81, 167, 177, 179-181, 183, 189, 199, 204, 213, 216, 268, 270
dissertation team 53, 79-80, 82, 275
dissertation topic 63, 75, 85, 88-90, 106, 276
dissertation wellness checks 248
dissertation writing blues 195, 280
doctoral advising 13, 58
doctoral education vii, 1-2, 5, 10, 52, 58, 74, 76, 102, 119-120, 146, 154, 213, 243, 247, 251, 280

E

editing 7, 19-20, 22, 31-33, 35-37, 71-73, 84, 114, 116, 121-123, 127-130, 132, 134-136, 138, 148, 152, 183, 196, 206, 215, 221, 240, 250, 261, 265, 270, 273-274, 277-278
editing expectations 31, 273
editorial commentary 7, 12, 20, 31, 33, 42, 60, 63, 72, 80, 121-123, 128-131, 137, 273, 277
Ericsson and Pool 253-256, 260, 262-263

G

Golde 1, 74, 76, 256, 272

F

facilitated review 36, 73
failure 24, 48, 50-51, 109-110, 121, 126, 142, 144, 147, 149, 153, 155, 163, 172, 196, 208, 210, 232, 237, 241, 266, 274
forming a committee 53, 274

H

Human Subjects Institutional Review Board (HSIRB)/protocol 138, 145, 165-175, 217, 264, 278-279

I

insecurity 8, 11, 33
isolation 6, 14, 101, 187, 190, 192-193, 196, 244, 248, 251, 273, 279-280
Institutional Review Board 36, 165, 216-217, 278

L

leadership 7, 48, 52, 74, 113, 245-246, 274
literature review 12, 72, 85-97, 99, 109, 111, 152, 165, 179, 220, 223, 232, 249, 270, 272, 276
Lovitts 1, 28, 30, 58, 66, 75, 77, 100-102, 120, 154, 157, 164, 259-260, 272

M

managerial style 61, 63, 158
mentoring 2, 10, 26, 58, 66, 84, 216, 222, 248
Microsoft SharePoint 21, 63, 134-136, 278
mosaics and modular patterns 94, 276

N

naming conventions 131-132, 277
"No Asshole Rule" 13, 15, 137, 150

O

Olson and Drew 21-22, 27-28, 106
oral defense 177-178, 279

P

paradigms 219, 280
plagiarism 228-242, 260-262, 281
preliminary literature review 84, 88-90, 276
proposal 6, 9, 14, 17-19, 25, 47, 62, 74, 83-84, 99, 100, 103-104, 108, 113, 115, 117, 126, 128, 137-138, 145-146, 158-161, 165-168, 170, 173, 175, 189, 196, 234, 240, 242-247, 249, 264, 267, 275, 277-278
proposal defense 18-19, 126, 167, 175, 278
prospectus 41, 101-106, 108, 167

Q

quality circle review 99-100, 114-119, 276

R

resources 26, 66, 70, 80-81, 86, 87, 89-90, 107
retention 1, 28-29, 50, 74, 81, 119, 242, 247, 251, 281, 283
rules of engagement 16-18, 31, 33, 62-63, 98, 121, 146, 149, 215, 273

S

secondary literature review 90-92, 99, 275
selection of the committee – for students 55
selecting an advisor 69
statistics 2, 6, 23, 81, 179, 229, 245
STEM 6, 45 46, 70, 73, 79, 83, 88-89, 102, 114, 132-133, 134-135, 144, 168, 196-197, 249, 257, 269, 280

T

technology 22, 43, 69, 79, 83, 88, 96, 102, 109, 121, 132-135, 182, 196, 224-226, 238, 248, 277, 280
time to degree (TTD) vii, 2, 36, 39, 40, 44, 57, 89, 102
toxic committee 39, 274

V

Versatile Ph.D. 39-40, 209-210
vetting the committee 83, 275

www.ingramcontent.com/pod-product-compliance
Lightning Source LLC
Chambersburg PA
CBHW050338230426
43663CB00010B/1907